D0205574

Panamanian Militarism

A Historical Interpretation

Panamanian Militarism

A Historical Interpretation

Carlos Guevara Mann

Ohio University Center For International Studies
Monographs in International Studies
Latin American Series Number 25
Athens • *1996*

LIBRARY
THE UNIVERSITY OF TEXAS
AT BROWNSVILLE
Brownsville, TX 78520-4991

© 1996 by the
Center for International Studies
Ohio University
Printed in the United States of America
All rights reserved
02 01 00 99 98 97 96   5 4 3 2 1

The books in the Center for International Studies Monograph Series
are printed on acid-free paper ∞

Library of Congress Cataloging-in-Publication Data

Guevara Mann, Carlos.
    Panamanian militarism : a historical interpretation / Carlos
Guevara Mann.
        p. cm. — (Monographs in international studies. Latin
American series ; no. 25)
    Includes bibliographical references and index.
    ISBN 0-89680-189-6 (pbk. : alk. paper)
    1. Panama—Politics and government. 2. Military government—
Panama—History. 3. Panama—Armed Forces—Political activity—
History. 4. Civil-military relations—Panama—History. 5. Panama—
Relations—United States. 6. United States—Relations—Panama.
I. Title. II. Series.
F1566.G85 1996
322'.5'097287—dc20   95-40747
                                                                CIP

This series of publications on Africa, Latin America, and Southeast Asia is designed
to present significant research, translation, and opinion to area specialists and to a
wide community of persons interested in world affairs. The editor seeks manuscripts
of quality on any subject and can generally make a decision regarding publication
within three months of receipt of the original work. Production methods generally permit a work to appear within one year of acceptance. The editor works closely with
authors to produce a high quality book. The series appears in a paperback format and
is distributed worldwide. For more information, contact the executive editor at Ohio
University Press, Scott Quadrangle, University Terrace, Athens, Ohio 45701.

Executive editor: Gillian Berchowitz
AREA CONSULTANTS
Africa: Diane Ciekawy
Latin America: Thomas Walker
Southeast Asia: James L. Cobban

Cover and text designed by Chiquita Babb
Cover illustration based on a drawing by Víctor Ramos

The Monographs in International Studies series is published for the Center for
International Studies by the Ohio University Press. The views expressed in individual monographs are those of the authors and should not be considered to represent the
policies or beliefs of the Center for International Studies, the Ohio University Press,
or Ohio University.

Contents

Illustrations

Preface

My interest in Panamanian history and politics is more than academic. As a native of the isthmus who has lived under an oppressive and corrupt military dictatorship, I have long endeavored to find a scientific explanation for the general phenomenom of militarism and its particular manifestation in Panama. The opportunity for so ambitious a purpose presented itself when, favored by a Fulbright scholarship, I began my graduate studies at Ohio University in Athens, Ohio.

This study has its origins in graduate research at Ohio University's Center for International Studies under the guidance of three outstanding academics: Dr. Michael Grow, who supervised the thesis project, Dr. Thomas W. Walker, my academic advisor, and Dr. Chester J. Pach, Jr., a historian of US diplomacy. I am most grateful to them for their guidance, their interest in my goal, and their faith in my capabilities.

I have endeavored to be objective in my use of sources and assessment of information, without undermining my convictions and opinions about the topic. The reader will therefore find that, despite my reference to authors subscribing to diverse ideologies, I make my points with vehemence.

It is thus mandatory to dedicate a few lines to my sources. For the interpretation of Latin American history in general, as well as for the analysis of US-Latin American relations, I have consulted authors who subscribe to the three fundamental paradigms of Latin American studies: the liberal school, which exalts capitalism and US-style representative democracy; the dependency theory, which attributes Latin American historical development to a capitalist conspiracy to maintain the region in socio-economic underdevelopment; and the corporatist model, which explains Latin American history as a result of the Iberic-American experience. The works of Howard Wiarda, Claudio Véliz, and James Malloy fall into this latter classification. My academic advisor Thomas W. Walker, Walter LaFeber, Jan Knippers Black, and José Comblin subscribe to the dependency paradigm. Of liberal tendency is the work of David Bushnell. Several authors have attempted a combination of models: my thesis director Michael Grow, David Healy, Lester D. Langley, Alain Rouquié, and Augusto Varas.

It is far more difficult to classify my sources on Panamanian history, for unfortunately, of the sum of Panama's historical studies, few conform to the scientific method. Among those exceptions which I found useful were the works of Omar Jaén Suárez, Alfredo Figueroa Navarro, and Alex Pérez Venero, as well as *Panama at the Crossroads: Economic Development and Political Change in the Twentieth Century*, an interesting economic history of the republic, by Andrew Zimbalist and John Weeks, and *Panama and the United States: The Forced Alliance*, a recent interpretation of US-Panamanian relations, by Michael Conniff. Other books that I found useful were William McCain's classic *The United States and the Republic of Panama*, Gustavo Mellander's *The United States in Panamanian Politics: The Intriguing Formative Years*, and Carlos Bolívar Pedreschi's *De la protección del canal a la militarización del país*.

The work of Humberto Ricord, Julio E. Linares, and Celestino Andrés Araúz and Patricia Pizzurno is remarkable for its detail and perceptive observations that contributed to the shaping of my analytical framework. Among the chronologies of Panamanian history, none is yet as complete as that of Juan Bautista Sosa and Enrique J. Arce, esential reading, despite its antiquity, for anyone interested in the events that occurred prior to 1903. Another informative work is that of Larry LaRae Pippin, who examined the so-called "Remón Era." I also consulted personal testimonies, such as the memoirs of

Liberal patrician Mariano Arosemena, military commander Esteban Huertas, and Conservative politician Tomás Arias, all of them principal actors in Panamanian history.

The historiography of the 1968–1989 military dictatorship deserves a paragraph by itself. I have yet to find a scientific analysis covering the period in its entirety. Although I have received favorable reports of the book *Panama protesta: En nuestras propias palabras* by Brittmarie Janson Pérez, I was not able to consult it while conducting the research which led to the publication of this study. Among the sources at my disposal, it is my view that despite its novelistic style—which distances it from the academic format—the book *In the Time of the Tyrants: Panama, 1968–1990* by Richard M. Koster and Guillermo Sánchez Borbón is by far the most authoritative source on the history of the period. The reader will thus understand my frequent references to Koster's and Sánchez's work.

I also consulted texts by apologists for the military regime, such as George Priestley, Renato Pereira, Juan Materno Vásquez, Michele Labrut, and Luis Puleio. As regards the books on the "crisis" years (1987–1989) and the US invasion of 1989, most of them are journalistic in nature. Margaret Scranton's *The Noriega Years: U.S.-Panamanian Relations, 1981–1990* stands out, however, within the "crisis/invasion" genre.

Finally, consulting primary sources proved invaluable. Thanks to the resources of Ohio University's Alden Library and to the assistance of family and friends, I was able to examine a wide range of official US and Panamanian government documents, as well as reports of international agencies and newspaper articles.

It would not be fair to end this preface without expressing my gratefulness to those who, in addition to my professors at Ohio University, helped make the publication of this study a reality: my wife Vivian and our children, Francisco and Cristina, my parents Carlos and Teresa, my uncle and former OAS official Francisco Céspedes, and historian Rodrigo Miró Grimaldo; journalists

Roberto Eisenmann, Guillermo Sánchez Borbón, and Rita Moreno de Valdés of *La Prensa*, Mario Lewis Morgan of *Epocas*, and Tatiana Padilla of *El Siglo*; Gillian Berchowitz and the staff at Ohio University Press; and my colleagues Alejandro M. Alonso, Pablo Pascual González, and Richard E. Clinton, Jr. To all of them, my gratitude is eternal.

Carlos Guevara Mann

Introduction

Militarism is the involvement of the military in the political life of the state. Depending on the circumstances, this involvement may take diverse forms: it may range from *pronunciamientos* and barracks uprisings to military coups d'état and outright dictatorship by the armed forces. The common denominator that defines all these manifestations as militarism, however, is that all are a reversal of the proper role of the military as an arm of the state in which the legitimate exercise of force is vested for the purpose of defending the state's integrity.[1] Whereas according to Western tradition the military is subordinated to the authorities of the state, in a situation of militarism the state is subordinated, in varying degrees, to the military.

This study aims at analyzing the influence of militarism in Panamanian political history and assessing its impact on Panamanian national development. The overall concept that informs the emergence of militarism in Panamanian history is that of *legitimacy,* or the absence of it, in the political process.

Legitimacy, as defined here, is the populace's generalized satisfaction with the political *status quo*. This definition transcends the usual meaning of the word, disseminated by US foreign policy (and accepted, without major objections, by Latin Americans throughout the region), which considers as legitimate a government chosen in more or less free elections. Neither should legitimacy be exclusively identified with a liberal democratic political system of the North Atlantic type. Although liberal democracy is, in our day and age, considered the regime most apt to generate political legitimacy, differences in cultures and tradition may, in fact, render such a system illegitimate. In the past, for example, this has frequently been the case in Latin America. On the other hand, an undemocratic, absolutist regime, such as the Spanish monarchy, may be perfectly legitimate.

Legitimacy is, therefore, the quality assigned to a political system by popular consensus. As such, it indicates the populace's agreement that the political system is acceptable and viable for the fulfillment of the objectives of the state; in consequence, it generates a sense of loyalty and respect for the political system. Legitimacy is thus indicated by the prolonged stability of the political system—in other words, by the absence of uncontrolled violence or violent change in the political process of a country.[2] It follows that illegitimacy obstructs the normal functioning of the state. Militarism is a consequence of a country's illegitimacy problem—a common one, it might be added, in the Iberic-American world.

The study of Panamanian, or, for that matter, Latin American, militarism requires that a distinction be made between *predatory* and *institutional* militarism. The term *predatory* was assigned by French political scientist Alain Rouquié to the type of militarism observable in Spanish America following independence from the metropolis in the early 1800s and prior to the so-called *professionalization* of the armed forces. The expression *predatory militarism* serves to describe a more primitive phenomenon in which armies at the service of local *caudillos* or parties became involved in politics and attempted to subordinate the state to their goals. A tradition of authoritarianism, coupled with an environment of illegitimacy and chaos, produced militarist responses to political problems. For in spite of the formally liberal democratic accouterments of the new states, force, in the Latin American setting, proved more effective than civil politics.

Predatory militarism precedes the consolidation of the state, since one of the distinguishing traits of statehood is a monopoly over collective force. Nineteenth-century Latin America saw the concentration of military power, not in formal, organized institutions, but in the hands of *caudillos* or *ad hoc* party armies. *Caudillos* and the leaders of these armies were usually civilians with little or no formal military instruction: the bureaucratic antithesis of modern day career officers.[3]

Considered in this thesis to be the antecedent to twentieth-century, or institutional, militarism, predatory militarism frequently manifested itself in civil war. Examples are provided in nineteenth-century Colombia—of which the present Republic of Panama formed a part —by, among others, the 1839–1841 War of the Supremes; the 1854 coup by José María Melo; the armed uprising which occurred between 1859 and 1862; the 1876 Conservative and 1885 Liberal insurrections; and the 1899–1902 Thousand Days' War. The rebel armies which thus became involved in politics lacked many of the characteristics associated in our time with the military, especially the monopoly of force for the defense of national integrity, which grants modern armies their institutional character.

Twentieth-century militarism, on the other hand, is mostly characterized by the subordination of the state to a national military institution in which the monopoly of force is vested. The rise of institutional armies is directly linked to the integration of Latin America into the international economy, a process which generally became evident in the second half of the nineteenth century and was consolidated by the early 1900s. The appearance of national militaries was one of the most significant responses of Latin American leaders to the problem of instability evidenced in part by predatory militarism (but not to the problem of legitimacy which *caused* predatory militarism). By strengthening the state's hold over the national territory and population, organisms entrusted with the monopoly of force were efficacious in maintaining a relatively higher degree of stability than the one previously regnant; a new order, in fact, more conducive to the role performed by each country in the international division of labor. The newly acquired stability, however, failed to last long in the face of continued political illegitimacy.

Given that Latin American political stabilization—as well as the sale of war *matériel*—was also in the interest of international capital, the advanced industrialized countries abetted the institutionalization of the Latin American armies. A salient example of this foreign support is the establishment of military missions, mainly of German, French, and US origin, which have undertaken the professionalization of the Latin American armed forces since the late nineteenth century. Professionalization transformed the informal nineteenth-century armed bands into self-regulated, independent bureaucracies. But in the absence of political legitimacy, professionalizing the army and granting it *de facto* or *de jure* autonomy provided the military with the means to intervene, free from civilian direction, in national politics.[4] After the military institutions became professionalized, they assumed power in most Latin American countries. While they succeeded in imposing some degree of stability, they did not, however, resolve the issue of legitimacy. Institutional military dictatorships have in fact proven capable only of perpetuating, and frequently aggravating, their countries' legitimacy crises.

By underlining the continuity of the militarist consequences of illegitimacy, this study intends to demonstrate that Panamanian militarism is not an isolated phenomenon of the late twentieth century. Incidents of predatory militarism that occurred after the breakdown of colonial legitimacy following the collapse of Spanish monarchical absolutism give evidence in this regard. After the establishment of the Republic of Panama in 1903, and to a large extent because of the initial US opposition to a domestic army, institutional militarism was a latecomer to the scene: it was not until the 1940s that a militarized constabulary began to have a say in the conduct of public affairs. Belatedness, however, did not preclude the subjection of the country to direct military rule from 1968 to 1989. As of today, despite the fact that the Panamanian Defense Forces were abolished after the US invasion of December 1989, and although the state's security apparatus has since been placed under civilian direction, lack of legitimacy—the characteristic which informs military involvement in politics —still persists. Militarism, therefore, may well reappear if the Panamanian polity fails to achieve legitimacy.

The evolution of Panamanian militarism is conditioned by two determinants: an internal factor of causation shaped by the domestic, Iberic-American experience, and an external one conditioned by US hegemony. The cultural-historical factor includes those characteristics of the Panamanian political tradition inherited from previous centuries: an authoritarian albeit paternalist—*"pan o palo,"* or "bread or the club"—approach to government; limited social mobility predetermined by birth and wealth; personalism or *caudillismo,* the charismatic attachment to a political figure, coupled with the *caudillo's* subordination of the common interest to personal goals; and the concept of the state as loot, which produced a permissive attitude toward official graft. Defining hegemony as "the establishment by a dominant power of limits for the behavior of other actors beyond which direct control by force will be invoked,"[5] US interest, the second determinant of Panamanian historical evolution, is described as the political demands of the Northern Colossus in economic and security matters. Depending on Washington's policy, US hegemony has played a decisive role in either enhancing or diminishing Panamanian militarism.

This study contains three major subdivisions. Part I examines the historical determinants more closely: while chapter 1 looks at the socio-political heritage and the way in which it generated illegitimacy, chapter 2 provides an overview of North American policy toward the Isthmian military in the context of US hegemony over Panama. For it was in pursuit of hegemony that Washington initially opposed political involvement by the Panamanian military, a policy that later gave way to toleration of and support for domestic militarism.

Part II deals with the antecedents of Panamanian institutional militarism. The incidents of predatory militarism occurring during the period of union with Colombia are analyzed in chapter 3. The following chapter surveys the militarization of the National Police, the institution which held the domestic monopoly of force for fifty years after the establishment of the Republic of Panama in 1903.

Part III focuses on institutional militarism *per se* in the light of local events and the international context of escalating bi-polar tensions. Chapter 5 peruses the evolution and political involvement, from 1953 to 1968, of a National Guard technically subordinated to the state. Chapter 6 examines the 1968 coup which led the National Guard to power, and the rise of Omar Torrijos, the first military dictator. The populist, inclusionist measures of Torrijos and his dictatorship's relationship to the United States are the subject of chapter 7. Chapter 8 examines Torrijos' repressive measures and the legacy of the military regime's first phase. The subsequent chapter analyzes the strengthening and eventual demise of the military regime during its second phase under Manuel Noriega. Lastly, an epilogue is devoted to Panamanian security policy and the possibilities for a future militarization of national politics in the present context of civilian rule and continued US hegemony.

The conclusion reiterates the proposal that militarism has appeared on the political scene precisely because the Panamanian political system has not yet achieved legitimacy. Paradoxically, however, due to its natural antagonism to the achievement of popular consensus, Panamanian militarism has served to perpetuate political illegitimacy. Aside from domestic determinants, local militarism has also been encouraged and to some extent shaped by the United States as a consequence of that country's hegemony in the area. All in all, the consequences of militarism have been basically negative for Panama's political and socioeconomic development.

Notes

1. Alain Rouquié, *The Military and the State in Latin America*, trans. Paul Sigmund (Berkeley: University of California Press, 1987), p. 73.

2. Lars Schoultz, *National Security and United States Policy Toward Latin America* (Princeton: Princeton University Press, 1987), p. 37 (note 7).

3. Rouquié, *The Military and the State*, chap. 2.

4. Ibid., chaps. 2 and 3.

5. Kenneth M. Coleman, "The Political Mythology of the Monroe Doctrine: Reflections on the Social Psychology of Hegemony," in *Latin America, the United States, and the Inter American System*, ed. John D. Martz and Lars Schoultz (Boulder: Westview Press, 1980), p. 95.

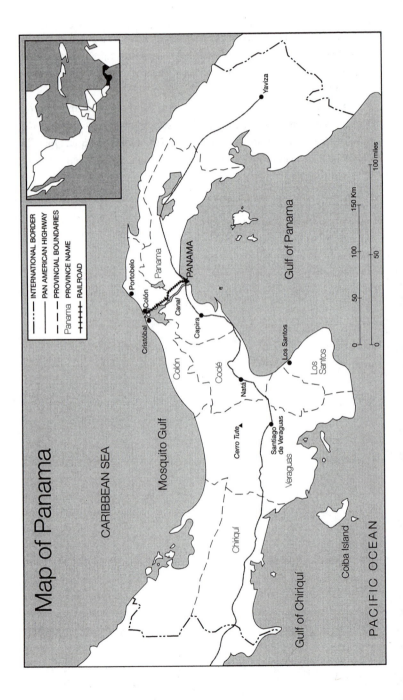

Map of Panama

CARIBBEAN SEA

Mosquito Gulf

Portobelo

Colón

Cristóbal

Canal

Panama

PANAMA

Capira

Gulf of Panama

Colón

Coclé

Natá

Los Santos

Los Santos

Cerro Tute ▲

Santiago de Veraguas

Veraguas

Chiriquí

Gulf of Chiriquí

Coiba Island

PACIFIC OCEAN

Yaviza

INTERNATIONAL BORDER
PAN AMERICAN HIGHWAY
PROVINCIAL BOUNDARIES
Panama   PROVINCE NAME
RAILROAD

0   50   100   150 Km
0   50   100 miles

Part I

The Determinants

Chapter 1

The Colonial Heritage, 1500–1821

IT WOULD BE ambitious to trace the origins of the twentieth-century Isthmian military to the establishment of locally-staffed Spanish colonial armies, as a Panamanian Defense Forces publication implied in 1987.[1] In actuality, it was not until 1953 that a professional, institutionalized military force was formally created. Examining Panama's colonial experience is, however, useful in our study of Panamanian militarism, for it was Spanish colonialism that, to a large extent, shaped domestic society and imprinted upon it many characteristics that are helpful in understanding the phenomenon of twentieth-century militarism.

Among these traits, the most salient are an authoritarian political system, the use of force to resolve political deadlocks, the Spanish juridical privileges which placed the local military above the reach of ordinary law, the role of the army as one of the few avenues for the advancement of ambitious individuals from the masses, and the participation of government employees, including the military, in graft. Above all, a careful reading of Panama's colonial history is important for understanding the origins of the illegitimacy crisis that has obstructed national development since the early nineteenth century and gave rise to institutional militarism in the second half of the twentieth century.

THE EARLY MODERN (*ca.* 1500 A.D.) Iberian concept of the state was distinguished by an effort to preserve harmony within a post-feudal order, in which resources were controlled by a small dominant class that directed the activities of a large majority. For this purpose, the sovereignty of the state was vested in an absolute monarch whose power was deemed to derive directly from God, to stabilize and pre-serve the social order and guarantee the welfare of its components. Divine right, accepted by an overwhelming majority of society, legit-imized the Spanish polity. This centralized, absolutist system origi-nated with the accession of Queen Isabella the Catholic to the throne of Castile in 1474 and lasted until the death of Ferdinand VII in 1833.[2]

Several factors contributed to popular acceptance of this form of authoritarianism, the most substantial being the support lent it by the Catholic Church and a general isolation from liberal ideologies, coupled with the absence of an intellectual revolution comparable to the Northern European Enlightenment. Moreover, due to the corpo-rate-absolutist nature of the state, political dissent was seen as a men-ace to the system, to be answered with legitimate force. Spanish absolutism had in place a loyal security apparatus to keep threats to the system in check.

Sixteenth-century conquest transplanted the Iberic tradition, of which the military is a pillar, to the New World. Here it was implant-ed through the processes of permanent settlement and colonization by *Peninsulares*. The use of military power for purposes of internal stabilization has thus characterized Latin America since the Iberian conquest. This regional characteristic stands in sharp contrast to the countries of the North Atlantic Basin, whose modern history has seen a relegation of the military to essentially defensive tasks under civilian direction, and a rise in popular participation, stemming from notions of equality and individual liberty, in governmental decision-making processes.

The Iberian concept of the state became a part of Panama's political culture rather late compared to other Latin American countries. Due to the transit role the isthmus played since the early colonial period, a lasting, rooted creole class did not emerge until the eighteenth and early nineteenth centuries, when legal trade almost came to a standstill. The few descendants of Spaniards who remained during this period of economic depression either took to the land or continued to engage in limited commercial activities, licit or illicit. In the words of two Panamanian historians,

> while Panama sank into economic asphyxia the commercial class, agglutinated in the *cabildo,* fought to prevent the wasting away of the isthmus. The *cabildo's* incessant petitions to the metropolis for the establishment of a regime of free trade, however, were almost always ignored. But this situation developed among the creoles of Panama City and Portobelo a spirit of social, political, economic, and cultural cohesion, which in turn helped them to survive in the midst of penury, mainly because of their ability to infiltrate the civil and military ranks of the colonial administration, which they astutely combined with contraband.[3]

Concurrently in the eighteenth century, growing security threats throughout its American realms posed by increasingly frequent creole and Indian rebellions, and hostile activities by pirates and contrabandists, led the crown to strengthen colonial defenses through military reform. These changes underpinned the importance of regular army units and colonial militias, both now largely staffed by the king's American subjects. Panama was given a larger geostrategic role within the empire, which translated into an increment in Spain's military presence on the isthmus, especially after the issuance of royal decrees in 1773 ordering the reorganization of local army units.[4]

It is at this time that, for Panamanian sociologist Omar Jaén Suárez, a sense of nationality first emerged on the isthmus. Jaén links the emerging nationalism to the process of permanent settlement by descendants of *Peninsulares,* of which the permanent settlement of Spanish military officers was an important constituent. Both the establishment of military lineages and the creation of urban and rural militias of creoles and *pardos* contributed significantly to the "trickle down" of the Iberic political tradition.[5] Their permanent settlement on the isthmus abetted the metropolis' authoritarianism and validated the use of force for the resolution of political conflicts, for as US historian Allan Kuethe has noted, the colonial militias were reorganized "not only to defend the empire from foreign aggression but to maintain order and to support the government as well; in the long run, the latter proved the more compelling objective."[6] Actually, one of the factors that prevented an earlier Panamanian declaration of independence from Spain was precisely, in the first-hand opinion of nineteenth-century patrician Mariano Arosemena, the presence on the isthmus of a substantial military force loyal to the crown.[7]

As elsewhere in the Spanish empire, in Panama the colonial army also served as an avenue for lower-caste social advancement and as a source of privilege for its members. Open not only to creoles but to free individuals of the *castas* (who found few other ways of acquiring status), the racially-integrated armed forces "quickly displayed signs of becoming an elite political and social institution."[8] Quintessential indicators of military elitism were the corporate privileges that the crown bestowed upon its soldiers, including "immunities from certain municipal taxes, levies, and responsibilities,"[9] especially the *fuero de guerra militar,* "a judicial prerogative that conveyed the right to present causes before military tribunals rather than before royal, or ordinary, tribunals."[10] This legal privilege "conveyed prestige and distinction, and like other fueros it set the holder above and apart from the remainder of society in varying degrees."[11] The fact that large numbers of creoles and *castas,* as well as their families, were included in the *fuero* was a significant departure from previous colonial policy and soon pitted military officers against civilian authorities:

6

In both Panama and the district of Nata, extensive feuding ... erupted in 1774 between the militia and the cabildos. As a result the deputy governor of Panama, Joaquin Cabrejo, a civilian, petitioned Santa Fe [Santa Fe de Bogotá, seat of the viceregal court] on behalf of ordinary justice, asking for a clarification of the cases of desafuero [infraction of the law by the military], and particularly for a firm statement emphasizing the occurrence of desafuero in instances of abuse of royal justice. As at Cartagena, the cabildo complained of recurrent humiliations.... However, although clarifying the items of desafuero, the viceregency vacillated.[12]

Another aspect of the Iberic tradition that effectively "trickled down" during Spanish colonialism was a generalized attitude of permissiveness toward official corruption. Because of Madrid's ineffective colonial policies, civil servants and military personnel entrusted with colonial administration on the isthmus actively engaged in graft and contraband. Difficult to quantify and record due to their illegal nature, these activities soon came to be regarded as perquisites complementing government salaries. An example occurred during the Portobelo fair of 1722, when British contraband merchants bribed the governor, the royal prosecutor, and other colonial officials of the city, including the commander of the Spanish fleet entrusted by the crown with the transport of the goods that were to be legally exchanged at the fair. Such palm-greasing permitted the contrabandists to freely participate in the event, and contributed to its failure. Furthermore, during the 1739–1748 War of Jenkin's Ear, an indignant (and presumably scrupulous) royal officer reported to the crown the effrontery of the contrabandists, who openly introduced their wares via the gates of Panama City—secured by the local garrison, it might be added—in broad daylight *("así de día como de noche")*.[13]

In spite of its reformist zeal, the Bourbon military reorganization failed to achieve the objective of protecting the integrity of the Spanish empire. The slow invasion of North Atlantic liberal ideas proved a foe too strong to counter with divine-right theories and, in case these failed, brute force. The crown's legitimacy rapidly dwindled after Napoleon Bonaparte's invasion of the Iberian peninsula in 1808, and the ensuing abdications of Charles IV and Ferdinand VII signaled the end of the Spanish empire in the Indies. It also initiated a long period, which could well be said to extend into the twentieth century, of political instability originating from a contradiction between liberalism and conservatism, in a political context lacking a general sentiment of loyalty toward the rule of law, the institution which theoretically replaced the monarchy. A Spanish analyst's assessment of the situation prevalent in Spain after 1808 may be applied to all of Spanish America, Panama included, to demonstrate the shared experiences transoceanic societies underwent as a consequence of the demise of traditional, monarchical legitimacy:

> Nineteenth-century Spanish history translated into a constant struggle between an illustrated, aggressive liberalism with little respect for the populace, and a majoritarian, yet intransigent, traditionalism. Dogmatic and authoritarian, both assayed to impose their beliefs with an unnecessary and, in many cases, unjustifiable violence.[14]

The collapse of monarchical absolutist legitimacy produced in Latin America the emergence of personalist politics and predatory militarism, phenomena which were frequently intertwined. While personalism represented an attempt by local *caudillos* to assume the king's legitimacy, predatory militarism surfaced as the instrument of personalist leaders or political parties for conquering the state. The fact that the new polities, especially in the former colonies of South America, were the product of armed struggle, furthered predatory militarism in the area.[15]

Albeit belatedly and in its own fashion, Panama followed the lead of its Latin American sister societies. In late 1821, several factors seemed to indicate the convenience of severing Panama's links to Spain. Following a declaration of independence in the interior village of Los Santos, on 28 November the directing class of the capital pronounced the isthmus independent of Spain and chose to join Bolívar's Gran República de Colombia, which eventually was to bring together the present-day states of Colombia, Ecuador, Panama, and Venezuela. The fact that the peaceful declaration of independence was made possible by the distribution of bribes among the soldiers of Panama City's garrison, underscores the fact that corruption was a pervasive characteristic of the Iberian heritage.[15]

THE CRUCIAL PERIOD between the 1750s and the 1820s saw the rooting in Panama of opposing elements that would later produce a breakdown of legitimacy and foment the emergence of militarism as a consequence. On the one hand, an authoritarian political tradition "trickled down," its functioning dependent exclusively on the divine-right legitimacy rendered the crown by its subjects. On the other, the influx of new liberal ideologies that were in contradiction to the Iberic-American political philosophy won enthusiastic support from many of the directing class. Even if after independence from Spain the Panamanian colonial militias failed to survive into the succeeding era of republicanism, such features as authoritarianism, recourse to force, interest-group privilege and status, official corruption, and *caudillismo,* proved resilient and contributed to shaping, in times to come, the corporate self-image of the Panamanian military. Yet another factor—a foreign one, however, over which Isthmians had little control—would begin to exert influence on Panamanian life in the 1850s. It is this factor—US hegemony, and its conditioning of Isthmian militarism—to which we now turn.

Notes

1. Fuerzas de Defensa de Panamá, *Fuerzas de Defensa: Fuerzas Armadas de Panamá* (Santiago de Chile: Editorial Sipimex, 1987), p. 13. This publication, in fact, claims for the Defense Forces direct descent from the warring

bands of the Cueva Indian nation which inhabited the isthmus in pre-Columbian times.

2. See especially Howard Wiarda's works *Corporatism and National Development in Latin America* (Boulder: Westview Press, 1981), and "Toward a Framework for the Study of Political Change in the Iberic Latin Tradition: The Corporative Model," *World Politics* (January 1973): 206–35. Also contributive are Augusto Varas, *Militarization and the International Arms Race in Latin America* (Boulder: Westview Press, 1985), pp. 1–14; and Claudio Véliz, *The Centralist Tradition of Latin America* (Princeton: Princeton University Press, 1980), Chap. 1.

3. Celestino Andrés Araúz and Patricia Pizzurno, *El Panamá hispano (1501–1821)* (Panama: Diario La Prensa, 1991), p. 252.

4. Omar Jaén Suárez, "El siglo XVIII y las permanencias estructurales," in "Visión de la nacionalidad panameña," a supplement to *La Prensa*, 6 August 1991. Allan J. Kuethe, *Military Reform and Society in New Granada, 1773–1808* (Gainesville: The University Presses of Florida, 1978), p.13.

Jaén provides a long list of family names, many of which are shared today by members of Panama's upper class, which he indicates constituted "important military lineages": Aldrete, Alvarez, Amandarro, Barranco, Barrera, Berguido, Bernal, Calvo Bustillos, Castro, Chiari, Díaz de Vivar, Estrada, Fábrega, Fernández, Flores, García de Paredes, Gómez Grimaldo, Govea, Goytía, Herrera, Jiménez, Linares, Miró, Martínez de Tapia, Mata, Meyner, Obaldía, Palazuelos, Ponce de León, Pujol, Remón, Rubini, Vallarino, Velarde, Vieto. Jaén, "El siglo XVIII", pp. 13–14.

Pursuant to the military reforms decreed by Charles III on 11 January and 12 February 1773, in 1806 Panama's security apparatus consisted of regular army units and the colonial militia, both substantially manned by locals. The regular army included a 679-man infantry Battalion of Panama, the 82-man light infantry of Chimán, the 29-man infantry detachment of Chagres, the 109-man infantry company of *pardos* of South Darién, and a 150-man Royal Artillery Corps company of Panama. The colonial militia included an 800-man infantry Regiment of Panama and Natá, an 800-man infantry battalion of *pardos* of Panama and Natá, a 400-man corps of light infantry of Portobelo and the margins of the Chagres River, a 100-man artillery company of *pardos* of Panama, and a 70-man artillery company of *pardos* of Portobelo. The total number of military thus added up to 3,219. Kuethe, *Military Reform*, pp. 217–18.

5. Jaén, "El siglo XVIII", pp. 13–14.

6. Kuethe, *Military Reform*, p. 41.

7. Mariano Arosemena, *Apuntamientos históricos (1801–1840)*, ed. Ernesto J. Castillero R. (Panama: Ministerio de Educación, 1949), pp. 70–71.

8. Kuethe, *Military Reform*, p. 25.

9. Ibid.

10. Ibid., p. 26

11. Ibid.

12. Ibid., p. 37.

13. Araúz and Pizzurno, *El Panamá hispano*, pp. 212, 217.

14. Vicente Cantarino, *Civilización y cultura de España*, 2d ed., (New York: Macmillan Publishing Company, 1988), p. 267.

15. Varas, *Militarization and the Arms Race*, pp. 5-8.

16. See Mariano Arosemena, *Apuntamientos históricos*; Isidro Beluche, *Independencia y secesión de Panamá* (Panama: By the Author, 1965); Alex Pérez Venero, *Before the Five Frontiers: Panama From 1821–1903* (New York: AMS Press, 1978), pp. 1–6.

Chapter 2

The Rise of the Colossus

THE INFLUENCE OF the United States on Panama's national development emanates specifically from the Isthmian republic's geographic location, and must be understood within the context of North American hegemony in the Western Hemisphere. US hegemony has influenced the development of Panamanian militarism by demanding that stability be maintained in Panama and that Panamanian leaders be responsive, at all times, to US interests. While Washington policy makers' specific interests, as well as their perceptions of the proper ways in which stability and responsiveness should be assured, have varied throughout the 150-year history of US-Panamanian relations, these policy objectives *per se,* as well as the fact of US hegemony, have been constant. Thus, depending on specific US policy, the United States has either discouraged or stimulated Panamanian militarism.[1]

THE NORTHERN COLOSSUS has exerted political leverage in Panama since the mid-nineteenth century. The motives which prompted the rise of US hegemony are many and complex. They are all, however, related to the ascent of the United States to the status of a modern great power. With a liberal political and economic development model firmly in place prior to independence, the United States followed, from its inception onward, a policy of outward expansion attributable to the inherently expansive nature of capitalism. This policy, which first assumed territorial, and later economic, trappings, has long been coupled with a foreign agenda based on containing powers which might pose a threat to the North American development model.

Both expansion and containment have been rationalized by a self-righteous and ethnocentric "missionary impulse" which developed in colonial New England. Later, in the nineteenth century, Social Darwinism contributed new rationalizations for North American expansionism, as did a yearning for imperial status to match the country's economic growth. Given that the North American paradigm was continuously successful, it was believed to be the correct one—one which, if applied to the undeveloped regions of the world, was certain to succeed there also. The United States—the New Jerusalem—had the duty of spreading its gospel of liberal, capitalist development beyond national boundaries.[2]

Economic expansion, ideology, and security, together with the proximity and vulnerability of weak southern neighbors, led to the establishment of US hegemony. Initially concentrated in the Caribbean Basin, Yankee leverage later extended into South America, with the globalization of US interests after the Second World War.

Two basic ideas propelled the establishment of US hegemony. The first focused on expanding North American trade and investment opportunities; the second on preventing hostile powers from acquiring beachheads from which they could threaten US territory or interests. This seemed a ready possibility due to the instability and weakness of the Caribbean Basin states, which could, it was thought, be easily subverted by foreign powers. The case for US hegemony over Panama was strengthened by the isthmus' strategic geographical location, ideal for the construction of a passage between the Atlantic and the Pacific. Such a waterway would significantly boost US trade and reinforce US defense capabilities.

Within this framework, three phases stand out in the history of US hegemony over Panama. The first, between 1846 and 1903, was characterized by the extension of North American hegemony to the isthmus, to the exclusion of Great Britain. This era stands out for US opposition, through direct military interventionism, to domestic predatory militarism, with a view to preserving stability. A stable environment was deemed essential for the protection of specific US interests, namely the Panama Railroad and the isthmus' potential as a canal route.

A second stage, between 1903 and 1936, witnessed the consolidation of Washington's hegemony over Panama. With the purpose of producing a lasting climate of stability, this period was distinguished by US efforts to reform and professionalize the Panamanian security force, although direct military intervention for stabilizing purposes was not rejected. Stability was now sought to preserve the security of the canal, the primary US interest in Panama.

Finally, during the third phase, which extends from 1936 to the present, the United States has been preoccupied mostly with defending US hegemony in Panama from foreign (especially Soviet) encroachment. Instability, still believed conducive to the establishment of foreign beachheads, was also avoided with a view to preserving the security of US military bases, now Washington's main interest on the isthmus. Concerned with the maintenance of stability, the United States now rejected direct military intervention except under the most extreme circumstances. Washington replaced intervention with a close bilateral relationship with the Isthmian military, and enhanced the latter's repressive capabilities with a view to guaranteeing Panama's stability and internal security.

The Extension of Hegemony, 1846-1903

This stage in US relations with Panama found a source of inspiration in Social Darwinism and the concept of Manifest Destiny, "which holds that U.S. expansion into Latin America is unavoidable since the natural law of social evolution inexorably leads higher civilizations (such as the United States) to rule primitive areas (such as Latin America)."[3] More tangible predecessors are the 1811 No-Transfer Resolution, the 1823 Monroe Doctrine, and the 1845 Polk Corollary thereto.

A resolution of the US Congress unilaterally prohibiting the transfer of American territory from one European colonial power to another, the 1811 document is considered a precursor to the Monroe Doctrine. President James Monroe's message to the Congress in 1823 included an equally unilateral prohibition to European recolonization of any territory in the Western Hemisphere. Two decades later, in another message to the Congress, President James Polk broadened the prohibition "by stating that henceforth Latin nations could not *voluntarily* accept European dominion."[4] The Polk Corollary had a certain significance in the case of Panama, where some years earlier a secessionist party had proposed the creation of a Hanseatic Republic under the joint protection of Britain and the United States.[5]

US interest in the Isthmus of Panama intensified in the 1840s. The importance of securing an interoceanic route increased dramatically after the US acquisition of California in 1848 and the discovery of gold shortly thereafter, for no safe and expeditious overland route to the Western territories yet existed. The Treaty of Peace, Amity, Commerce and Navigation, more commonly known as the Bidlack-Mallarino Treaty, signed in 1846 between Colombia and the United States and approved two years later by the US Senate, marks the beginning of the special US-Panamanian relationship.

In exchange for nondiscriminatory commercial treatment by

Colombia, the United States pledged to guarantee the neutrality of the Isthmus of Panama "with the view that the free transit from one to the other sea, may not be interrupted or embarrassed in any future time" as well as to "ensure the rights of sovereignty and property which New Granada [Colombia] has and possesses over the said territory."[6] In actuality, the treaty created a de facto US protectorate with concomitant security commitments in Panama, thus inaugurating Washington's hegemony. Both the neutrality provision and the maintenance of Colombian sovereignty were understood as preserving stability on the isthmus, and the means to maintain it included the frequent use of direct US military force to restrain local outbreaks of predatory militarism.[7]

During the second half of the nineteenth century and culminating with Panama's separation from Colombia in 1903, the isthmus was brought more and more under Yankee tutelage, with increased interest in the northern republic for US construction and control of an interoceanic canal, to the exclusion of other actors. By the Clayton-Bulwer Treaty of 1850 the United States and Britain agreed to provide joint protection to a future canal and guarantee its neutrality, and to renounce exclusive domination of the waterway by either country. Thus did Washington diplomatically avoid unilateral action by the British in Panama, a development the US was unable to prevent militarily at the time. Also in 1850, a group of New York capitalists began the construction of the trans-Isthmian Panama Railroad, completed in 1855. A tangible investment by a US corporation was now in place; it would be the duty of the marines to protect it.

As a result of the remarkable expansion of US economic power which followed the Civil War, the North American urge for building an interoceanic canal reached new heights in the 1890s. A waterway through the Central American isthmus would benefit both the US merchant marine and navy and set the ground for their expansion by enhancing US commercial and security possibilities in Latin America and the Far East. Control of a canal would strengthen US security: through the establishment of naval bases to protect the route, the US defensive perimeter would be substantially extended to the south. And furthermore, a canal would permit swift movements of the US fleet, as needed in case of emergency, from one coast to the other. Because of the French failure in Panama, however, it was evident that the building of a canal was an enterprise of such magnitude that it required governmental initiative.[8]

Reinforced by the Olney Declaration of 1895, by which the US secretary of state warned that the advantages of US superiority were "imperiled if the principle be admitted that European powers may convert American states into colonies or provinces of their own,"[9] as well as by the US military victory over Spain in 1898, the Roosevelt Administration finally cleared the scene of outside interference. In 1901 the Hay-Pauncefote Treaty between the United States and Britain stipulated that an interoceanic canal could be built, administered, and fortified by the United States to the exclusion of any other foreign power. When a 1902 report of the Isthmian Canal Commission (created by the US Congress to study the feasibility of building a canal) recommended the Panama route, the US Congress passed the Spooner Act, which authorized the US president to acquire the French canal rights and to negotiate a canal treaty with Colombia, to whose nominal sovereignty Panama was still subject.[10]

But Panamanian instability was a serious obstacle to Washington's plans. The preceding half century had seen numerous uprisings, many of which appeared to threaten US interests. By one count, there were thirteen US military interventions in Panama between 1846 and 1902, the most significant perhaps being those that occurred during the 1885 and 1899–1902 civil wars.[11] The need to stabilize the isthmus was therefore urgent for the United States, which saw the root of the evil of instability in the domestic use of military power for political purposes. After the formalization of US hegemony, Washington would experiment with means other than the traditional landing of marines in an effort to produce lasting stability.

LIBRARY
THE UNIVERSITY OF TEXAS
AT BROWNSVILLE
Brownsville, TX 78520-4991

The Consolidation of Hegemony, 1903–1936

A second stage in US-Panamanian relations began in 1903, with Panama's independence from Colombia, and lasted until the implementation of the Good Neighbor Policy in the 1930s. Still another phase of North American expansion, it saw the formalization of US leverage in Panama. The period was furthermore marked by a concern for stabilizing the new Isthmian republic through US-led reform and—in case this policy did not work—direct military intervention.

When the Colombian Senate's rejection of the proposed canal treaty stood in the way of President Theodore Roosevelt's unbending determination to build a canal under US direction and control, Washington resorted to supporting a Panamanian separatist conspiracy, which culminated in independence on 3 November 1903. The Isthmian Canal Convention or Hay-Bunau-Varilla Treaty, which allowed for the realization of Roosevelt's plans, was signed by the Republic of Panama and the United States the following month.

As evidence of its importance to the Department of State, the issue of stability in the transit area figured prominently in the treaty. The convention included prerogatives granting the United States the right to intervene to reestablish order in Panama City as well as in Colón. The treaty also committed the United States to guaranteeing and maintaining the independence of the Isthmian republic. Additionally, Panama's deputies to the February 1904 Constituent Convention inserted Article 136, modeled on the Cuban Platt Amendment, into the republic's constitution, in order to legalize US intervention with the purpose of maintaining "public peace and constitutional order" throughout the isthmus.[12]

Thus authorized, and further inspired by the 1904 Roosevelt Corollary to the Monroe Doctrine (which stated that "chronic wrongdoing" by subordinate Caribbean nations would be subject to US "police power"[13]), the United States launched a policy aimed at eliminating predatory militarism in Panama. With strong US support, the new Panamanian government abolished its restless (but otherwise innocuous) army in November of 1904. Thereafter, the United States endeavored to avoid political violence through reform, in an approach similar to that pursued in Cuba, the Dominican Republic, Nicaragua, and Haiti during the period. Believing that US models were the key to safeguarding expanded US interests represented primarily by the canal, Washington's proconsuls strove to bring about at least a semblance of US-style liberal democracy in Panama. Encouraging honest electoral processes, fiscal efficiency, and police professionalization were the preferred means. But when reform failed to assure the stability desired by the United States, its policy makers opted for more forceful tactics, such as occupation by US troops.[14]

By imposing the rule of law and placing the monopoly of force under the strict surveillance of a civilian constitutional government, US policymakers hoped to assure stability and responsiveness. The policy, however, represented imposition from outside; furthermore, it did not take into account the lack of legitimacy of Panama's political system. In consequence, US-guided reformism was not successful in permanently stabilizing the Panamanian polity.[15]

The Defense of Hegemony, 1936–present

A third stage in the US-Panamanian relationship, focusing on the protection of acquired US hegemony, is usually said to have been initiated with President Franklin D. Roosevelt's Good Neighbor Policy. Conceived during the early 1930s to contribute to the recuperation of the North American economy, the policy was subsequently directed toward containing threats from German fascism and—after World War II—Soviet communism.[16] Washington maintained an interest in preserving stability, but rejected US military intervention as a means to achieve it except under the most extreme circumstances. "Out of the experience in Nicaragua," writes Walter LaFeber, "came the conclusion that local police (such as Somoza's Guard) could relieve the marines of maintaining order."[17] Washington strove to cultivate more affable relations with the Panamanian government and, beginning in the 1940s, with a National Police steadily exercising its lawful monopoly over force and submerged in the process of professionalizing into a National Guard.

The origins of the Good Neighbor Policy, however, are to be found in the Coolidge (1923–29) and Hoover (1929–33) administrations. In the 1920s and early 1930s the United States concluded that an alternative to military interventionism, which had become overwhelmingly unpopular both at home and abroad, had to be found. Furthermore, explains LaFeber, military interventionism "never corrected the fundamental problems." For these reasons, Washington "decided that the system could run better on its own without those intermittent, costly military adjustments."[18] With President Roosevelt's desire for increased trade with Latin America added to the preceding policy reformulations, the United States formally committed to nonintervention in the affairs of other Western Hemisphere states, and negotiated a new canal treaty with Panama.

The Alfaro-Hull Treaty, signed in 1936 but not approved by the US Senate until 1939, abrogated the clauses of the Isthmian Canal Convention regarding the US guarantees of protection and maintenance of order. It also evidenced an increasing US interest in the military bases versus the canal itself. These bases, in effect, soon came to represent the primary North American interest in Panama, and would continue to do so into the 1990s.[19]

The US emphases on security and partnership, within a context of hegemony, intensified during World War II and the Cold War. To forestall the threat of Nazi encroachments in Latin America, in 1938 the Roosevelt Administration devised the policy of hemispheric solidarity. Later complemented with lend-lease aid to some of the countries of the region, hemispheric solidarity inaugurated an era of

US–Latin American military cooperation. The Inter-American Defense Board, which brought together representatives from each of the Western Hemisphere countries, was established in 1942 to coordinate the defense of the continent and to standardize military equipment, training, and organization along US lines. In the same year, a bilateral agreement between Panama and Washington permitted the establishment of numerous US defense sites throughout the isthmus; still another 1942 accord provided for the detail of a US military officer as adviser to the Panamanian foreign office. Though it had little practical effect at the moment, this latter agreement served in 1962 as the basis for the establishment of a US military mission on the isthmus.[20]

Following the beginning of the Cold War, the United States concentrated on maintaining an open channel with the Latin American armies in order to enlist their support in the global struggle against Soviet communism. To defend the newly acquired US global preponderance in the face of the Soviet threat, the National Security Act of 1947 created the National Security Council (NSC) and the Central Intelligence Agency (CIA). Both institutions were destined to play fundamental roles in the protection of US interests. Also in 1947, the United States and the Latin American republics signed the Inter-American Reciprocal Assistance Treaty, also known as Rio Treaty, which provided for the peaceful settlement of disputes among signatories, as well as for collective self-defense in the event any of its parties suffered external attack. The following year, the Ninth International Conference of American States, held in Bogotá, Colombia, established the Organization of American States, whose charter encompassed the defensive principles set forth in the 1947 Rio Treaty.

With the purpose of training Latin American military personnel and generating "inter-American military fraternity,"[21] in 1949 the Pentagon established the Army Caribbean School, predecessor of the School of the Americas, in the Panama Canal Zone. The Mutual

Defense Assistance Act of 1949, which inaugurated the Military Assistance Program (MAP) for the provision of military aid to Third World countries throughout the globe, significantly expanded the scope of US containment objectives.[22]

Pursuant to these developments, the United States initiated a policy of providing the Latin American republics with military scholarships, army training missions, and grants and credits for the purchase of weaponry. As an analyst of the early Cold War has emphasized,

> the main impetus for the startling growth of military aid during the late 1940s was the belief that it would provide critical political and psychological reassurance to friendly nations. Whatever the ultimate military objectives of these programs, their most important and immediate goals were raising foreign morale, solidifying the will to resist Communist expansion, and demonstrating American resolve and reliability.[23]

Preoccupied with the evolution of nationalism in Panama, which seemed to create potential opportunities for Soviet communism to gain inroads and thus threaten US control of the military bases and the canal, the United States signed a new treaty in 1955, in which Panama achieved mostly economic rectifications, while the Pentagon retained the right to operate the military bases. But even as a new canal agreement failed to appease local nationalists, the triumph of Fidel Castro in 1959 added fuel to the fire. When a small group of Cuban-inspired insurgents attempted to launch a Panamanian revolution in 1959, Washington was quick to receive the signal: despite the large US military presence on the isthmus, Panama was not immune to contagion from the Cuban Revolution.

In the light of these new regional and local developments, the Kennedy Administration launched a broad program of capitalist economic development and internal security aimed at reducing the threat of Marxist revolution throughout the hemisphere. On the one hand, economic goals were to be achieved through the Alliance for Progress; on the other, US military missions were to train Latin

American soldiers for internal security, as opposed to a previous emphasis on hemispheric defense. Through the assistance programs the Pentagon began diffusing counterinsurgency theory and setting up civic action projects with the purpose of undermining communist insurgency. Above all, US policy makers sought to preserve and increase Yankee leverage with the Latin American armies, whose political preponderance Washington recognized. As stated by a deputy assistant secretary of defense in 1964,

> When the chips get down and you see who is supporting a U.S. position, whether it be in the U.N. or in some dispute that is going on in the country, or whether it be a problem of a new government and its attitude toward the United States; we can see—I think I can report confidently—that those who have been trained here have a greater friendliness for us.[24]

Thus did the United States, in 1961, inaugurate a policy of direct support for and assistance to the Panamanian National Guard. The policy focused on increasing the reliability of the guard in the protection of US assets, and was deemed of exceptional importance after a particularly bloody outbreak of anti-US violence in January 1964. In this regard, the US consulate in Panama reported to the Department of State in March of 1964 that "MAP does help influence local military (Guardia Nacional) be pro-US and pro-West."[25]

After these riots the United States finally took note of the necessity to overhaul its relationship with Panama through a new canal treaty. Its close association with the domestic military was intended as yet another guarantee that US interests in the country would remain secure. In this spirit, Washington continued its support for the Panamanian military even after the National Guard deposed the constitutional regime and assumed power in a 1968 military coup. US assistance was augmented after the signing of the new Panama Canal treaties in 1977, which contemplated Panama's increasing participation not only in the administration of the waterway but in its defense.[26]

The close relationship between the US and Panamanian military establishments lasted until the late 1980s, by which time local and regional developments had once more rendered domestic militarism a threat to US hegemonic pursuits. As proof of yet another policy change, in 1989 Washington launched Operation Just Cause, a military invasion that dismantled the Panamanian Defense Forces.

THROUGHOUT ITS 150-year history, the relationship between Panama and the United States has been characterized by Washington's efforts to exert hegemony over the isthmus. US hegemonic pursuits have basically sought stability in Panama in order to safeguard US interests, which have varied from railroad to canal to military bases. Likewise, the policies implemented by Washington to preserve its interests have also varied, from an initial, staunch opposition to predatory militarism, to a close association with and abettance of institutional militarism. While from our late twentieth- century perspective the different US policies toward the Isthmian military may seem contradictory, they are readily understandable in the light of the changing regional and global contexts and, above all, the constant reality of hegemony and its accompanying requirement of stability.

Notes

1. For a framework of US foreign policy based on the concepts of stability and influence, see Jan Knippers Black, *Sentinels of Empire: The United States and Latin American Militarism* (New York: Greenwood Press, 1986).

2. Jules R. Benjamin, "The Framework of U.S. Relations with Latin America in the Twentieth Century: An Interpretive Essay," *Diplomatic History* 11 (Spring 1987): 91–93; Kenneth M. Coleman, "The Political Mythology of the Monroe Doctrine: Reflections on the Social Psychology of Hegemony," *Latin America, the United States, and the Inter American System*, eds. John D. Martz and Lars Schoultz (Boulder: Westview Press, 1980), pp. 105–09.

3. James Petras, H. Michael Erisman, and Charles Mills, "The Monroe Doctrine and U.S. Hegemony in Latin America," *Latin America: From Dependence to Revolution*, ed. James Petras (New York: John Wiley & Sons, 1973), p. 233.

4. Ibid., p. 238.

5. Alex Pérez-Venero, *Before the Five Frontiers: Panama From 1821–1903* (New York: AMS Press, 1978), p. 26. A second suggestion for a protectorate came in 1860 when Panamanian Governor José de Obaldía proposed that, if the Granadine Confederation (Colombia) disintegrated as a result of the current civil war, Panama should seek the joint protection of the United States, Great Britain, and France. Juan B. Sosa and Enrique J. Arce, *Compendio de historia de Panamá* (Panama: Editorial Universitaria, 1971), pp. 247–48.

6. US Department of State, *Treaties and Other International Agreements of the United States of America, 1776–1949*, vol. 6 (Washington: GPO, 1971), pp. 879–80.

7. Michael L. Conniff, *Panama and the United States: The Forced Alliance* (Athens: University of Georgia Press, 1992), pp. 19–20.

8. David Healy, *Drive to Hegemony: The United States in the Caribbean, 1898–1917* (Madison: University of Wisconsin Press, 1988), pp. 29, 31.

9. Petras, "The Monroe Doctrine," p. 240.

10. Julio E. Linares, *Enrique Linares en la historia política de Panamá, 1869–1949: Calvario de un pueblo por afianzar su soberanía* (Panama: By the Author, 1989), pp. 32–33.

11. Conniff, *Panama and the United States*, pp. 34, 50–51. See chapter III of this book for information on the civil war and US interventionism during the 1846–1903 period.

12. Linares, *Enrique Linares*, pp. 130, 155.

13. Petras, "The Monroe Doctrine," p. 242.

14. On measures implemented to stabilize US protectorates elsewhere in the Caribbean, see Healy, *Drive to Hegemony*, especially chapter 13. US interventionism during the 1903–36 period will be dealt with more fully in chapter 4 of this book.

15. See Healy, *Drive to Hegemony*, chaps. 9 and 11.

16. For an analysis of motivations behind the Good Neighbor Policy, see Michael Grow, *The Good Neighbor Policy and Authoritarianism in*

Paraguay: United States Economic Expansion and Great Power Rivalry (Lawrence: Regents Press of Kansas, 1981).

17. Walter LaFeber, *Inevitable Revolutions: The United States in Central America* (New York: W.W. Norton, 1984), pp. 79, 80.

18. Ibid., p. 63.

19. Conniff, *Panama and the United States*, p. 90.

20. US Department of State, *Treaties and Other International Agreements of the United States of America, 1776–1949*, vol. 10 (Washington: GPO, 1972), pp. 809, 817–80. US Department of State, *U.S. Treaties and Other International Agreements*, vol. 3, pt. 4, 1952 (Washington: GPO, 1955), pp. 4962–66.

21. Conniff, *Panama and the United States*, p. 150.

22. José Comblin, *The Church and the National Security State* (Maryknoll, New York: Orbis Books, 1979), p. 64. International Institute for Strategic Studies, *The Military Balance 1990–1991* (London: Brassey's, 1990), p. 182. For a discussion of the US military assistance program, see Philip J. Farley, Stephen S. Kaplan, and William H. Lewis, *Arms Across the Sea* (Washington The Brookings Institution, 1978).

23. Chester J. Pach, Jr., *Arming the Free World: The Origins of the United States Military Assistance Program, 1945–1950* (Chapel Hill: The University of North Carolina Press, 1991), p. 5.

24. Lars Schoultz, *Human Rights and United States Policy toward Latin America* (Princeton: Princeton University Press, 1981), p. 235.

25. US Department of State, Telegram, Taylor to Assistant Secretary of State Thomas Mann, 5 March 1964 (available through the Declassified Documents Reference System, document No. 1981–572C).

26. US Department of State, *American Foreign Policy: Basic Documents, 1977–1980*, part 13 (Washington, GPO, 1983), p. 1386.

Part II

The Antecedents

Chapter 3

Predatory Militarism under Colombian Sovereignty, 1821–1903

GIVEN THAT THE issue of political legitimacy remained unsolved during the eighty-two years of Panama's union to Colombia, instability was the salient characteristic of the period. This lack of stability was evident at two levels: the national, or Colombian, and the local, or Panamanian. At both levels purported solutions to the unceasing ferment were numerous and wide ranging, including Panamanian separatism, national and local political reformism through the frequent modification of constitutional arrangements, and Colombian and Isthmian attempts at forcible change through armed uprisings or coups d'état. Because none of these solutions dealt seriously with the problem of political legitimacy, however, they all failed to bring about the lasting stability which characterizes legitimate polities. Mid-century saw the emergence of US military intervention, pursuant to the Bidlack-Mallarino Treaty of 1846, in an effort to curb local predatory militarism. But foreign imposition, which failed to take heed of domestic political illegitimacy, also failed to produce enduring stability.[1]

At the national level, political reformism translated into numerous constitutional conventions which produced the Colombian charters of 1819, 1821, 1830, 1832, 1843, 1853, 1858, 1863, and 1886. Military coups also occurred against presidents Joaquín Mosquera (1830) and José María Obando (1854). Uprisings by opposition armies, which in many occasions resulted in prolonged and bloody civil wars, were more frequent and destructive. National civil wars, in fact, were waged in 1839–1841, 1860–1861, 1876, 1885, 1895, and 1899–1902. To greater or lesser degrees, all of these incidents affected Panamanian political life.[2]

The local level replicated these developments, in addition to separatist moves and US interventionism. Panama thrice proclaimed its independence—in 1830, 1831, and 1840—and gave serious consideration to separation on at least two other occasions. Under the Colombian federal arrangement, in force on the isthmus between 1855 and 1885, the State of Panama enacted six constitutions: those of 1855, 1863, 1865, 1868, 1873, and 1875. And in spite of the avowed preference for civilian politics reiterated by Panama's urban directing class, incidents of predatory militarism particularly characterized the 1855–85 federal regime.

Separatism and Militarism, 1830, 1831

Stimulated by a lack of governmental legitimacy produced by the central government's negligence and the disintegration of Bolívar's polity, Panama's first militarist experiences occurred shortly after independence from Spain.[3] The two episodes of *caudillismo* were characterized by authoritarian, personalist politics, and reveal the use of the military as an avenue for social advancement. Protagonist of the first was José Domingo Espinar, a mulatto from the Santa Ana slum of Panama City who had acquired celebrity as an aide to Simón Bolívar during the Wars of Independence. In mid-1830 Espinar returned to the isthmus as the newly-appointed commandant of the local detachment of the Colombian national army. Advocating the reestablishment of Bolívar's national rule, as well as Panamanian economic and political aspirations, the commandant declared a state of siege, deposed the local governor, and briefly separated the isthmus from Gran Colombia in September of 1830. The fledgling dictator did not act solely out of patriotism, however, for he held a grudge against Colombian President Joaquín Mosquera who, after commissioning Espinar to Panama City, had changed his mind and ordered the commander's transfer to a backwater garrison.

During his short tenure Espinar persecuted and exiled prominent local members of the anti-Bolívar faction. He also imposed new tributes, seized ecclesiastical funds, and promoted supporters to superior military ranks. The Liberator's recommendations, however, led Espinar, a loyal Bolivarian, to reunite Panama with Colombia in December of the same year. His local dictatorship expired in March of 1831, when Juan Eligio Alzuru, one of Panama City's garrison chiefs, deposed and exiled his commander.

In July of 1831, Alzuru personally assumed the government of the isthmus, putting into practice during his short-lived reign the most repugnant characteristics of Latin American militarism. The usurper was instigated toward military authoritarianism by a coterie of disaffected, unemployed veterans of the Wars of Independence, directed by a certain Luis Urdaneta. Alzuru, a Venezuelan like Urdaneta, engaged many of the latter's cronies in the local bureaucracy, to the displeasure of Panamanian-born civil servants. In order to maintain power, Alzuru attracted soldiers and local thugs by providing cash rewards and appointing the most notorious to officer status. He also created a paramilitary force, appropriately called Compañía de Desguazadores (Company of Axemen) to terrorize the population. An army loyal to Colombia, led by the Isthmian military hero Tomás Herrera, finally captured and shot Alzuru in late August 1831.

Federalism and Militarism, 1855–1885[4]

When the centralist Colombian regime to which Panama was subjugated gave way in 1855 to a federal arrangement, chiefly through the efforts of an eminent Panamanian jurist, Justo Arosemena, many were confident that a new era had dawned for the isthmus. A stronger dose of liberalism, however, proved no panacea for political illegitimacy and the now deeply-rooted recourse to force. On the contrary, liberalism exacerbated the legitimacy question. The 1855–1885 period was ironically the most unstable of Panama's history, and instability was undoubtedly aggravated by the disposition whereby Colombia's federal states were empowered to raise their own militias, which became little more than tools of factions competing for the spoils of office.

Even among Colombia's other federal states, Panama gained notoriety for its barracks coups and the "immorality of its politics."[5] Of thirty-three chiefs of state who assumed power between 1855 and 1885, only five completed their terms. In the same period, four of the seven constitutions enacted by the State of Panama were the result of de facto situations. A group of prominent Panamanian historians have blamed this turbulence on a pervasive "lack of adequate civic education,"[6] as the prevalent culture opposed the absolute submission to the law required by political liberalism. Such a view reiterates the population's disagreement with or indifference toward the new regime, underscoring its illegitimacy, which ultimately doomed it to failure.[7]

An attempt to subvert constitutional order in 1856 through election fraud was followed in 1862 by the first insurrection against an elected chief magistrate of the State of Panama. Panamanian neutrality during the 1860–1861 Colombian civil war had incurred the wrath of the victorious armed Liberal faction of Tomás Cipriano de Mosquera, the national president at the end of the conflict, who sent an armed force to the isthmus to secure his rule. Thus bolstered, a

Buenaventura Correoso (1831–1911). *From a painting by Epifanio Garay. By courtesy of Mario Lewis Morgan, Panamá.*

local Mosquera adherent and Liberal chieftain, Buenaventura Correoso, issued a *pronunciamiento* against Conservative Governor Santiago de la Guardia y Arrue. Correoso had the support of militant Isthmian partisans of Mosquera, and his action spurred an armed confrontation with Guardia's Conservatives. Following the death of Santiago de la Guardia on the battlefield, Correoso's selection for governor assumed office.

In 1865 local Liberals and Conservatives, outraged by the reputed dishonesty of the incumbent Calancha administration, convinced the Tiradores Battalion of the Colombian army, stationed in Panama, to overthrow the state's chief executive. José Leonardo Calancha was replaced by Gil Colunje, who in his short tenure (1865–1866) faced a Tiradores conspiracy, an invasion from Cauca by his deposed rival, and a plot by President Mosquera involving the Santander national battalion serving in Panama City.

Buenaventura Correoso returned to the scene in 1868 with still another *pronunciamiento*, on 5 July, this time against the administration of Juan José Díaz, who was deposed in favor of his deputy, Fernando Ponce, a Colombian army officer. Correoso intended to bar the Conservatives from assuming office after the coming elections, which—led by their candidate, Dr. Manuel Amador Guerrero —they were almost certain to win, but the coup sparked an uprising in the rural areas. Shortly after Ponce returned from suppressing this revolt, he was deposed by the local militia. As Ponce's deputy, Correoso now assumed power in early September 1868; tranquility, however, failed to return to the isthmus as a group of Conservatives rose in rebellion in Chiriquí Province in October. At the battle of Hatillo, near Santiago de Veraguas, on 12 November 1868, Correoso defeated the rebellious Conservatives after a fierce one-month campaign. In the midst of this agitation, the United States deployed a marine detachment to preserve the security of the Panama Railroad Company. Buenaventura Correoso was forced to face still another insurrection in 1871, which he also suppressed.

Irreconcilable differences of principle between Conservatives and Liberals, in addition to the personal ambitions of national and local politicians, continued to engender armed strife in the following years. In 1873 Gabriel Neira, Panama's chief magistrate, was removed by another Liberal warlord, Rafael Aizpuru, with the assistance of the local militia and the Pichincha Battalion of the national army. Dámaso Cervera, Neira's replacement, rewarded Aizpuru by appointing him to head the state militia. But Cervera's rule was short-lived, for Colombian President Manuel Murillo Toro instigated a successful military conspiracy against him. When a revolt by Buenaventura Correoso ensued, US marines landed to restore order.[8]

Two years later, in 1875, Rafael Aizpuru issued a *pronunciamiento* against Panamanian chief executive Gregorio Miró. The uprising was not yet defeated when Miró's term expired, so his successor, Pablo Arosemena, confronted the unpleasant challenge. To aggravate matters, Sergio Camargo, a Colombian army officer, arrived in the isthmus at the head of a large force. Camargo ultimately deposed Arosemena and replaced him with Aizpuru.

In 1879 the national battalion Tercero de Línea, encouraged by bribes from a Panamanian opposition party, rose against the administration of Jose Ricardo Casorla. Casorla managed to put down the rebellion with the help of the state militia and a group of volunteers. Shortly afterwards, Casorla subdued yet another revolt by Aizpuru and Benjamín Ruiz.

While all Colombian political factions contributed, through their incessant squabbles, to the collapse of the Colombian federal system, a bloody civil war in 1885 ultimately ended the liberal experiment. In Colombia, a group of radical Liberals rebelled against national President Rafael Núñez, accusing him of plotting against the federal regime. On the isthmus, Rafael Aizpuru, a *caudillo* popular with Panama City's masses, and Pedro Prestán, a mulatto leader of Colón, rose on behalf of federalism, at the head of a local insurgency of the radical Liberal faction. Prestán's actions in Colón merited the dispatch of a contingent of loyal Núñez soldiers from Panama City, which defeated the rebels. A huge fire attributed to Prestán by his opponents subsequently broke out in the Caribbean port and destroyed most of it. Meanwhile, in the absence of troops to defend the state capital, Rafael Aizpuru took Panama City and proclaimed himself civil and military chief of the isthmus. A substantial US force of approximately 1,000 marines then disembarked in Colón, at the request of the Colombian minister in Washington. The Yankee troops marched to the state capital and imprisoned the rebel chief Aizpuru when he initiated preparations to defend Panama City from an invasion by government forces loyal to Rafael Núñez. The marines released Aizpuru only after he promised not to confront the invading force within the radius of the city; he eventually surrendered to the loyalist invaders. Núñez's forces restored order in the capital and in Colón, where Pedro Prestán and two of his followers, accused of arson, were found guilty by a military tribunal and hanged.

The victorious national administration of Núñez then proceeded to institute the so-called *Regeneración,* or the regeneration of Colombia, for which purpose it wrote a new constitution. The 1886 charter reinstated centralism, concentrated powers in the executive branch, abolished the local militias, and curtailed individual rights. The new measures now excluded the Liberal opposition from participating in the political system (just as during the past three decades the Liberals had governed by excluding the Conservative opposition). The repressive atmosphere created by the Conservative reaction after 1886 ultimately ignited the most destructive explosion of predatory militarism in Colombia's history, the Thousand Days' or Three Years' War.[9]

The Thousand Days' War

Dissatisfaction with the lack of legitimacy of the Colombian "regeneration" erupted in unparalleled violence in 1899. The civil war broke out in an authoritarian, corrupt polity permeated by ideological antagonism between the traditional Iberic-American political system and Northern-Hemisphere-style liberalism. Battles took place throughout the territory of the republic; in the Department of Panama the Liberals won significant victories. As a showcase of early

Belisario Porras (1856–1942). *From a painting by Carlos Endara. By courtesy of Mario Lewis Morgan, Panamá.*

Latin American military involvement in politics, the war is relevant not only because it occurred due to the lack of legitimacy of the political system, but also because it demonstrates the nefarious consequences of predatory militarism and illustrates the exertion of

Yankee hegemony during this stage of US-Latin American relations.

Rafael Núñez's reaction tried to stabilize Colombia, which by 1886 had endured approximately three decades of unending anarchy, by reproducing in a somewhat modified form the traditional, absolutist, Iberic-American political system. *La Regeneración* tried to generate legitimacy by relying on a strong executive and the Catholic Church. Formal dissent was stifled through strict control of the press, with a view to halting the spread of liberal ideas, and the state's security apparatus was strengthened to deal with threats of subversion.

The system, however, did not succeed in gaining legitimacy. Not only was it ineffective in assimilating substantial sectors of the Liberal party, it ostracized large segments of the population by its repressive, exclusionary, and venal nature, which intensified after Núñez's death in 1892.[10] A historian of nineteenth-century Panama illustrates the situation prevailing throughout Colombia as follows:

> conditions leading to the revolt of the Liberals in 1899 were many indeed. Until 1880 gold and silver had been the medium of exchange. The government withdrew this supply and replaced it with almost worthless paper money. Commerce and industry suffered because of this depreciated money. Colombia's treasury was empty.
>
> In addition, prior to 1899 Liberals had been imprisoned for opposing the Conservative government. At Panopticon, the state prison in Bogota, some three thousand political prisoners were being held. Here and in other prisons throughout Colombia torture was freely used. Government troops almost daily committed atrocities against the Liberals. According to one eye-witness, he saw "women sawn in halves by rawhide ropes because they refused to tell where their revolutionist husbands were hidden. I have seen children tortured and flogged to death, and wounded men killed mercilessly on the field of battle."[11]

With access to power closed to the Liberals through repression and government-directed electoral fraud, and after the rapid defeat of

Domingo Díaz de Obaldía (1841–1912). *From the book* Domingo Díaz Arosemena: una vida ejemplar, *ed. by Nadhji Arjona (Panamá: 1975). Reproduced with authorization from Mrs. Temístocles Díaz Quelquejeu, Panama.*

a rebellion they launched in 1895, several prominent members of the opposition party initiated preparations for a large-scale insurrection, a procedure in which they, like their counterparts, were not inexperienced. Armed combat began on 17 October 1899 in the Department of Santander; although firmly confronted by the government, the germ of insurrection spread rapidly throughout Colombia. "The hope for peace," writes Panamanian scholar Humberto Ricord, "vanished completely," for even pacifist Liberals soon "recognized that if they failed to take up arms, Panopticon awaited them."[12]

Discontent in Panama ran high at the time. An economic depression had followed the collapse of the French canal enterprise, and had been aggravated by the repeal of the regime of free trade that the isthmus had enjoyed under the federal arrangement, as well as by the central government's increased taxation. Persecution against Liberals was also resented, for according to British Consul Sir Claude Mallet, approximately 80 percent of Panama's male population adhered to the Liberal Party. The Isthmian rural masses were also hard-pressed by governmental abuses and exactions. It was therefore not surprising that a representative cross-section of the department's population rallied under the Liberal banner when the rebels' Panamanian operations were initiated in early 1900.[13]

The war on the isthmus witnessed three stages. The first, preceded by small-scale guerrilla activities, started with an invasion of Panama by Colombian and Panamanian Liberals on 31 March 1900. Launched from Nicaragua, the invasion was directed by Isthmian Liberal leader Belisario Porras and Colombian commander Emiliano Herrera. Despite successive victories, the Liberals were disastrously defeated by Conservative forces at a Panama City battle on 26 July 1900.

Although the rebels agreed in the subsequent peace treaty to lay down their arms, the Conservative regime's persecution against known opposition sympathizers and collaborators, as well as the continuation of the war in Colombia, fanned the will of Panama's Liberals to continue the fight. A new Liberal army under Domingo Díaz de Obaldía captured Colón on 19 November 1901, but suffered a defeat by the Conservatives in the outskirts of the city nine days later. This loss, in addition to the warning issued by the US consul in Panama City that his government, in accordance with the Bidlack Treaty, would not permit fighting to interrupt free transit along the railroad, led to a Liberal surrender on the 28th. Prompted not only by a desire to protect US economic and security interests, but also by interventionist requests of Colombian and Panamanian Conservatives, Yankee admonitions were backed by the landing of marines.[14]

The last stage of the war on the isthmus began with a second Liberal invasion, this time led by the Colombian rebel commander Benjamín Herrera, whom his party bosses named "supreme director for war" in Cauca and Panama. Although the Liberals had consolidated their superiority in the whole area west of Panama City by August 1902, the end of the war in Colombia (formalized by the signing of the Treaty of Nerlandia, or Neerlandia, on 28 October), the Conservative government's preparations for a large invasion of the isthmus and renewed threats of US intervention forced Herrera to agree to peace talks. Signed on board the USS *Wisconsin,* the final Conservative-Liberal peace treaty of 21 November 1902 concluded the state of war on the isthmus.[15]

Despite the unparalleled destruction it brought, the Thousand Days' War failed to produce political results of substance. Except for promises of amnesty for the insurgents and of "free and legal" elections to integrate a new national congress—which was scheduled to debate, among other affairs, the canal treaty negotiations then developing in Washington—nothing was left to compensate for the protracted and intense bloodletting. The number of deaths is estimated at between 50,000 and 100,000, or roughly between one and 2.5 percent of Colombia's total population.[16] Economic activities came nearly to a halt and government finances were left in a shambles as a consequence of high military expenditures financed with repeated currency devaluations.

Nearly 5,000 Panamanians, out of an Isthmian population of approximately 300,000—1.6% of the population—lost their lives during the conflict. The isthmus indeed witnessed its share of "persecution, murder, depredation by both belligerents, destruction, and horror"[17] sanctioned by the "war-to-the-death" decree issued by

Bogotá on 18 February 1901. And the predatory nature of the government forces was documented by the French consul in Panama City, who in 1902 wrote his superiors that the

> garrisons are composed of very undisciplined, almost savage, elements, which survive through plunder. The officers who direct them are worth no more: there are thirty generals, and the number of colonels and other officers is proportionate. They care little about their troops, who are frequently found carousing in the streets.[18]

The civil war also seriously disrupted the economy of the isthmus: cattle-raising and agriculture were practically abandoned, and impoverishment, caused by repeated exactions from both bands, became widespread.

FOLLOWING THE COLLAPSE of colonial legitimacy in the early 1820s, the ensuing illegitimacy resulted in political upheaval and instability throughout the nineteenth century. Because political actors did not faithfully subscribe to the formal liberal democratic arrangements of the polity, recourse to force—in the Latin American setting—became a valid instrument for resolving political deadlocks. Violent politics translated into predatory militarism, especially evident on the isthmus during the 1855–1885 federal regime and, not least of all, during the 1899–1902 Thousand Days' War. Further episodes of militarism, in fact, were contained only by the United States, whose exercise of hegemony over the isthmus was formally inaugurated in 1846 with the signing of the Bidlack-Mallarino Treaty. Washington viewed predatory militarism as a destabilizing force antithetical to US hegemonic requirements of stability, and continued to regard political recourse to force with suspicion well into the twentieth century.

Nineteenth-century Panamanian predatory militarism also reflected the traditions of authoritarianism, venality, and *caudillismo* inherited from the Iberic-American past. Proving their resilience, these characteristics would project into twentieth-century Panamanian politics.

Notes

1. The state of lawlessness created by many North American roguish types who used the Isthmian route, especially during the California gold rush (1849–1869), must also be taken into account in assessing Panamanian instability during the nineteenth century. Never very effective, even under normal circumstances, in enforcing law and maintaining order, local authorities were overwhelmed by the influx of thousands of travelers, many of disreputable and troublemaking nature, as well as by the wave of criminality provoked by an economic boom amidst domestic squalor. Several clashes between Panamanians and foreigners also occurred during this period, the most notable of these being the Watermelon War *(Incidente de la tajada de sandía)* of 1856, which prompted US military intervention. See in this regard Michael Conniff, *Panama and the United States: The Forced Alliance* (Athens: The University of Georgia Press, 1992), chap. 2; and Alex Pérez Venero, *Before the Five Frontiers: Panama from 1821–1903* (New York, AMS Press, 1978), chap. 4.

2. See David Bushnell, *The Making of Modern Colombia: A Nation in Spite of Itself* (Berkeley: University of California Press, 1993).

3. Information in this section is taken from Ricardo J. Alfaro, *Vida del general Tomás Herrera*, edición conmemorativa (Panama: Universidad de Panamá, 1960), pp. 73–109; Mariano Arosemena, *Apuntamientos históricos (1801–1840)*, ed. Ernesto J. Castillero R. (Panama, Ministerio de Educación, 1949), pp. 200–30; Alfredo Figueroa Navarro, *Dominio y sociedad en el Panamá colombiano*, 3d ed. (Panama: Editorial Universitaria, 1982), pp. 245–49; Pérez Venero, op. cit., pp. 11–16; and Juan B. Sosa and Enrique J. Arce, *Compendio de historia de Panamá*, ed. Carlos Manuel Gasteazoro (Panama: Editorial Universitaria, 1971), pp. 209–12.

4. Except when otherwise indicated, information in this section is taken from Sosa and Arce, *Compendio*, pp. 236–84, and Victor F. Goytía, Las constituciones de Panamá, 2d. ed. (Panama: By the author's estate, 1987), pp. 101–299.

5. Celestino Andrés Araúz and Patricia Pizzurno, "Historia de Panamá: El Estado Federal de Panamá," a supplement to *La Prensa*, 8 January 1992, p. 11.

6. Carlos Manuel Gasteazoro, Celestino Andrés Araúz, and Armando Muñoz Pinzón, *La historia de Panamá en sus textos*, tomo I (Panama: Editorial Universitaria, 1980), p. 39.

7. Pérez Venero, *Before the Five Frontiers*, pp. 110–11. See also Celestino Andrés Araúz and Patricia Pizzurno, "Historia de Panamá: El Estado Federal de Panamá."

8. US marines, in fact, were deployed twice during 1873. Conniff, *Panama and the United States*, p. 34.

9. Bushnell, *The Making of Modern Colombia*, p. 143.

10. Celestino Andrés Araúz and Patricia Pizzurno, "Historia de Panamá: La Guerra de los Mil Días en Panamá," a supplement to *La Prensa*, 8 April 1992, p. 2.

11. Pérez Venero, *Before the Five Frontiers*, p. 120.

12. Humberto E. Ricord, *Panamá en la Guerra de los Mil Días* (Panama: By the Author, 1989), pp. 43, 44, 58.

13. The account of the war is basically taken from Pérez Venero, *Before the Five Frontiers*, chap. 6; Ricord, *Panamá en la Guerra de los Mil Días*, pp. 73–238; and Celestino Andrés Araúz and Patricia Pizzurno, "Historia de Panamá: La Guerra de los Mil Días en Panamá."

14. In August 1901 the US Navy had sent the gunboats *Machias, Ranger,* and *Iowa* to Panamanian waters. At the request of Conservative Colombian Governor Carlos Albán, US and French forces agreed on 15 October to occupy Panama City in case government troops had to abandon the city to pursue rebel forces. The following month the US North Atlantic Squadron arrived in Colón. After the Liberals entered Colón, a group of marines from the USS *Machias* occupied the railroad stations at Panama City and Colón and undertook the escort of trains traveling between both cities. With French participation, this intervention was expanded on 29 November. Celestino Andrés Araúz and Patricia Pizzurno, "Historia de Panamá: La Guerra de los Mil Días en Panamá," pp. 9–11.

15. In January 1902 the US consul in Panama City had warned the army of Benjamín Herrera that the US government would not allow Liberal attacks on Panama City or Colón. Two months later, Governor Víctor

Salazar notified the US consul of his incapacity to maintain free transit. As a consequence, US troops disembarked in Colón.

New requests for intervention came after the Liberal victory in Aguadulce, in August of 1902. In that month, Colombian War Minister Aristides Fernández and Lorenzo Marroquín, son of the Colombian acting president, held an interview with the US minister in Bogotá, seeking US military intervention to put an end to the conflict in Panama, in exchange for Colombian expediency in approving a canal treaty. The following month the Colombian government instructed its minister in Washington to request US military intervention in Panama, to which the minister refused. Nevertheless, the USS *Cincinnati* was dispatched to the isthmus with instructions to preserve "free transit" on the railroad line. Marines once again disembarked on 17 September. In the following days two more warships, the USS *Panther* and the USS *Wisconsin,* arrived in Panamanian waters. Their respective crews became involved in policing actions on the isthmus, which even led to confrontations with forces of the Conservative government. Finally, charged by his government with mediating between the factions in order to end the civil war, the commander of the USS *Wisconsin* addressed both Salazar and Benjamín Herrera, inviting them to enter into a peace accord, which materialized in November of 1902. With its naval presence on the isthmus, Washington in effect prevented a Liberal invasion of Panama City after August of 1902. Celestino Andrés Araúz and Patricia Pizzurno, "Historia de Panamá: La Guerra de los Mil Días en Panamá," pp. 9–11; Ricord, *Panamá en la Guerra de los Mil Días*, pp. 227–29.

16. Colombian historian Diego Montaña Cuéllar claimed that deaths amounted to one hundred thousand. Bushnell, however, considers this figure high, but does not offer an estimate. Diego Montaña Cuéllar, *Colombia: País formal y país real* (Buenos Aires: Editorial Platina, 1963), p. 86. Bushnell, *The Making of Modern Colombia*, p. 151.

17. Ricord, *Panamá en la Guerra de los Mil Días*, pp. 16, 70.

18. Celestino Andrés Araúz and Patricia Pizzurno, "Historia de Panamá: La Guerra de los Mil Días en Panamá," p. 6.

Chapter 4

The Civilian, Liberal Republic, 1903–1953

PANAMA JOINED THE community of independent states under favorable auspices. The junta which led the separatist movement was a coalition of Liberals and Conservatives, with seemingly conciliatory policies. Through honest and efficient leadership, the country might have achieved political legitimacy and authentic development. In spite of commendable efforts in this regard—a fairly liberal constitution adopted in February 1904, and early and constant government support for popular education and public works—discouraging aspects of the Iberic-American tradition persisted, continually reinforced as they had been during the nineteenth century. The view of the state as booty, *caudillismo,* political violence, and a tendency towards authoritarianism, all in a system formally conceived as liberal-democratic, generated conflictive situations that have characterized the Panamanian state, to greater or lesser degrees, since its early years.

Predatory militarism resulting from the illegitimacy problem was curbed only by the United States, which after having consolidated its hegemonic role on the isthmus imposed stability by assuming an arbitrating political role. As in the preceding half century, however,

US-imposed solutions did not contribute to legitimizing the system. Militarism thus returned, in institutionalized fashion, after the United States abandoned a policy of direct interventionism for one of more subtle, disguised control.

The Army of the Republic, 1903–1904

With US underwriting, peaceful independence on 3 November 1903 signaled the isthmus' full incorporation into the international division of labor, in the role of world crossroads.[1] The consummation of such a role required a stable environment, and the United States, which sponsored Panama's development as path between the seas, was determined to impose stability. But economic self-interest or national security were not Washington's sole motivations. US historian David Healy has pointed out the importance of ideological-political stimuli in the exercise of Yankee hegemony:

One of the features of Caribbean life which regularly outraged Yankee observers was the use of military power for political purposes. As elsewhere in Latin America, Caribbean regimes were often overthrown by force, which might reside in a national army turning on its own government, or in ad hoc political armies, hired mercenaries, or armed mobs. To North Americans, all were equally unacceptable. In the United States, the military service had always been properly subordinated to civil control. They had been as politically neutral in practice as in theory, their nonpolitical nature taken as a given. Furthermore, there had been no rival military forces in the United States capable of challenging those of the state. The sole exception, the Confederate army, had been the creation of a new civil polity, not a case of a military insubordinate to its state. This record represented the only proper state of affairs, in Yankee eyes, and it was natural that the very different situation in the Caribbean should provoke efforts at reform. If the devil of revolution was to be exorcised, the region's armed forces must be reduced to their proper role of instruments of the civil state. The goal was to create professional, nonpolitical armed forces strong enough to protect their governments against armed revolt, and to disband or destroy any rival forces which might challenge these depoliticized armies.[2]

At the time, the possibilities in Panama for armed revolt rested essentially with the Army of the Republic. Established by the provisional government junta on 5 November 1903, the creation of the army represented a reward to the Colombia Battalion for its inaction during the separatist events, and a response to the threats of Colombian retaliation in the early and confused aftermath of Panama's separation. Prior to independence in November of 1903, the 500-man battalion, commanded by Esteban Huertas, a Colombian general, was the sole security force of importance stationed on the isthmus. And even though its commander was then administratively subordinate to Francisco de Paula Castro, military chief of Panama, Huertas was deemed the strongman of the department.[3]

Although the junta had rejected military action on their part to bring about their separatist objective, the presence of the local military was a reality they had to deal with. They needed to keep the Colombia Battalion inactive because its potential capacity for terror was substantial. Accordingly, the separatist plan was in part a replay of 1821. The military chief and his men were bribed and co-opted, not a difficult task given Huertas' personality and his grip on the battalion.[4]

Huertas was the product of a stratified society in which opportunities for advancement were limited and a military career provided one of the few avenues for social ascent, if merely for the opportunities for plunder it offered. Like those who would succeed him as military commanders, Huertas amassed significant power and leverage, and permitted a craving for wealth, recognition, and power to determine his official actions. Born in 1876 to peasant parents in the Colombian Department of Boyacá, the future commander joined the armed forces at the age of eight. The army of *la Regeneración* was,

Esteban Huertas (1876–1941). *From the book* La guerra en el Istmo, *by Donaldo Velasco (Panamá: Star & Herald, 1902). By courtesy of Mario Lewis Morgan, Panama.*

indeed, his home and school. And he proved a worthy scion, rising rapidly through the ranks. After losing an arm during the Thousand Days' War, he was promoted to general at the age of twenty-six. Huertas had initially come to Panama in 1890, as a sergeant, and on the isthmus he acquired some measure of social acceptance. He was appointed to head the Colombia Battalion shortly after the end of the civil war.[5]

Enticed by the junta's promises of riches and glory, and fearing transfer to the inhospitable Venezuelan border, demotion, or even death at the hands of his superiors for his avowed sympathy towards Panama, Huertas threw his lot in with the separatists. On the morning of 3 November, a prominent Colombian military officer arrived in Panama City from Colón. The Colombian government had assigned Generalissimo Juan B. Tovar as commander of the Tiradores battalion, with the purpose of crushing Panamanian separatism. Tovar, "chief of the Colombian armies"[6] and reputedly one of Colombia's bravest warriors, was charged with relieving Huertas of his command and assuming the office of governor, with civil and military powers. The sagacious *generalissimo,* however, was duped by the US railroad superintendent in Colón into making the trip in a comfortable coach, unaccompanied by his troops. Tovar therefore depended on Huertas' loyalty until the Tiradores Battalion arrived in Panama City.

Visions of splendor, however, had eroded Huertas' military honor. On the afternoon of 3 November, he ordered a subordinate to place Tovar and his entourage under arrest, "in justice, and to avoid my imprisonment and death, for those were the true intentions" of Tovar and his staff, he later wrote.[7] When word of the arrest reached the separatist junta and the *caudillos,* who by that time had assembled the populace to the city's plazas, independence from Colombia was proclaimed.[8]

With the creation of the Army of the Republic of Panama the provisional junta provided an official solution to the issues of how to co-opt the Colombia Battalion and its commander after independence was achieved, and of how to face a much rumored Colombian invasion. Curiously enough, the army never fulfilled the purposes for which it was created. Regarding security threats, the institution never had any real capacity to defend the new republic and never engaged in combat. Moreover, actual, non-US threats to the territorial integrity of the Republic of Panama disintegrated after the formalization of US hegemony, by virtue of the Isthmian Canal Convention, which the US Senate approved on 23 February 1904. And in the first regard, instead of satisfying and appeasing its commander, the army became an instrument through which Huertas expected to realize his increased ambitions.[9]

Authoritarianism, corruption, and personalism reappeared on the scene following the approval of the canal treaty. With the Panamanian government's dependent relationship to the United States now formalized to the benefit of the group in power, the government had little need for conciliatory domestic politics. Antagonism between the dominant members of the separatist junta and a disgruntled sector of the directing class that gravitated around the leaders of the Liberal Party surfaced shortly after the Conservative Manuel Amador Guerrero assumed the presidency on 20 February 1904.[10]

Although President Amador appointed some prominent Liberals, and others were elected, to positions of relative importance, in essence they were excluded from the inner, decision-making circle. A historian of the period points out that they "were irked over the lack of patronage proffered by Amador."[11] In other words, they demanded a larger share of what present-day Panamanian politicians refer to as *espacio político,* a euphemism used to indicate a larger share of the spoils. Aggravating the opposition's discontent was Article 136 of the constitution. As mentioned in chapter 2, the article authorized US intervention throughout the national territory to reestablish "public peace and constitutional order in case they were disturbed."[12] The opposition believed this disposition had been inserted to assure the perpetuation of the ruling clique. Those desirous of constitutional guarantees of stability by the United States, however, claimed they wished to prevent future outbursts of predatory militarism.[13]

Panamanian politics thus factionalized into two power-contending bands: the "civilists," including those who clung to their appointments but did not have a substantial popular base, and the "militarists," those with popular support but lacking sufficient *espacio político* to meet their demands. They each sought a vigorous backer: the "civilists," as expected, continued to cultivate the local US representatives, pretending that because they were members of an elected administration they had the right to impose their will. In this endeavor they had no major problems, for US proconsuls distrusted Huertas and his army as potential instigators of predatory militarism. The first US minister to Panama, William I. Buchanan, suggested to Secretary of State John Hay on 4 January 1904 that the army "be disbanded and formed into a *guardia rural* after the ratification of the Hay-Bunau-Varilla Treaty"[14] by the United States Senate. The minister's reasoning was that once treaty approval was extended the United States would be officially committed to preserving Panamanian independence, and thus an institution charged with the republic's defense against external attacks would no longer be required. "The men should be armed only with revolvers," Buchanan continued, "and spread over the republic in order that no faction might use them collectively to intimidate the government."[15] Buchanan returned to the subject on 1 February, informing the State Department "that there were too many young officers strutting around Panama" and indicated his apprehension about a possible military coup.[16]

On the other hand, the "militarists," as indicated by their name, nurtured Esteban Huertas in hopes of a coup that would permit their rise to power. Their opportunity for an even closer rapprochement with the commander came when the National Assembly passed a law reducing the army to 250 men, including officers. Because the law, signed by President Amador on 21 March 1904, in effect cut the army by half, the "militarists" interpreted it as proof of the civilist plan to undermine Huertas and, indirectly, the opposition.[17]

In the interim, the commander had been utilizing his position as a vehicle for personal advancement. Delusions of grandeur led him to believe that Panama's prosperity and well-being depended on the army and his direction of it. During the first year of independence, he consistently held that because he led not only the armed force, but also "the people who had *liberated* the isthmus," the *"first place"*[18] corresponded to him and the army. He meddled in politics, issuing political proclamations, recommending administrative appointments, talking for and engaging the military without regard for his civilian superiors, and threatening to take "effective action" when government procedures countered his interests or those of the army.[19]

Rumors of a coup against President Amador began to circulate in May of 1904 and became more intense after Huertas' return from a "military mission" to Europe on 7 September.[20] Thereafter, the commander's behavior became unacceptable to civilian authorities. Amador attributed the political confrontation to the Liberal "itch for the $6,000,000,"[21] referring to the portion of the $10,000,000 paid by the United States as compensation for the canal concession, which had been invested in US securities. Huertas, on the other hand, argued that even as the military were being reduced, "consuls, vice-consuls, chancellors, and embassy secretaries" were being added to the foreign service.[22] Sympathizers of the ruling party, he maintained, monopolized the new positions.[23]

On 28 October Huertas wrote to the president demanding the resignations of Tomás Arias and Nicolás Victoria Jaén, the two "civilist" secretaries in the four-portfolio cabinet. Both complied, but the president, intent on bargaining with the opposition, accepted only Arias' resignation, replacing him with Santiago de la Guardia y Fábrega, "much to the displeasure of the Liberals," according to William McCain, for Guardia "was a staunch conservative, an ambitious presidential possibility and a friend of the United States."[24]

A second letter to the president followed. Dated 13 November, it was addressed in terms more amazing . . . than the first. [Huertas] was . . . displeased that Victoria was still in office. Victoria, a stranger to dignity, honor, gratefulness, and decency, and a fraud in whose "jaundiced features" hypocrisy and perfidy were seen clearly, had to be dismissed.[25]

President Amador now turned anxiously to the US diplomatic representatives. Chargé Joseph Lee and Minister John Barrett, believing that buttressing the constitutional government would be more convenient to US requirements of political stability, encouraged Amador to disband the army, offering US support if difficulties arose. Lee even warned first the opposition leaders, and later Huertas himself, that the United States would not allow a coup against the constitutional authorities. Finally, on 18 November the president, with US backing, asked Huertas for his resignation; in response, the commander issued threats of insubordination. Secretary Guardia, in conjunction with US diplomatic representatives Lee and Barrett, managed the situation thereafter, confronting the military with the bugaboo of US military intervention. In the following days the government disbanded the Army of the Republic. The National Police, created in 1903 to succeed the former departmental police force, absorbed the troops, and Huertas was comfortably pensioned at five hundred dollars a month.[26]

McCain writes that "the business community and the government were reported as being most grateful for the attitude of the American legation and military officials."[27] The Roosevelt administration was also pleased. During his visit to Panama between 27 November and 6 December, US Secretary of War William H. Taft "commented on the blessings of an orderly constitutional government and congratulated the Panamanians that their junta had set up no dictatorship and that they had chosen civilians rather than soldiers for their important government posts."[28]

The National Police, 1904–1930

The US-supported elimination of the Army of the Republic, within the context of official US commitments to protect the independence of and maintain order in Panama, had a decisive repercussion in the domestic political field from 1904 to 1930. To local power contenders, the incident pointedly demonstrated that the age of predatory militarism was over, and that in spite of the minor uses the National Police could be put to in political disputes, real power brokerage rested with the North American legation.

Meanwhile, political traditions inherited from the colonial and Colombian past continued to perpetuate themselves in the Panamanian national environment. The lack of pluralist politics was repeatedly evidenced in the parties' reluctance to admit defeat. Whenever contending groups feared their political fortunes were in decline, they solicited US mediation. This accounts for the repeated requests for election supervision that both government and opposition made throughout the period. Along with further subjecting Panama to the status of Yankee protectorate, these actions produced additional, uninvited US interventions, the most noteworthy of which occurred in 1918. In the midst of a convoluted electoral process, while the opposition requested US supervision of the voting, President Ciro Luis Urriola, with the obvious purpose of retaining power, postponed the municipal and legislative elections indefinitely. Urriola's action sparked the US military occupation of Panama City and Colón, as well as Chiriquí and Veraguas provinces. The elections were eventually held under US inspection.[29]

Because the National Police held little attraction to members of the urban propertied class as a source of employment except at the highest echelons, the force was staffed principally by individuals of the masses. Overshadowed by the US exercise of mediating powers, the police played a relatively insignificant role in national life until the 1930s. In the early years of the republic, North American authorities regularly accused the force of abusive conduct against US military personnel stationed in Panama. The fact that the National Police was inefficient is underlined by the urgent call for reform of the force in 1916 by several prominent Panamanians. To be fair, however, it should be stressed that most US-Panamanian security problems arose from the "disorderly conduct of Canal Zone employees and American soldiers and sailors."[30] At the time, US haughtiness towards Panamanian authorities was legendary. Particularly repugnant to Panamanians were the visits of the US fleet, whose sailors would descend upon Panama City and Colón in a manner reminiscent of Morgan's pirates. Regarding the disturbances in which Yankee military and Isthmian police were involved, a distinguished Panamanian attorney, Horacio Alfaro, stated: "we all know that they have been provoked by US soldiers."[31]

This was one of the arguments advanced by Panamanian Foreign Secretary Ernesto T. Lefevre in his endeavor to resist Washington's humiliating demand that the police in Panama City and Colón be disarmed of high-powered rifles. Seeking to minimize the encounters between native police and Yankee military, which occasionally resulted in the death of North Americans, on 9 May 1916 US Minister William Jennings Price presented the foreign office with the disarmament request, to which Panama reluctantly assented.[32]

A concerted effort by the United States to professionalize the police then followed. The Northern Colossus, in fact, had long expressed a desire to place the force under the command of a US citizen experienced in security matters, but Panama continually procrastinated. Finally yielding to US pressure, the administration of Ramón Maximiliano Valdés in 1917 appointed a US instructor. The choice fell upon Albert Lamb, of the Washington, D.C. police.[33]

In July of 1918, following the Yankee occupation triggered by President Urriola's attempt to postpone the elections, the US legation in Panama had suggested to the Department of State that a bill be introduced in the Panamanian National Assembly providing for the appointment of a US police commissioner with full powers "to control, instruct, and guard the police force of the Republic"; significantly, at the same time the appointment of a US "fiscal agent" was also suggested.[34] A special attorney for the Panama Canal—that is, a US citizen—had been instructed to prepare the draft of the bill. Writing shortly after Minister Price's dispatch, Secretary of State Robert Lansing communicated to the Panamanian minister in Washington, Dr. Belisario Porras, his desire to see a "US instructor of the Panamanian police placed under the direct orders of the President of the Republic," independent of the Department of Government and Justice.[35] Lansing also indicated his wish that the police as well as the police courts be

> removed from political influence . . . The police of the entire Republic should be under the Instructor and the Instructor should have complete control over the punishing and rewarding of his force. . . . He and his force must be absolutely and permanently withdrawn from all political influences. . . . The reform of the Police Courts should, it is believed, be undertaken only after consultation and in cooperation with the American Police Instructor.[36]

In the following months the US-prepared draft was presented to the National Assembly. After the bill's approval, Albert Lamb was appointed to head the force, as inspector general, on 19 February 1919. He exercised maximum authority over the police until 1924, when the Panamanian government, chafing under Yankee control over its sole security force, put another bill through the assembly which placed the police once more under the direction of a Panamanian commander. Lamb, however, was retained as advisor to the force until 1928.[37]

The results of US professionalization are difficult to assess, mainly for lack of research on the issue. Unlike what US training produced in Nicaragua, Cuba, Haiti, or the Dominican Republic, the Panamanian police did not become militarized under Lamb's direction. The fact that the instructor was a policeman and not a military officer could account for this. On the other hand, confrontations between Yankee military and Panamanian police, the matter of most interest to local US representatives, subsided. Professionalization and subsidence of US-Panamanian clashes prompted President Harmodio Arias Madrid in 1936 to declare proudly that "our humble police agent is no longer the object of ridicule or mockery, but of the community's respect."[38] But seizure of the presidential house in early 1931 by a militant group of nationalists demonstrated that—Mr. Lamb's enlightened efforts notwithstanding—the institution's effectiveness did not, in fact, merit excessive praise.

The First Coup and Its Aftermath, 1931–1953

On 2 January 1931 the nationalist political society Acción Comunal overthrew President Florencio Harmodio Arosemena, who had been elected to serve the 1928–1932 term. That the coup enjoyed widespread support, at least in the capital city, is indicative of the discontent the populace felt toward the administration. Seen as a mere puppet of his predecessor, Liberal *caudillo* Rodolfo Chiari, *don Floro* was perceived as a weak, inefficient president, inordinately permissive of nepotism and graft. Arosemena, moreover, presided over a period of increasing social ferment, brought about by modernization, urbanization, and resentment against US hegemony. The economic depression which began with the new decade, in addition to the unceasing political bickering within the government, further alienated large segments of the population from the president.[39]

Above all, the 1931 coup evidenced the body politic's lack of legitimacy. Acción Comunal, by then a significant actor in Panamanian politics, did not feel an unbreakable commitment—essential to legal legitimacy—toward the constitution. The nationalist group did not regard the existing constitutional arrangements as an impediment to removing, through extra-legal means, the president who held office according to the rule of law.

Due to the absence among Panama's political actors of a feeling of loyalty toward the system, such a move most likely would have occurred earlier had it not been for the direct arbitral role, backed by military force, the United States assumed. It has been seen that as early as 1904 the opposition conspired with the army chief to overthrow the elected president, to which development US proconsuls responded by warning the plotters not to tamper with the constitutional regime. But by the early 1930s, despite President Arosemena's beliefs to the contrary, North American hegemonic behavior had changed. The US minister, Roy Tasco Davis, declined the president's requests for armed intervention in favor of his administration with a rationale reflecting the new modus operandi:

> I doubted the advisability of injecting the United States into a problem which had to do with political policies in Panama. [Moreover,] it was apparent that, if American troops should enter Panama, there would have been a bloody skirmish with considerable loss of life. Bitter feelings would have resulted in the relations between the United States and Panama which would have lasted for years; and it also appeared probable that such action would be severely criticized at home and abroad.[40]

The new US policy approach continued to focus on stability, but relied on more subtle, diplomatic means to assure the maintenance of a stable environment. Washington could afford new approaches because its hegemony was already consolidated. In consequence, with US diplomatic encouragement, but without US military intervention, the coup was window-dressed by the Supreme Court. The magistrates accepted President Arosemena's resignation and, in a resolution of suspect constitutionality, called on Dr. Ricardo J. Alfaro, elected *primer designado* for a vice-presidential period which had already expired, to assume the presidency. Thus did the court inaugurate a time-honored tradition of legalizing de facto situations.[41]

Panamanian politicians were quick to derive a lesson from the

Arnulfo Arias Madrid (1901–1988). *Photograph by Foto El Halcón, Panamá.*

success of the coup and US disinclination for military intervention, a lesson, however, related not to political legitimacy but to the monopoly of force. A strong, effective National Police would be required in the future to protect the power of the incumbent. A steady effort toward strengthening the police now began. In consequence, after 1931 illegitimacy and militarization became mutually reinforcing phenomena.

In July 1935 Police Commandant Aurelio Guardia, brother-in-law to President Harmodio Arias, headed an uprising apparently directed more against Government and Justice Secretary Galileo Solís than against the rebel's political relative. The action, however, was firmly contained by Arias, with no other consequences than the resignations of Solís and Guardia. The following year the Arias Administration utilized every means within its reach, including police manipulation, to impose the candidacy of Juan Demóstenes Arosemena. The massive vote fraud frustrated the opposition and intensified the legitimacy crisis. Consequently, President Arosemena was forced to rely more than his predecessors on the National Police, which he significantly endowed. During the 1940 elections, the administration of Augusto Samuel Boyd unleashed the police on the opponents of the government-endorsed candidate, Arnulfo Arias Madrid (Harmodio's brother). Once in office, to support his regime President Arias reorganized the secret service and National Police.[42]

Arnulfo Arias was innovative in more than his security policy. Inspired by *Panameñismo,* the physician-turned-*caudillo*'s nationalist and populist political creed, the new president's guiding principle was "Panama for the Panamanians." Dr. Arias presided over a period of swift and far-reaching reform, aimed at "awakening the civic conscience from the lethargy in which it has thus far been subsumed."[43] The Arias administration fostered national development and social redistribution through the creation of a number of government agencies, most saliently the Social Security Administration; it reorganized the executive and judicial branches; it commendably promoted national culture, generating in Panamanians a proud sense of nationality. Last but not least, Arias wrote a new constitution, which entered into force in January 1941.

The *Panameñista* charter strengthened presidential powers and, in a typically Iberic-American reaction to the perceived excesses of Marxism and liberalism, resorted to state intervention in the economy and proclaimed the preponderance of social interest over individual rights. The 1941 Constitution also withdrew Panamanian nationality from all citizens whose parents belonged to races of "prohibited immigration," except for cases in which one of the parents was a Panamanian citizen by birth. Institutionalized racial discrimination was directed against non-Spanish speaking blacks, Semites, and Asians.

In October 1941, with US instigation and police backing, Minister for Government and Justice Ricardo Adolfo de la Guardia overthrew President Arnulfo Arias. Because Arias' domestic policies threatened the status of important political actors, not least of all, the National Police, his legitimacy became questionable vis à vis these sectors. In an effort to subject the police to his increasingly personal rule, the president appointed an unpopular Guatemalan army officer as inspector general. Moreover, the growing independence of Arias' international policy countered Yankee hegemonic interests in the context of World War II. The president rejected a US request for arming Panamanian-registered merchant vessels, which Dr. Arias considered inconsistent with the isthmus' neutrality during the war. Consequently, when the president left Panama incognito on 7 October from Cristóbal, on US-controlled territory in the Atlantic terminus of the canal, US intelligence tipped Guardia and Second Police Commandant Rogelio Fábrega, who proceeded to police headquarters to assume direct command of the force and to order the arrest of the most prominent of Arias' supporters. Convened once more, as in 1931, to whitewash the coup, the Supreme Court proclaimed the national presidency vacant and, through legal juggling, swore in Ricardo Adolfo de la Guardia as president of the republic. The new chief executive, as expected, promptly dismissed the Guatemalan military advisor and authorized the arming of Panamanian vessels.[44]

The October coup also triggered the rise to power of José Antonio Remón, Panama's first professionally-trained military officer. Born in 1908, Remón was the offspring of an impoverished family of Spanish-colonial ancestry. Through his mother's resourcefulness, he was awarded a scholarship to Mexico's military academy, from which he graduated as a tactical officer with the rank of lieutenant. Appointed to the police as a subordinate chief in December of 1931, in 1935 Remón was dismissed from the force by President Harmodio Arias for favoring Domingo Díaz Arosemena, the opposition candidate in the 1936 elections. Re-entering the force in 1940, the military officer was immediately removed from the scene by President Arnulfo Arias, who dispatched him to Fort Riley, Kansas, to participate in a basic cavalry course. Soon after taking over in 1941, President Ricardo Adolfo de la Guardia appointed him second commandant of the police.[45]

In his study of the Latin American military, Alain Rouquié has emphasized the importance of formal military education, explaining how it develops a sense of military identity and superiority, which in turn produces a deeply-rooted corporate spirit.[46] This is precisely what Remón contributed to Panamanian militarism. Remón began instilling in the force a military spirit consistent with his training. Concurrently, he embarked on the task of building a personal power base in the police, culminating in his appointment as first commandant—and actual strongman—in 1947. Through his control of this office he manipulated his election to the presidency in 1952.

Throughout his tenure as commandant and president, Remón, a pro-US opportunist, was committed to improving the "prestige" of the police, with a view to raising it to military status. A student of this period of Panama's history underlines how "Remon sensed that, in

José Antonio Remón assuming the national presidency, 1 October 1952. Taking the oath is his brother Alejandro Remón, president of the National Assembly. First Vice-President José Ramón Guizado is in the background. *Photograph by courtesy of Tatiana Padilla / El Siglo, Panamá.*

José Antonio Remón saluting President Domingo Díaz Arosemena on the former's assumption of the national presidency, 1 October 1948. Second Vice-President Roberto F. Chiari is in the background. *Photograph by courtesy of Tatiana Padilla / El Siglo, Panamá.*

Bolívar Vallarino (1916–). *Photograph by courtesy of Tatiana Padilla / El Siglo, Panamá.*

military circles, a Panamanian delegate who was just a police officer lacked prestige. Remon thought of himself as an army officer. He was not satisfied with being just a policeman."[47] Hence as police chief he encouraged many Panamanians to go abroad for military training. One of them, Bolívar Vallarino, a graduate of Chorrillos Military Academy in Peru, was appointed third commandant in 1947 and promoted to second commandant the following year. At the same time, recognizing the role of the force as a medium of advancement for many individuals of the masses—and seeking to co-opt these elements—Remón cultivated officers who had risen through the ranks.

The commandant inundated his civilian superiors with requests for additional barracks, instructors, drill fields, arms, and vehicles. A gymnasium, low-cost police housing, improvements in radio communications, special health care, and increased administrative autonomy were also required to satisfy the needs of an organization that, according to Remón's most vehement desires, would in the near future become Panama's national army.

The strengthening of the National Police generated the emergence among its members of a corporate spirit embodying elements of the Iberic-American past as well as more recent additions. Empowered with a monopoly of force and an arbitral political role as a consequence of the manifest US reluctance to intervene militarily, the police force now evidenced the stepped-up discipline, increased professionalism, and political and economic involvement characteristic of the Latin American military. Police commandants and subordinate chiefs began to figure in national life, with Remón himself achieving the presidency in 1952. Larry Pippin, an analyst of midcentury Panama, characterized Remón's personal standing toward the end of his life as follows:

> Power brought Remon wealth and social status. The Police Chief was reported to have accumulated a multimillion dollar fortune. Some operations were known; more were not. Remon owned a gasoline station from which the police purchased the gasoline needed to keep its equipment operating. . . . [He] exercised [control] over the slaughter of cattle. . . . It was the Police Chief who authorized urban, commercial bus routes—an activity that was particularly graft-ridden. Remon was said to be a part-owner of at least the choice house of prostitution in the capital city. . . . Apartment houses, farms, and race horses were included among his holdings. Remon was one of the stockholders of the daily newspaper La Nacion, of Liberal tendency. He was involved to an extent unknown to most Panamanians in the movement of narcotics through the Isthmus on the way from their source areas to consumption centers in other areas of the world, normally from Bolivia to the United States.[48]

After Remón's appointment as first commandant in 1947, police meddling in politics assumed proportions which recalled the Colombian federal period (1855–1885), except for the fact that a century later only one official institution possessed the monopoly of force.

This involvement reflects the preponderance of a militarized constabulary in national life and is an early manifestation of Panamanian institutional militarism.

In July of 1948, the commandant's support for yet another scandalous vote swindle prepared the way for Domingo Díaz Arosemena's assumption of the presidency, to the detriment of Arnulfo Arias. Following President Díaz's death the next year, his successor Daniel Chanis requested Remón's resignation based on the latter's graft-related activities, especially the illegal slaughterhouse monopoly which he shared with a son of the deceased chief executive and other associates. Remón responded by overthrowing Dr. Chanis and handing over power to Second Vice-President Roberto Chiari (who, incidentally, was a first cousin to the police chief). But when the Supreme Court (remarkably) sustained Daniel Chanis' right to the presidency, Acting President Chiari notified the commandant that he would honor the ruling.

Remón was determined not to permit Dr. Chanis' return to office; at the same time, however, he had to face widespread popular indignation against police encroachment in politics. "The intensity of the people's repugnance for the police leadership," reported Pippin, "was reflected in a protest strike" which paralyzed urban life.[49] Seeking a way out of the crisis, Remón opportunistically fetched Arnulfo Arias and installed him in the presidency, which the *Panameñista* leader assumed for the second time on 24 November 1949. This action was justified with a recount of the ballots cast in 1948. It turned out that the *caudillo* had in effect won the election, but Domingo Díaz had "mistakenly" been declared victor. With Arnulfo Arias' connivance, therefore, Remón's militarism—more defined, even in its primitiveness, than popular, momentary anti-militarism—emerged victorious from its first match with the populace.

By 1951 President Arias had once more antagonized substantial segments of the population, not least because he decreed the replacement of the 1946 Constitution with his 1941 charter. On 8 May a large crowd demanded that the police chief remove the president. Remón hesitated until the National Assembly impeached Arias and elevated Vice-President Alcibíades Arosemena to the presidency, in a move sustained by the Supreme Court. Thus backed, Remón sent a police detachment to the presidential house; after a prolonged exchange of gunfire with Arias' supporters, the police finally succeeded in forcing the impeached president's surrender.

Increased repression by the force against dissenting elements of society also characterized this period of transition from innocuous police to militarized constabulary. Remón was especially keen on suppressing nationalist protests, if for no other reason than to substantiate his pro-US, anti-Communist stance in the wake of the Cold War. Notorious incidents of police repression occurred in December 1947 and April 1948, against opponents of a new lease on military bases, and an air convention with the United States, respectively. Remón was also hard-handed against those who disputed his political supremacy, especially during the 1949 events, when he unleashed the police on anti-militarist protesters.

US policy toward Panama in the late 1940s and early 1950s was seemingly caught between a dislike for the commandant's crude methods and a need to protect US hegemony vis à vis the feared Soviet threat. "Remon is not well educated and lacks experience in international affairs, but is strongly anti-Communist and is considered pro-United States," read a briefing paper prepared for President Dwight Eisenhower.[50] Yankee hegemonic interests also explain the local US commander's astonishing praise of Remón, in 1948, for the Panamanian commandant's "known adherence to the ideals of democracy and . . . furtherance of the common interests of our two republics," even as Remón's police were beating up nationalist protesters.[51]

But although the United States worried about the rise of nationalism and communism on the isthmus, and sought to "strengthen the pro-US elements in Panama,"[52] Washington did not, at the time, foment the militarization of Panama's security force. Lend-lease, for example, was never made available to the republic, and when an agreement for the detail of a military advisor was signed in 1942, the

US officer was assigned to the foreign office and the agriculture ministry, to serve additionally as head of a veterinary mission.[53] Moreover, when in January of 1946 the US Department of War recommended furnishing Panama with one AT-6 and two PTs aircraft, the US ambassador to the isthmus indicated that "no planes should be allocated to Panama at this time," the reason being that Panama had no army and was not expected to be able to finance the creation of an armed force in the near future.[54] Because of the strong US military presence on the isthmus, the United States did not share, at the time, Remón's grandiose military plans.[55] Regional and local developments would, however, later change the point of view of Washington policy makers.

BY THE EARLY 1950s, Panamanian political illegitimacy and US unwillingness to involve its forces in domestic political disputes had triggered the strengthening of the National Police, as well as the latter's assumption of a well-defined arbitrating role in local politics. Coupled with the incorporation into the force of professionally-trained military graduates—especially José Antonio Remón, who became first commandant of the police in 1947—these arbitrating powers were soon to transform the formerly immaterial force into an institutional military, the National Guard. Although the process of militarization was not directly abetted by the United States, Washington's hegemonic pursuits, in a reputedly non-interventionist context, stipulated recognition of the pre-eminent political role played by the Panamanian militarized constabulary, as well as maintenance of cordial relations with the force. When toward the end of the decade a serious blow to US hegemony in the Western Hemisphere indicated to Washington policymakers the need to boost the US position in Latin America, the cordial relationship developed during the first half of the twentieth century between Yankee representatives and Panamanian military would make the latter a dependable guarantor of domestic stability and US hegemony.

Notes

1. A detailed account of Panama's independence is impossible here. For an informative chronology of events in the Spanish language, see Julio E. Linares, *Enrique Linares en la historia política de Panamá, 1869–1949: Calvario de un pueblo por afianzar su soberanía* (Panama: By the Author, 1989), chapters 3–7. William D. McCain's *The United States and the Republic of Panama* (Durham: Duke University Press, 1937), pp. 11–18, provides a good, more concise account in English.

2. David Healy, *Drive to Hegemony: The United States in the Caribbean, 1898–1917* (Madison: The University of Wisconsin Press, 1988), pp. 220–21.

3. Esteban Huertas Ponce, ed., *Memorias y bosquejo biográfico del general Esteban Huertas, prócer de la gesta del 3 de noviembre de 1903* (Panama: Ediciones Continentales, 1959), pp. 49, 51. Linares, *Enrique Linares*, pp. 71, 83, 98–101, 104. Other security forces were the departmental police, of which there were detachments in Panama City and Colón, and a fire brigade of 287 men, which could be mobilized for security purposes. In November of 1903, a Colombian flotilla of three warships was also anchored in the Bay of Panama.

4. Tomás Arias, *Memorias de don Tomás Arias, fundador de la República y triunviro* (Panama: Talleres Gráficos de Trejos Hnos., Sucs., 1977), pp. 27, 52. Linares, *Enrique Linares*, p. 84. Two episodes of military brutality had occurred on the isthmus shortly before independence. In May of 1903 a military court over which Esteban Huertas presided, condemned Victoriano Lorenzo, a guerrilla in the Thousand Days' War, to death. This occurred in contravention of the Wisconsin Peace Treaty, which granted amnesty to all insurrectionists. On 25 July an armed force acting under the instructions of José Vásquez Cobo, military chief of Panama and brother of the Colombian war minister, vandalized an opposition press and arrested several government officials, including the governor. Juan B. Sosa and Enrique J. Arce, *Compendio de historia de Panamá*, ed. Carlos Manuel Gasteazoro (Panama: Editorial Universitaria, 1971), p. 308. Huertas, *Memorias*, p. 34. Linares, *Enrique Linares*, pp. 53–54.

5. Huertas, *Memorias*, pp. 8–32. In his memoirs, Huertas is keen on underlining his marriage into the distinguished Ponce family, his valuable social relations with the urban patriciate and the popular *caudillos*, and the

esteem with which he believed himself to be held by the populace and the troops.

6. Huertas, *Memorias*, p. 60.

7. Ibid., p. 78.

8. Linares, *Enrique Linares*, p. 95.

9. The Hay-Bunau-Varilla Treaty was approved by the Panamanian Provisional Government Junta on 2 December 1903. Prior to US-Senate approval in February 1904, security threats included the presence in Colón of the 466-man Colombian *Tiradores* battalion, which never reached Panama City. Several factors persuaded the *Tiradores'* commanding officer, on the evening of 5 November, to embark his troops on the Royal Mail steamer *Orinoco*—among them his hesitancy to confront US military reinforcements which were expected shortly, and payment of US$8,000 by the provisional junta to assume the transportation costs of his battalion.

Other potential security threats included the presence of part of the *Colombia* battalion—a 250-man force ignorant of the events in the capital—in the rural district of Penonomé, as well as rumors of an invasion from Colombia. The latter persisted even after the arrival, on the night of 6 November, of the US fleet dispatched to back Panama's independence. In fact, four military expeditions were organized in Colombia, between December, 1903, and January, 1904, with the purpose of restoring Panama to Colombian rule by force. To further complicate matters for the junta, several leaders of the Liberal Party who had fought in the campaigns of the Thousand Days' War had taken the lead from the provisional government, collaborating with Huertas since the night of the third to organize the defense of Panama City against a possible attack by forces loyal to Colombia. Given the security threats and the Liberal interest in the military, all in the undefined period between the declaration of independence on 3 November and official US recognition (which coincided with the arrival of US warships) on 6 November, it would have been dangerous, if not suicidal, for the provisional junta not to recognize the status of Huertas and his troops.

The threats to Panama's security, however, rapidly subsided. As to the situation in the interior, the soldiers in Penonomé, once informed of the events, adhered to the secessionist movement. And the Colombian military expeditions were all frustrated, not only by fear of US retaliation, but also by the then impenetrable Darién jungle. See Ernesto J. Castillero, *Panamá y Colombia, historia de su reconciliación: Capítulos de historia diplomática en los albores de la República de Panamá* (Panama: Instituto Nacional de Cultura, 1974), pp. 27–45; Huertas, *Memorias*, pp. 40–98; Linares, *Enrique Linares*, pp. 107–52; and McCain, *The United States and the Republic of Panama*, p. 52.

10. A provisional triumvirate, entrusted with the new republic's executive and legislative powers until February, 1904, was, like the separatist junta, a bipartisan coalition. This was also the case with the constitutional convention, whose seats were equally divided among Conservatives and Liberals. Manuel Amador Guerrero was unanimously elected by the constitutional convention to serve the 1904–1908 presidential term. Linares, *Enrique Linares*, chapter 3.

11. Gustavo A. Mellander, *The United States in Panamanian Politics: The Intriguing Formative Years* (Danville, Illinois: The Interstate Printers & Publishers, 1971), p. 62.

12. Ramón E. Fábrega and Mario Boyd Galindo, *Constituciones de la República de Panamá: 1972, 1946, 1941, 1904* (Panama: By the Authors, 1981), p. 288.

13. See the defense of Article 136 by Conservative Tomás Arias, and the protests against it by Liberal Buenaventura Correoso, in Carlos Manuel Gasteazoro, Celestino Andrés Araúz, and Armando Muñoz Pinzón, *La historia de Panamá en sus textos*, vol. II (Panama: Editorial Universitaria, 1980), pp. 31–36.

14. McCain, *The United States and the Republic of Panama*, p. 49.

15. Ibid.

16. Mellander, *The United States in Panamanian Politics*, p. 65.

17. Another law authorized the executive branch to auction a number of Colombian war vessels Panama had taken over, which composed the navy of the new state. Linares, *Enrique Linares*, p. 161.

18. Huertas, *Memorias*, p. 114; emphasis added.

19. Ibid., p. 121.

20. In late May of 1904, in a further opposition effort to woo the commander, Liberal *caudillo* Domingo Díaz de Obaldía asked a number of his party's deputies to the Constituent Convention to sponsor a bill with the purpose of sending the commander-in-chief on a "special military mission"

to the United States, France, and Germany, for which fifty thousand gold pesos were to be allocated. The bill was unanimously approved by the convention. Huertas, *Memorias*, pp. 149–52.

While the purpose of such a mission remains obscure—for if the army was being officially reduced, there was no logic in it—one supposes that the government, by that time intent on annihilating the army, took advantage of the Liberal initiative and instructed responsive deputies to vote in favor of the bill with the intention of getting Huertas out of the way and moving against the army. Soon after Huertas went on holiday on 17 July, President Amador assumed direct command of the military, a maneuver which, however, did not produce any tangible results. Huertas' activities during his European tour are also illustrative of the more venal aspects of Latin American militarism. The fifty thousand pesos were spent returning the "high honors" he received from the governments and peoples he visited, in addition to paying the expenses of the military commander's three *aides-de-camp* (his *compadre* Pastor Jiménez, Harmodio Arosemena, and José Agustín Arango Jované), buying new German uniforms for the army, and purchasing various Holstein cattle and Berkshire swine for the general's *finca*. Huertas, *Memorias*, pp. 153, 166, 181.

21. McCain, *The United States and the Republic of Panama*, p. 51.

22. Huertas, *Memorias*, p. 144.

23. Ibid.

24. McCain, *The United States and the Republic of Panama*, pp. 53, 54.

25. Ibid., p. 54.

26. Ibid. Huertas, *Memorias*, pp. 185, 187–88. Linares, *Enrique Linares*, pp. 163, 164. Mellander, *The United States in Panamanian Politics*, p. 65.

27. McCain, *The United States and the Republic of Panama*, p. 59.

28. Ibid., p. 42.

29. Representatives of either the ruling or opposition parties requested US supervision of the Panamanian elections in 1906, 1908, 1912, 1916, 1918, 1920, 1924, and 1928 (and thereafter as well). US inspection materialized on three occasions, in 1908, 1912, and 1918. See Celestino Andrés Araúz, *Belisario Porras y las relaciones de Panamá con los Estados Unidos* (Panama: Ediciones Formato Dieciséis, 1988).

Dr. Ciro Luis Urriola assumed office in his capacity as *primer designado*, or first vice-president, upon the death of President Ramón Maximiliano

Valdés on 3 June 1918. Legislative elections were due shortly afterwards and, according to the constitution, the elected assembly had the task of choosing the president for the remaining two-year period of the 1916–20 term. By canceling the elections, Dr. Urriola hoped to prolong his incumbency. Linares, *Enrique Linares*, pp. 202–4. McCain, *The United States and the Republic of Panama*, pp. 62–77.

Although the troops soon withdrew from Panama City, Colón, and Veraguas Province, they remained in Chiriquí Province until August of 1920. US forces occupied the province with the ostensible purpose of supervising the elections subsequent to a US demand that they be held. However, after the elections, the US presence in Chiriquí was reinforced, the excuse being that US nationals resident there required military protection. It later transpired that a US citizen was involved in a feud with a Chiriquí family over a considerable extension of land, and that the US military expedition had been launched to force the Panamanian authorities to recognize the claim of the US citizen. Linares, *Enrique Linares*, pp. 203–4.

30. McCain, *The United States and the Republic of Panama*, p. 78.

31. Carlos Iván Zúñiga, *El desarme de la Policía Nacional de 1916* (Panama: Ediciones Cartillas Patrióticas, 1973), p. 17.

32. Linares, *Enrique Linares*, 191–92. Zúñiga, *El desarme*.

33. US Department of State, *Records of the Department of State Relating to Internal Affairs of Panama, 1910–1929*, available in the Department of State Decimal File (Washington: National Archives Microfilm Publications, 1965), microfilm, M-607, roll No. 1, p. 234.

34. US Department of State, *Foreign Relations of the United States, 1919*, vol. 2 (Washington: GPO, 1934), pp. 679-80. In its quest for Caribbean stability, the US government resorted to several mechanisms, none of which was lastingly effective. Political initiatives included supervision of elections and the encouragement of liberal democracy, as well as the little-known promotion of a Central American peace system. Economic measures encompassed the stimulation of US investments, which would purportedly bring about the creation and fair redistribution of wealth, as well as US control of a country's customs, in so-called "customs receiverships," implemented to avoid graft and partisan disputes for control of the state's resources. Last but not least, US administrations resorted to direct military intervention, unilaterally sanctioned by the 1904 Roosevelt Corollary to the Monroe

Doctrine and in some cases (e.g., Cuba and Panama) authorized by national constitutions.

While none of the above approaches achieved the US goal of keeping the Caribbean Basin quiescent, Washington also resorted to the creation of unified, "professional" constabularies, supposedly obedient to elected civilian authorities and the rule of law. Coming from a country in which the army had always been subordinated to elected officials, US proconsuls endeavored to impose a comparable state of affairs in the areas under their supervision, with the purpose of protecting elected governments responsive to US designs from the threat of insurrection. Although the option did produce an increased measure of stability in comparison to the status quo ante, its consequences were disastrous for the peoples involved and, ultimately, highly embarrassing and problematic for the United States. See Healy, *Drive to Hegemony*, especially chaps. 8, 9, 10, 11, 13.

35. US Department of State, *Foreign Relations of the United States, 1919*, vol. 2 (Washington: GPO, 1934), p. 680.

36. Ibid.

37. US Department of State, *Records of the Department of State Relating to Internal Affairs of Panama, 1910–1929*, microfilm, M-607, roll No. 1, p. 243.

38. Mélida Ruth Sepúlveda, *Harmodio Arias Madrid: El hombre, el estadista y el periodista* (Panama: Editorial Universitaria, 1983), p. 183.

39. Linares, *Enrique Linares*, chaps. 16–17, gives a detailed account of these events and a favorable judgement of the administration of Florencio Harmodio Arosemena. See also Celestino Andrés Araúz and Patricia Pizzurno, "Historia de Panamá: Años de crisis y el golpe de Acción Comunal (1928–32), a supplement to *La Prensa*, 9 December 1992.

40. US Department of State, *Foreign Relations of the United States, 1931*, vol. II (Washington: GPO, 1946), p. 896.

41. Linares, *Enrique Linares*, pp. 312–15. For the role of US Minister Roy Tasco Davis during the 1931 coup, see US Department of State, *Foreign Relations of the United States, 1931*, vol. II (Washington: GPO, 1946), pp. 890–904.

42. Carlos Manuel Gasteazoro, Celestino Andrés Araúz, and Armando Muñoz Pinzón, *La historia de Panamá en sus textos*, vol. II, pp. 11, 187. Celestino Andrés Araúz and Patricia Pizzurno, "Historia de Panamá:

Harmodio Arias y la consolidación de la República," a supplement to *La Prensa*, 17 February 1993. Idem, "Historia de Panamá: Convulsión y reformismo (1936–1941)," a supplement to *La Prensa*, 17 March 1993. Linares, *Enrique Linares*, pp.367–68.

43. Linares, *Enrique Linares*, p. 369.

44. Ibid., pp. 367–92.

45. Except when otherwise indicated, information on Remón's career, his command of the National Police, and his political involvement, is taken from Richard M. Koster and Guillermo Sánchez Borbón, *In the Time of the Tyrants: Panama 1968–1990* (New York: W.W. Norton & Co., 1990), pp. 52–55, and Larry LaRae Pippin, *The Remon Era: An Analysis of a Decade of Events in Panama, 1947–1957* (Stanford: Institute of Hispanic American and Luso-Brazilian Studies, 1964), pp. 1–8.

46. Alain Rouquié, *The Military and the State in Latin America*, trans. Paul E. Sigmund (Berkeley: University of California Press, 1987), p. 87.

47. Pippin, *The Remon Era*, p. 6 (note 2).

48. Ibid., p. 8.

49. Ibid., p. 53.

50. Conniff, *Panama and the United States*, p. 106.

51. Pippin, *The Remon Era*, p. 38 (note 1).

52. US Department of State, *Foreign Relations of the United States, 1950*, vol. 2 (Washington: GPO, 1976), p. 975.

53. US Department of State, *Treaties and Other Agreements of the United States of America: 1776–1949*, vol. 10 (Washington: GPO, 1972), p. 817. US Department of State, *US Treaties and Other International Agreements*, vol. 3, pt. 4, 1952 (Washington: GPO, 1955), pp. 4962–66.

54. US Department of State, *Foreign Relations of the United States, 1946*, vol. XI (Washington GPO, 1969), p. 92.

55. Between 1942 and 1948 the United States, by virtue of the Defense Sites Agreement with Panama of July 1942, had occupied nearly 100 defense sites throughout the republic. After the Panamanian National Assembly's rejection in December 1947 of a new convention regulating the defense sites issue, the United States concentrated its military presence in the Canal Zone. Humberto E. Ricord, *Noriega y Panama: orgía y aplastamiento de la narcodictadura* (México: By the Author, 1991), p. 617.

Part III

Institutional Militarism

Chapter 5

The National Guard, 1953–1968

THE CHANGE IN name of Panama's security force, from National Police to National Guard, represents the institutionalization of the force's role as political arbiter. The 1953–68 period witnessed a reinforcement of the guard's corporate self-image and a strengthening of its repressive and coercive apparatus, due to internal and external factors. In the domestic arena, the exercise and jealous preservation of privileges acquired under José Antonio Remón, in addition to the courting of the force by politicians, boosted the guard's self-confidence. The external component lies with the favor the National Guard found with Washington policy makers in the context of Cold War containment. With a view to preserving stability on the isthmus and responsiveness to US interests under at least the semblance of constitutional democracy, the new institution began receiving US assistance in the form of grants for training and purchases of weapons. Emboldened by privilege, courting, and US support, the guard assumed direct political power for the first time in 1968, and retained it for the following two decades.

Legitimacy and the Guard

At the instigation of José Antonio Remón, who became president in 1952, the National Assembly approved Law 44 of 1953, which converted the 2,500-member police force into Panama's National Guard. The new legislation reflected Remón's punctilio in military matters. It divided the country into military zones and provincial sections, and mandated that these divisions be headed by officers with the ranks of major and captain, respectively; it decreed military honors for guard members who "met death in acts of heroism" or while undertaking official duties; and it provided for the punishment of any citizen who verbally "mocked, insulted, or offended" a national guardsman, or even of anyone who utilized a National Guard whistle without being duly authorized. The provisions were, indeed, evocative of the colonial *fuero de guerra militar*.[1]

Remón resigned from the police in October 1951 to launch his presidential candidacy, and one year later assumed the country's highest office. Throughout his incumbency, until his violent death on 2 January 1955, he retained firm control of the security force, whose membership he increased to 3,000. After becoming first commandant in 1951, Bolívar Vallarino, a loyal subordinate, oversaw the constabulary for his former boss. Like Remón, Vallarino belonged to a family of impoverished creoles and had received formal military schooling.[2]

Somewhat influenced by Argentine *Justicialismo*, President Remón inaugurated a populist government, in which his wife Cecilia played a prominent role. Authoritarian and efficient, his rule was based on the military and the masses, incorporating, at the same time, the propertied class. Stability was maintained through a *pan o palo* policy: adversaries were either co-opted or outlawed. Arnulfo Arias had been banished from the political scene in 1951, after being deposed and tried by the assembly, which deprived him of political rights. Now Remón moved against party proliferation, putting through the legislature a law which denied recognition to any group which failed to receive at least 45,000 votes in the past election.[3] A law declaring "illicit and violating the national constitution those totalitarian activities such as communism"[4] was also passed in December 1953 and, together with informal press censorship, permitted increased control over the opposition. In economic matters, Remón imposed fiscal discipline and favored a development model combining state intervention and private investment, which focused especially on agricultural development. Finally, Remón negotiated a new canal convention, labeled Treaty of Mutual Understanding and Cooperation, in which Panama gained some economic concessions and leased the Río Hato Military Base to the United States for fifteen years.[5]

Remón's assassination in 1955—reputedly for his involvement in the narcotics traffic—marked the end of a short interregnum of political stability. The return of instability indicated Panama's continued failure in achieving legitimacy, and further projected the National Guard into politics, despite the relatively less conspicuous political involvement of First Commandant Vallarino. Less than two weeks after Remón's death, the National Assembly impeached President José Ramón Guizado (first vice-president under Remón) and replaced him with Second Vice-President Ricardo Arias Espinosa, more acceptable to Remón's supporters and the guard. And although the three succeeding presidents all completed their constitutional four-year terms, a feat unaccomplished since Harmodio Arias' 1932–1936 presidency, one of them, Marco Aurelio Robles (1964–1968), assumed office tainted with charges of electoral fraud. A short-lived 1959 insurgency in Veraguas Province, in addition to two purported invasions in the style of Fidel Castro, all shortly after the victory of the Cuban revolutionaries, indicated disillusionment with the political system. A rise in nationalist militancy, evidenced by violent anti-US demonstrations in 1958, 1959, and 1964, also pointed to disenchantment with Panama's relationship to the United States.[6]

Containment, Revolution, and US Aid

The United States had long worried about the rise of Isthmian nationalism, which it saw as an ideology inimical to its interests and, after World War II, one which additionally provided Soviet communism with opportunities for making inroads in Panama. In the 1950s and 1960s, nationalism was therefore nothing new to the isthmus; neither was communism, in spite of its almost negligible influence in domestic politics. A Communist Group, in fact, had been formed in 1921, a Stalinist Communist Party appeared in 1930, a Socialist Party three years later, and a Marxist-Leninist Labor Party in 1935. Acción Comunal, the nationalist organization which undertook Panama's first successful coup d'état, was founded in 1923.[7] In the aftermath of the 1931 coup, US Minister Roy Tasco Davis took care to inform Secretary of State Henry Stimson that the society was not "in any way connected with the International Communist movement,"[8] and the United States agreed to maintain relations with the Acción Comunal government only after Washington obtained informal representations that its interests would not be threatened.[9]

With the rise of Third World nationalism following 1945, however, Washington became increasingly apprehensive of parallel developments on the isthmus. The Frente Patriótico de la Juventud, a nationalist movement of students and middle-class intellectuals founded in the 1940s, played an instrumental role in the rejection of the proposed US-Panamanian Defense Sites Agreement in December 1947 and in the political stirrings of the following decade. Not surprisingly, therefore, a 1950 Department of State Policy Statement declared its preoccupation with Panamanian resentment against the United States which, it claimed, was "deliberately and artificially fostered in recent years by certain cynical elements in Panama for political advantage." These individuals, the statement continued, "have often cooperated with and attempted to make use of communist and subversive elements, which, while not important numerically, have at times exercised an undue influence in Panamanian political life."[10] Furthermore, in 1952 an interdepartmental Special Estimate concluded that the

> most dangerous aspect of Communism in Panamanian politics is the influence of individual communists ... among the intelligentsia. In these circles, in which philosophical Marxism is a respectable and widely accepted doctrine, Communism is not regarded as an alien menace. Communism exerts a strong influence upon both teachers and students at all levels of the Panamanian educational system and, through them, may eventually gain control of the Patriotic Front.[11]

By the early 1950s the Panamanian Marxist movement had converged into a local communist party, known as Partido del Pueblo. Despite President Remón's outlawing of "totalitarian" activities in 1953, the party continued to operate, clandestinely until the president's assassination, more openly thereafter. Fear of radical developments which the Marxists might trigger was, in fact, an important reason leading the United States to agree to new treaty negotiations with Remón. Accordingly, the Eisenhower Administration expected to quell Panamanian nationalism through the economic rectifications delivered in the treaty. The successful conclusion of a new convention abetted for a short while the confidence of US policy makers, one of whom, US Ambassador Julian Harrington, reported in 1957:

> We can foresee in the near future no probable change in the attitude of the Panamanian Government or people toward the maintenance of our defense operations in this area. The long-range Panamanian objective of undermining our sole control of the Canal and substituting some form of joint operation from which they would obtain greater benefits will no doubt continue to be pursued. Our position is so strong, however, that this attitude is not a serious threat under present conditions.[12]

At the same time, Washington recognized that "the stability of the government will depend on the continued support of the National Guard and control of the Guard will be the key to the political situation."[13]

The regional and local environments, however, changed before the end of the decade, giving the United States cause for renewed and intensified anxiety. The advent of Fidel Castro's successful revolutionary nationalism in the US "backyard," and the ensuing developments in Panama in 1959, inspired precautionary policies in Washington. In recognition of the National Guard's preponderant political role, the United States provided it with military assistance—in the form of a small $100,000 grant for training—for the first time in 1960.

At the time, most Panamanian officers who had received military schooling had graduated from Latin American academies, primarily in El Salvador, Nicaragua, Peru, and Venezuela. Although a rudimentary training center was created in 1956, Panama had not yet established a national military academy, despite José Antonio Remón's earlier suggestions in this regard. With the aforementioned US grant, Panamanian officers began training at the Canal Zone Army Caribbean School, renamed the US Army School of the Americas in 1963. It received 195 Panamanian students in 1960; by the end of 1964, the school had trained 1,420 National Guardsmen.[14]

Between 1960 and 1968 Panama received a total of $3.1 million in Military Assistance Program (MAP) grants. Most of the funds were destined for military training in counterinsurgency and civic action. During the same period, the republic also received $28.2 million of Security Supporting Assistance, an average of $3 million per annum ($10.2 million in 1967 alone).[15] This type of assistance included aid to supplement military assistance by contributing to the stability of countries "under stress or threat of conflict."[16] Although not technically military aid, Security Supporting Assistance was and is offered for purposes of defense, and recipient countries are not required to use it in any given way. In consequence, it has usually served as a mechanism to support the recipient's security expenditure.

Other developments during the decade testify to the National Guard's increasing professionalization and militarization under

Yankee auspices. In September 1961, the National Guard sent a representative to the first meeting of the Central American Armed Forces Chiefs of Staff, held in Guatemala. Promoted by the Pentagon, the meeting declared it the obligation of the region's armed forces "to unify and coordinate their efforts in defense of democratic interests . . . in the face of the totalitarian threat of Communism."[17] The Guatemala meeting ultimately produced CONDECA, the Central American Defense Council, in which Panama was given observer status.[18] The following year the structure of US military missions abroad underwent a thorough reorganization.[19] In Panama, at the proposal of the US embassy, the 1942 agreement for the detail of a US officer as advisor to the foreign office was amended to allow for a US military advisory group whose members would "serve as advisers to the Ministry of Government and Justice on subjects pertaining to the defense of the Republic of Panama, including military training."[20]

US concerns with Castroite communism in Panama approached paroxysm after January 1964, when the Panamanian nationalist issue exploded into what US Latin Americanist Michael Conniff has called "a spectacular venting of hatred and anger."[21] The incident originated on the 9th when a group of Panamanian students attempted to raise the national flag in the Canal Zone and were prevented by a group of Zonians. In the ensuing fray, the Isthmian flag was torn; when the events were reported, thousands of irate Panamanian demonstrators took to the Zone border, where they were confronted by US military personnel. While the National Guard remained conspicuously absent from the scene, the situation degenerated into vandalism and looting, directed principally against US-owned property in Panama City and Colón. Not until the 13th, by which time twenty-three Panamanians and four US military had already perished, did the guard reappear to restore order.

While intelligence reports of an imminent communist takeover in Panama flooded Washington, the Johnson Administration prepared to assist National Guard First Commandant Vallarino in forestalling the anticipated coup (which, the CIA's assurances notwithstanding, proved to be a misrepresentation of the Panamanian situation).[22] Commander Andrew P. O'Meara of the US Southern Command reported to the Joint Chiefs of Staff that "positive evidence exists that Castro-trained organizers seized control of the situation as soon as the first group of students returned from the flag incident to the Republic of Panama."[23] The alarming tone of SOUTHCOM's cables subsided with mention of the National Guard, for which the US military had nothing but praise:

> The activity of the Guardia Nacional was commendable. When they were permitted to act, they did so in a professional, competent manner. They worked closely with the U.S. military. On their own initiative, they helped many Americans to get safely to the Canal Zone.[24]

Commander O'Meara's concluded that in order to avert future outbreaks of violent nationalism, the personnel of the 3,400-man Panamanian security force should be augmented: "The Guardia Nacional is much too small to handle the grave responsibilities incumbent" on it. Its membership should therefore be "increased to 6,000 men."[25]

The bloody and embarrassing 1964 flag riots finally made Washington realize that the US-Panamanian relationship urgently required repair. The new agreement the State Department envisioned, however, was difficult to achieve, for it sought to stabilize US interests by removing Panamanian nationalist grievances. A Johnson Administration State Department report specifically defined the former as:

> 1. Guaranteeing transit through the canal to US vessels and ships of all nations;
>
> 2. Ensuring the safety of the waterway;
>
> 3. Securing a provision for the "construction, operation and defense of a sea level canal to meet the future needs of [the] United States";

4. Achieving a "political settlement" with Panama to boost the US position worldwide; and

5. Assuring access to US military bases in Panama, "not only to provide for the defense of the canal but also as a major element in our regional security arrangements and as a valuable communications center and tropical training and research area, supporting our world-wide security commitments."[26]

Hence while the United States could bring itself to recognize Isthmian sovereignty in the Canal Zone and accept Panamanian part-nership in canal management, Washington also insisted on legalizing its military presence on the isthmus. For a Northern Colossus immersed in a prolonged struggle for global supremacy with the Soviet Union, military bases on the isthmus were of utmost impor-tance, more so with the moral and material stimulus given to Marxist revolution in the Western Hemisphere by Fidel Castro's triumphant entry into Havana on New Year's Day, 1959.

Legalization of the Yankee bases as a "major element" in US regional security arrangements was, nevertheless, inconsistent with Panamanian objectives of national sovereignty and neutrality. Moreover, such legalization had never before been formally contem-plated in a canal treaty between the United States and Panama, for Panama's representatives had hitherto consented to the US military presence only for purposes of canal defense, not as an integral part of the US global security apparatus.[27] The essence of the problem faced by Washington was that the ultimate US objective—the main-tenance of hegemony—was in contradiction with the course of action required to achieve it—satisfaction of Panamanian nationalism. And while these contradictory goals were pursued, stability had to be maintained on the isthmus. In a worst case scenario, instability could invite takeover by a radical Castro-style leadership. Even if a drastic occurrence such as the one most feared by State policy makers failed to materialize, however, a repetition of the 1964 flag riots would most certainly endanger the lives and property of US citizens and—more importantly in a Cold War context—wreak havoc on the US image as leader of the "free" world, by exposing the Northern Colossus as an oppressive world power.

As a double insurance, therefore, while Washington demonstrated receptiveness toward Panamanian nationalism through willingness to negotiate, it also concentrated on strengthening a pro-US National Guard, with a view to maintaining hegemony to secure North American interests. The diplomatic-military efforts translated into new canal treaty negotiations and direct US financing of a 500-man increase in the guard, through security supporting assistance. The increase materialized in 1965, in the understanding that US taxpayers "would pick up the tab for salaries and allowances during FY1966 and the Panamanians thereafter."[28] But the build-up was not solely in the interest of the United States. In 1966 Panamanian Foreign Minister Fernando Eleta Almarán asked US Ambassador Robert Anderson for continued support for payment of National Guard salaries in the light of increased security problems, which recent riots in Colón had indicated. The Robles Administration, in effect, desired US funding for an additional increase of one thousand guardsmen. Although US patronage for intensified recruitment did not materialize, payroll support did continue, at least into 1968.[30]

In spite of the substantial difficulties treaty negotiations under the above-mentioned conditions implied, in July of 1967 a bilateral team produced the draft of a new arrangement in the so-called "three-in-one" treaties. The three separate documents addressed the existing canal, the military bases, and proposed plans for a sea-level waterway, respectively; they adequately protected US strategic interests and partially satisfied Panamanian demands of sovereignty. Ambassador Charles Adair described the major features of the proposed agreements as follows:

> The provisions of the draft treaties follow guidelines established by Presidents Johnson and Robles in a joint statement of September 24, 1965. At that time the two Presidents declared that the new agreements would abrogate the 1903 treaty with its perpetuity clause, and

would provide for Panamanian participation with the United States in the management of the canal. They further stated that the new treaties would provide for U.S. forces and military facilities to be maintained on the isthmus for the defense of the existing canal, and any sea level canal which may be constructed in Panama.[31]

The Robles and Johnson administrations were thus eager to obtain legislative approval prior to the coming elections in both countries. Panamanian nationalists, however, stirred up opposition to the drafts on the basis of their legalization of the US military bases. Their objections, in addition to the National Assembly's subsequent involvement in a bitter 1968 electoral dispute, caused the proposals to be shelved, presumably until a new Panamanian assembly convened in October of 1968.[32]

Corporate Self-Image and the 1968 Breakdown

Until 1968 Panama was governed by a political class which was heir to the Conservative-Liberal leadership of the Colombian era. The political class formally adhered to a liberal development model; hence the characterization of the 1903–1968 period as the "liberal republic." Although marred by illegitimacy, the regime had successfully withstood previous political crises as well as the *Panameñista* incursions of Arnulfo Arias and the authoritarian-populist experiment of José Antonio Remón. Despite the regime's outward instability, the negotiating abilities of the political class, as well as the fact that no one sector predominated, accounted for its longevity. During the latter half of the regime's existence, however, domestic politics and US support had unduly strengthened one of these political actors: the National Guard.

In this context, the deterioration of the political class's willingness to compromise with opponents triggered an unprecedented political crisis during the 1968 electoral process. Personalism played no small role, as sworn political enemies joined opposing coalitions. On one side, the official candidate, David Samudio, endeavored to appear as an Alliance for Progress champion, determined to continue implementing diffusionist economic measures, such as the tax reform he put through during his tenure as minister for finance under President Marco Robles (1964–1968). The prospects of taxation antagonized many propertied Robles partisans, who fled to the camp of opposition candidate Arnulfo Arias.[33] Also in evidence was an unmasked scramble for the spoils of office among the notoriously corrupt Liberal faction in power and some of President Robles' erstwhile supporters, now transformed into vehement partisans of Dr. Arias. Recognizing the need for military support in accomplishing their plans, representatives of both government and opposition sought the backing of the National Guard. Given the time-honored animosity between the physician-*caudillo* Arias and the military, however, the National Guard initially sided with Samudio.[34]

Favored with a newly acquired majority in the National Assembly, the opposition further aggravated the crisis by impeaching Robles for his blatant (and unconstitutional) support for Samudio. The March 1968 impeachment trial antagonized the opposing coalitions to the point at which a truce became impossible. The assembly voted to dismiss Robles, and called on First Vice-President Max Delvalle to assume the presidency. But based on the ruling of a lower-echelon judge, whose competence in the matter was at best dubious, the National Guard frustrated the deputies' maneuvering. In a military operation, the armed forces prevented Delvalle, who sided with Arnulfo Arias, from acceding. The troops beat and arrested supporters of the opposition, vandalized Arias' headquarters, and sealed the National Assembly building, de facto suspending the legislature's debates.[35]

In the midst of these developments, some of the officer corps repeatedly urged Bolívar Vallarino to launch a coup to end the crisis. But Washington, maintaining its leverage with the guard commandant, feared such a move would generate instability and hamper treaty approval, both in Panama and the United States. In consequence, Ambassador Adair discreetly pressured Vallarino not to disturb the constitutional order. While Washington claimed to be "prepared to work with any candidate chosen in free elections,"[36] its envoy in Panama reported to his superiors at Foggy Bottom that the "greatest hope for moderation and cooperation from the Guardia Nacional now and in the future as well as for free elections lies in Vallarino."[37] The US Embassy, in fact, feared an internal guard coup by anti-Arias officers headed by Omar Torrijos, executive secretary to the guard, whose "leftist and anti-US"[38] brother Moisés was running for deputy on the Samudio ticket. Moisés Torrijos had spoken out strongly against the draft treaties, US Ambassador Charles Adair informed Secretary of State Dean Rusk,

> and Omar is reported to have supported his position and referred to his brother as one of the few patriots who were protecting the country's interests. If [brother Moisés] ever becomes Omar's political counselor while Omar is first commandant of the Guardia Nacional, I would not expect a cordial or cooperative regime. Inasmuch as the Torrijos group is strongly anti-Arnulfo, a Guardia Nacional commanded by Torrijos should not be expected to promote free elections while Arnulfo is a candidate.[39]

Although US diplomatic efforts did avert a military coup in early 1968, they did not prevent the National Guard from openly and violently supporting the Samudio candidacy. Even so, Arnulfo Arias won the 12 May elections by a landslide. Adair's good offices now intensified. Because of the Panamanian *caudillo's* popularity, Yankee policy makers were betting on easy approval by the Panamanian assembly if Dr. Arias favored the "three-in-one" treaties. Indirect US pressure and fear of provoking civil strife if Samudio was imposed led Vallarino to reach an understanding with Arias. The deal included recognition of the *Panameñista* leader's victory and the commandant's voluntary retirement after the 1 October presidential inauguration. The president-elect also pledged to respect the guard's hierarchy. Thus did Vallarino hope to settle matters in a way satisfactory to the electorate, the military, and the US Embassy.[40]

The defeated Liberals, however, felt Vallarino had betrayed them. Their deception soon turned into frustration when in the following months Arias manipulated the results of the legislative elections to the detriment of several rightfully-elected deputies, one of whom was Moisés Torrijos. Many military officers who had been ordered to obstruct the opposition vote during the May contest now looked askance at their commandant's understanding with his nemesis. Vallarino had arranged his honorable retirement while abandoning his subordinates to the *caudillo*'s wrath. Amidst rumors that President Robles was encouraging a coup against himself to prevent Arnulfo Arias' rise to power, the Samudio press now launched virulent attacks against the guard's first commandant. One of the most outspoken journalists, Jaime Padilla Béliz, wrote a series of "Letters to the National Guard" in which, while candidly proposing a coup d'état, he in effect underlined the illegitimacy of the political system. "The young, middle-class officers of the guard," wrote Padilla, "must feel a certain preoccupation at being involved in the shameful spectacle of an abject marriage between their chiefs and the country's most reactionary forces." Encouraging them to correct, "before it is too late, the political and social" issues which "thrash us," Padilla went on to demand the rise of the guard as a "third force . . . free of ties to the creole oligarchy, emanating from the people and supportive of the people." How to achieve this if not through a military coup? the journalist asked. He then urged all "honest" officers of the guard to "give Panamanians a lesson in dignity and civics," by replacing the constitutional authorities with military rule.[41]

The content of Padilla's articles certainly must have appealed to the majority of officer corps, for as the "Letters" astutely implied, the guard's personnel was overwhelmingly middle and lower class. In 1968, in fact, only the first commandant and one other top officer,

Federico Boyd, belonged to the old political/propertied class. Along with the class appeal of the articles, the president-elect's *caudillismo* represented a threat to the National Guard: those officers who opposed Arnulfo Arias stood to lose their status, privileges, and perquisites, including their access to supplemental income through graft. It was this ensemble of circumstances that effectively favored the direct assumption of power by the National Guard.

BY 1968, DOMESTIC POLITICS and US hegemony had inadvertently prepared the National Guard for a prolonged exercise of absolute power. While crude ambition motivated many politicians' courting of the guard, the US obsession with Soviet-Castroite communism, in addition to Washington's hegemonic demands of stability, made the National Guard the object of US favor. These developments consistently enhanced the Panamanian military's strength and corporate consciousness, and effectively transformed the guard into the preponderant actor in national politics. When in October of 1968 the constitutional president moved to undermine the power of the guard as a politically deliberating institution, he met with invincible opposition from the officer corps, which ultimately resulted in the overthrow of the civilian, liberal regime.

Notes

1. República de Panamá, "Ley No. 44 de 23 de diciembre de 1953, por la cual se crea la Guardia Nacional y se subroga la Ley 79 de 1941," *Gaceta Oficial*, No. 12.255, 24 December 1953, pp. 2–3.

2. Larry LaRae Pippin, *The Remon Era: An Analysis of a Decade of Events in Panama, 1947–57* (Stanford: Institute of Hispanic American and Luso-Brazilian Studies, 1964), p. 84.

3. Ibid., chapters 8–9.

4. República de Panamá, "Ley No. 43 de 23 de diciembre de 1953, por la cual se declaran ilícitas y violatorias de la Constitución Nacional en la

República, las actividades totalitarias tales como el Comunismo," *Gaceta Oficial*, No. 12.255, 24 December 1953, p. 1. Prior to Remón's law, a Decree-Law issued in 1950, during the second presidency of Arnulfo Arias, had banned the Partido del Pueblo. Steve C. Ropp, *Panamanian Politics: From Guarded Nation to National Guard* (New York: Praeger, 1982), p. 86 (note 4).

5. Río Hato was the largest of the defense sites leased to the United States in 1942. It had been recovered by Panama after the rejection of the Defense Sites Agreement in 1947.

6. Michael L. Conniff, *Panama and the United States: The Forced Alliance* (Athens: The University of Georgia Press, 1992), p. 112. Humberto E. Ricord, *Los clanes de la oligarquía y el golpe militar de 1968* (Panama: By the Author, 1983), pp. 31–32. On Remón's assassination, see Pippin, *The Remon Era*, chap. 10.

7. Julio E. Linares, *Enrique Linares en la historia política de Panamá, 1869–1949: Calvario de un pueblo por afianzar su soberanía* (Panama: By the Author, 1989), pp. 227–28, 283, 359–60.

8. US Department of State. *Foreign Relations of the United States, 1931*, vol. II (Washington: GPO, 1946), p. 895.

9. Ibid., pp. 894–902.

10. Idem, *Foreign Relations of the United States, 1950*, vol. II (Washington: GPO, 1976), pp. 974–75.

11. Id., *Foreign Relations of the United States, 1952–1954*, vol. IV (Washington: GPO, 1983), p. 1395.

12. Id., *Foreign Relations of the United States, 1955–1957*, vol. VII (Washington: GPO, 1987), p. 334.

13. Ibid., p. 245.

14. Richard M. Koster and Guillermo Sánchez Borbón, *In the Time of the Tyrants: Panama, 1968–1990* (New York: W.W. Norton & Co., 1990), p. 54. Renato Pereira, *Panamá: Fuerzas armadas y política* (Panama: Ediciones Nueva Universidad, 1979), p. 153. US, Congress, House, Committee on Foreign Operations and Monetary Affairs, *Hearings Before the Subcommittee of the Committee on Government Operations: U.S. Aid Operations in Latin America*, 87th Cong., 1st sess., 9 December 1961, p. 254. Willard F. Barber and C. Neale Ronning, *Internal Security and Military Power: Counterinsurgency and Civic Action in Latin America* (Columbus: Ohio State University Press, 1966), p. 145.

15. US Agency for International Development, *US Overseas Loans and Grants and Assistance from International Organizations, July 1, 1945–June 30, 1975*. Washington GPO, 1976. All figures are expressed in current US dollars.

16. Philip J. Farley, Stephen S. Kaplan, and William H. Lewis, *Arms Across the Sea* (Washington: The Brookings Institution, 1978), p. 30.

17. US Department of State, *Report*, 1961 (available through the Declassified Documents Research System [hereafter DDRS] document No. 1983–2029).

18. Walter LaFeber, *Inevitable Revolutions: The United States in Central America* (New York: W.W. Norton & Co., 1984), p. 151.

19. Robert P. Case, "El entrenamiento de los militares latinoamericanos en los Estados Unidos," *Aportes* 6 (October 1967): 50.

20. US Department of State, *U.S. Treaties and Other International Agreements*, vol. 13, pt. 3, 1962 (Washington: GPO, 1963), pp. 2598–2604.

21. Conniff, *Panama and the United States*, pp. 120–21.

22. See US Central Intelligence Agency, *Agreement of Arnulfo Arias Madrid and the Communist Party for Joint Action Against the Government,* cable, 13 January 1964 (DDRS 1988-65); and US Central Intelligence Agency, *Involvement of Major Victor Mata of the National Guard in Coup Plans of Arnulfo Arias and the Communists*, cable, 13 January 1964 (DDRS 1988-67).

23. US Department of Defense, *Cable*, White House to the commander-in-chief of the Southern Command, January 1964 (DDRS 1983-1658).

24. Id., *Cable*, commander-in-chief of the Southern Command to the Joint Chiefs of Staff, January 1964 (DDRS 1983-1652).

25. Ibid.

26. US Department of State, *IRA/ARA Contingency Study: Panama*, undated (DDRS 1989-2180).

27. Carlos Bolívar Pedreschi, *De la protección del canal a la militarización del país*, (Panama: By the Author, 1987), p. 19.

28. US National Security Council, *Memorandum*, Walter W. Rostow to President Lyndon B. Johnson, undated (DDRS 1991-527).

29. Ibid.

30. Ricord, *Los clanes de la oligarquía*, p. 87.

31. US, Congress, House, Committee on Foreign Operations, *Hearings*

Before the Foreign Operations and Government Information Subcommittee: U.S. Aid Operations in Latin America Under the Alliance for Progress, 90th Cong., 2d sess., 24 January 1968, p. 4.

32. Conniff, *Panama and the United States*, pp. 121–25.

33. President Roberto F. Chiari had in 1960 restored Arnulfo Arias' political rights.

34. Conniff, *Panama and the United States*, p. 124. Ricord, *Los clanes de la oligarquía*, pp. 18–19.

35. Koster, *In the Time of the Tyrants*, p. 64. Ricord, *Los clanes de la oligarquía*, pp. 64–67.

36. US Department of State, *Telegram*, Secretary of State Dean Rusk to Ambassador Charles Adair, March 1968 (DDRS 1981-371C).

37. US Department of State, *Telegram*, Ambassador Charles Adair to Secretary of State Dean Rusk, March 1968 (DDRS 1981-372B).

38. US Department of State, *Telegram*, Ambassador Charles Adair to Secretary of State Dean Rusk, March 1968 (DDRS 1981-372A).

39. Ibid.

40. Ricord, *Los clanes de la oligarquía*, pp. 84–88.

41. Ibid., pp. 107–10.

Chapter 6

The 1968 Coup and the Rise of Omar Torrijos

ON 11 OCTOBER 1968 the National Guard overthrew the constitutionally elected government of Dr. Arnulfo Arias Madrid and inaugurated the first institutional military dictatorship in the republic's history. By the second half of the twentieth century, however, political instability and breaks with constitutionality (such as vote frauds and coups d'état) were nothing new to Panama's political history. The search for an explanation for both instability in general and the 1968 coup in particular leads directly to the issue of political illegitimacy.

The polity's lack of legitimacy explains the option for a break with constitutionality, in 1968 as well as previously. Because of its illegitimacy, the liberal democratic political system was disposable. But understanding what triggered the embrace of this option by the National Guard in October of 1968 requires a closer look at the military institution. The Panamanian guard had by the late 1960s evolved in a fashion similar to its Latin American counterparts. It was the depository of corporate privileges, represented by rank and hierarchy, and it provided opportunities for social advancement that its members, otherwise, most likely would be unable to achieve. When Dr. Arias interfered with "military honor," the guard overthrew him to preserve its privileged status.

The military regime instituted in 1968 evidenced important strains of the traditional political culture: a *pan o palo* approach to politics, the use of the National Guard as a vehicle for advancement, and the concept of the state as loot. Additionally, though institutional in nature—because it originated with and ultimately responded to the officer corps—the regime manifested a vein of *caudillismo* in the person of Omar Torrijos. In consequence, it is worthwhile to commence this chapter with a look at the military dictator's early career.

Omar Torrijos

Torrijos' military career, in which he fulfilled both *pan* and *palo* tasks, had a decisive influence in shaping the political approach his dictatorship would utilize after 1968. Influential in shaping the *pan* side were his association with opportunistic, pseudo-leftist politicians; his brief albeit significant relationship with Juan Domingo Perón; and his training at the US Army School of the Americas. The *palo* aspect he internalized through performance of routine duties as officer of the National Guard, which since the early 1940s had evolved as a repressive force that regularly involved itself in politics. Above all, the authoritarian, albeit paternalist, Panamanian political tradition, inherited from the colonial and Colombian past, provided the setting for a late twentieth-century version of the old Iberic-American style of governance.

Born in Santiago de Veraguas in 1929, Omar Torrijos was the seventh of the twelve offspring of a middle-class couple of rural schoolteachers. José María Torrijos, a one-time seminarian from Roldanillo, Colombia, was his father; Joaquina Herrera, his mother, came from Los Ruices, a village in the vicinity of Santiago, the

Omar Torrijos (1929–1981). *Photograph by courtesy of Tatiana Padilla/El Siglo, Panamá.*

provincial capital. Omar's early years elapsed amidst the placidity of his native colonial town and the financial penury of his parents. As an elementary-school student his performance was far from outstanding; Torrijos himself said in an interview: "I studied until sixth grade when stumbled against Mr. Future Pluperfect [*sic*]."[1] The dictator-to-be later meandered through Juan Demóstenes Arosemena School, then a prestigious Santiago high school, with little academic gain.[2]

In political matters, however, his acquaintance with militant fellow students would prove extremely useful in the future. The young Omar joined the Santiago chapter of the Federación de Estudiantes de Panamá (FEP), a nationalist student organization on the lines of the Frente Patriótico de la Juventud. "Having been a member of FEP is my greatest pride," he would say once in firm control of the ship of state, for in his view the student organization was "the greatest source of civic consciousness from which the present and future leaders of the country can obtain nourishment."[3] Also studying at Santiago at the time and a member of FEP was Juan Materno Vásquez, who became a close friend of Torrijos' and later matured as a leftist intellectual. Attorney to the National Guard in the 1960s, Vásquez acquired notoriety as one of the military regime's ideologues after the 1968 coup.

However active in FEP Torrijos might have been, his poor marks would have destined him to obscurity had it not been for a unique opportunity which came to his parents' attention in late 1946. Two scholarships to the Salvadoran Gerardo Barrios Military Academy were being offered to prospective Panamanian military officers. Competition was low, for military studies, least of all in El Salvador, had no attraction whatsoever for most talented or well-connected Isthmians in the 1940s. Omar obtained one of the scholarships, dropped out of Juan Demóstenes Arosemena School, and reinitiated high-school education in El Salvador at the belated age of eighteen.

Torrijos joined the National Police as a second lieutenant in 1952.

"Unencumbered by excess idealism or integrity," he "adapted well to soldiering Panamanian style"—which included utilizing one's commission for personal profit—"and floated upward."[4] A full lieutenant by 1955, Torrijos was entrusted with the security of former Argentine populist dictator Juan Domingo Perón during the latter's short exile on the isthmus. Perón made a "durable" impression on the future Panamanian leader: "I admired and loved Perón," Omar declared two decades later, and considered him "America's great leader."[5] The Torrijos regime, in effect, adopted numerous populist measures similar to those implemented by the Argentine *conductor*. The admiration seems to have been reciprocal and enduring, for Torrijos received an honorary doctorate in law from the University of Buenos Aires in 1974, during Perón's final comeback, and played host to a visit by the Peronist Youth to Panama in March of the same year.[6]

In 1959 Torrijos was sent as head of a mission to negotiate with a small group of invaders who purported to follow Fidel Castro's footsteps and to initiate a revolution on the isthmus. Promoted to major and assigned military command of Colón Province in 1960, Torrijos attended a year-long counterinsurgency course at the Army Caribbean School in 1962. The civic action component of the course had a lasting effect on the young officer who, once transformed into dictator, would apply the theories he imbibed from Alliance for Progress modernization to create a rural constituency.

The instruction he received at the School of the Americas' predecessor also awakened Torrijos' political skills: when in 1963 he was assigned as military chief to Chiriquí, he proved a worthy model of the "new" military advocated by Washington. Although far from brilliant by normal standards, Torrijos was a great listener who could, moreover, convey sincere concern for others' plights. Some years afterwards Jack Hood Vaughn, then US ambassador to Panama, provided an evaluation of Torrijos' civic-action performance in the following terms:

He (Torrijos) was specializing in his big political initiative then, which was to be seen as the savior, the benefactor, the caring leader. He would round up doctors and dentists and take them in a caravan, and they would go out overnight, two full days of pulling teeth and physical examinations and all sorts of feeding programs with the CARE people. He invited me to witness this, and I went up and spent a day with them.

Torrijos made five, six, seven speeches that day. Of all the military men I met in Latin America—and I met a lot of them—he was the most impressive speaker. I don't mean haranguing a multitude. Talking to fifty campesinos, a village. He didn't condescend, and yet he reached them, but I don't think the fire in the eye was the fire of compassion, to the betterment of the Panamanian people, because he screwed them up pretty badly . . .

Civic action did more to put the military in power than anything else we ever did. It was a concerted effort to get the troops out of the barracks, building roads and public showers, and suddenly ... for the first time in their lives, they were applauded by civilians ... We gave a lot of civic action money to Torrijos and company, and we put them in business.[7]

Torrijos served in Chiriquí until 1966 when, promoted to lieutenant colonel, he was appointed executive secretary to the National Guard and placed in charge of the civic action projects of the military.

The career of his elder brother Moisés also provided Omar with advantageous political relationships. Moisés Torrijos became a journalist and actively pursued politics throughout the 1950s and 1960s, posing as a "progressive." His political stance and his visit to the Soviet Union made him suspect to US Ambassador Charles Adair who, as we have seen, expressed his distrust to Secretary of State Dean Rusk in March 1968. That year Moisés Torrijos' candidacy to the National Assembly was supported by Panama's Moscow-oriented Partido del Pueblo. In one of those curious occurrences of Panamanian politics, however, Moisés Torrijos figured in the slate of official Liberal presidential candidate David Samudio, the country's professed Alliance for Progress champion.

In spite of the wariness with which the US embassy regarded him, especially for the activities of his brother Moisés, Omar had links to US army intelligence. This reveals the divisions among US policy makers in their dealings with Panama since at least the 1960s, which later, under the Noriega dictatorship, would have such dire consequences. Omar Torrijos was reportedly a collector of information for Efraín Angueira, the Southern Command liaison officer with the National Guard.[8]

The *palo* side of Torrijos' career showed up in 1959, when he was given command of repressive operations against the short-lived Cerro Tute guerrilla uprising in his native province, although it was his second-in-command Boris Martínez who actually obtained the insurgents' surrender. During his command in Chiriquí, in October of 1963 two guardsmen subordinate to Torrijos were brought to trial for murdering a labor organizer whose activities irritated the Chiriquí Land Company, a United Brands subsidiary with extensive operations in the province. Also suspected of participating in the assassination was Manuel Noriega, who served as lieutenant under Torrijos. Noriega's boss, however, covered up for him.[9]

With brother Moisés' candidacy and National Guard First Commandant Bolívar Vallarino's partiality in favor of the official slate, Omar Torrijos became deeply involved with the Samudio ticket during the 1968 electoral campaign. Torrijos directed the March operation against First Vice-President Max Delvalle, in which the troops tear-gassed, beat, and arrested opposition sympathizers. During the May elections Torrijos was charged with coordinating vote-buying for the Liberal slate in three of the republic's nine provinces. In this capacity he had many supporters of Arnulfo Arias arrested and jailed.[10]

When the Arias-Vallarino entente permitted the former's rise to the presidency, for the third time, on 1 October 1968, President Arias undertook to cleanse the guard of his opponents. Torrijos was one of those targeted for banishment, in his particular case to the post of military attaché in Guatemala and El Salvador. Those demoted or transferred by Arias would be unable to supplement their salaries with the kickbacks National Guard officers allegedly received in exchange for allowing the continued operation of such illegal activities as prostitution, gambling, and drug trafficking.[11] It was thus that Torrijos joined the crowd of resentful officers and politicians who, fearful of losing their perks, began contemplating Arias' ouster.

The October Coup

In the few months after the 1968 elections, Arnulfo Arias had managed to heat the political cauldron to boiling point. In civilian politics he manipulated the vote count, demanding that the Electoral Tribunal award deputy credentials to his candidates. Furthermore, in his dealings with the military, Arias humiliated the corporate-conscious National Guard. He ungraciously dismissed Second Commandant José María Pinilla, scheduled to assume the post of first commandant at Vallarino's retirement on 11 October, thus breaking the pact which had allowed the president-elect's rise to power. He appointed his barber as director of the secret police, and ordered the banishment or transfer of Samudista officers. The new president obviously strove to subordinate the military to his absolute control, which purpose, it was rumored, he had entrusted to Luis Carlos Díaz Duque, his aide-de-camp, a graduate of Chile's Police Academy but a civilian and an outsider to the armed institute.[12]

It was Boris Martínez, Torrijos' deputy in 1959 and, in October 1968, military commander of Chiriquí Province, who channeled the complaints of the estranged officers and Liberal politicians toward insubordination. On the night of 11 October 1968, Martínez coordinated the coup d'état from his David garrison, replacing his fellow officers' closet subversion with forceful action. While some of the officer corps purported to elevate First Vice-President Raúl Arango to the presidency, Martínez ordered the establishment of a military duumvirate. As the authors Koster and Sánchez point out, the major's choices for junta membership and guard leadership indicate his obsession with military punctilio, an obsession that his predecessors José Antonio Remón and Esteban Huertas also shared and that can be traced to the Spanish colonial militias. The duumvirate was composed of José María Pinilla as president and Bolívar Urrutia as "member." Pinilla had been second commandant since 1960 until his dismissal by President Arias on 9 October, and Urrutia had been third commandant also since 1960. On 13 October the duumvirs presided over a swearing-in ceremony for themselves and the new cabinet.[13] Moreover, on Martínez's instructions, the ranking guard officer, Aristides Hassán, was appointed National Guard commandant. Former President Arias' shuffling of the officer corps was reversed and fifteen *Arnulfista* officers were purged. A general staff was created, and the offices of second and third commandant were eliminated. Omar Torrijos, the officer following Hassán in rank, was appointed chief of staff, with Martínez as his deputy. Apart from correcting what in Martínez's view were President Arias' intentions of undermining the professionalism and institutional character of the National Guard, the changes and innovations purported to bring the guard in line with more "advanced" military institutions. A little more than a month later, on 5 December, Hassán retired from active duty. Torrijos assumed the post of guard commandant and Martínez that of chief of staff.[14]

An effort to appeal to the citizenry through promises of political reform and prompt elections was contained in a 12 October military proclamation justifying the coup. The new cabinet's chief of staff, Juan Materno Vásquez, wrote the communiqué in which the National Guard assumed the role of protector of a constitution it would soon dump. The junta accused Arnulfo Arias of pursuing "a systematic and well-known plan to destroy representative democracy and enthrone a dictatorial regime" under his "unlimited, unipersonal" authority. "Under such circumstances," the communiqué proceeded,

> the National Guard had no other alternative but to comply with its sworn duty: impose respect for the laws and Constitution of the Republic of Panama . . . . Thus was born the movement of 11 October, which places public power, provisionally, in the hands of the National Guard.[15]

Reformist pledges were reiterated in ten so-called "Postulates of the Revolution Without Dictatorship and Liberty With Order," made public on 20 October. The junta rejected communism, committed itself to a complete purification of the executive branch and the judiciary (including a reduction of the bureaucracy), assured that free and fair elections would be held promptly, and promised to remove the National Guard from politics.[16]

While the rebellious officers had united in their desire to preserve corporate privilege and status, the direct assumption of political power by the guard soon caused cleavages to arise within its ranks. Boris Martínez led a vehemently anti-Communist hard-line faction which sought dictatorship to create a "republic of virtue" under the lead of the military, immune from corruption and Marxism, as the dictatorship's "postulates" give evidence to. Not many officers sided with Martínez, as might be presumed given the guard's history of corruption. Most converged around Omar Torrijos, articulator and spokesman of a faction far more preoccupied with opportunities for personal gain than with the East-West struggle. Correspondingly, the Torrijos faction had little reticence about incorporating leftist intellectuals and, at the same time, warning against "Communist dangers," to ensure its aims.

Antagonized by Martínez's puritanism, Torrijos and his followers overthrew and exiled the opposing faction on 23 February 1969, accusing it of leading the country, through radical policies, toward communism. But Torrijos' undisputed reign had not yet begun, for in December of 1969, while on a private visit to Mexico, one of his subordinates attempted his overthrow and a return to civilian rule. Amado Sanjur had close links to the estranged civilian political class, believed it inappropriate for the National Guard to assume the republic's government, and took Torrijos' leftist discourse at face value. So did a now alarmed US Southern Command counterintelligence, which instigated or at least abetted Sanjur's action.[17] But most of the officer corps, as Sanjur explained two decades later, "were not prepared to return power. After having tasted [its] benefits, it was almost impossible to convince them to return to the barracks."[18] Also contributing to the movement's failure were disagreements among the rebels and CIA preference for Torrijos, which took the form of support from Manuel Noriega, the new military commander of Chiriquí. Noriega, a "prize asset" of the CIA, permitted Torrijos' emergency landing at an airstrip in Chiriquí, whence the military commander regained control of the country.[19]

"Deep Distress" Becomes "Play Ball"

The October military coup caught the Johnson Administration by surprise, and for a short time the State Department cooled relations with Panama. Washington had placed high hopes on Arnulfo Arias' presidency. Because of the *caudillo*'s popularity, US policy makers were counting on swift approval by the Isthmian legislature if the new president indicated his satisfaction with the three-in-one treaties. The US embassy, in fact, feared that denial of Arnulfo's electoral triumph through fraud or a preventive military coup would generate uncontrollable instability and forestall treaty approval.[20] Secretary of State Dean Rusk's "deep distress" over the coup, which he declared in a statement issued on 12 October 1968, was therefore not totally unexpected. Rusk justified the administration's concern by citing the "close relationship with Panama and [the US] stake in the stability of the isthmus in view of our presence there as stewards of the vital Panama Canal."[21] The preceding night Arnulfo Arias and a number of followers had taken refuge in the US-controlled Canal Zone.

In the month that followed, however, Washington's outlook changed. Zone officials asked Arnulfo Arias to leave the territory, which he did on the 21st, and on 13 November Washington formally recognized the military junta. "The United States took this action," according to a Foggy Bottom statement, "after extensive consultations with other members of the Organization of American States." Washington had given "careful consideration to the publicly declared intention of the Panamanian Government to hold elections, to return to constitutional government, to respect human rights, and to observe Panama's international obligations."[22]

Other factors that influenced the diplomatic normalization can only be extrapolated. Except for an isolated and little-known insurgent outburst in Chiriquí,[23] the regime had succeeded in maintaining stability throughout the country, one of the essential international-relations criteria for establishing normal diplomatic relations (the other being compliance with international obligations, which the new government, according to the State Department, duly acknowledged). National Guard officers, some of whom were on the US intelligence payroll, most probably reiterated their steadfastness to their respective control officers. Boris Martínez's calls for an anti-Communist crusade must have impressed the embassy favorably. And although Ambassador Adair suspected Omar Torrijos because of his brother Moisés' "progressiveness," Efraín Angueira, of Southern Command intelligence, certainly must have vouched for Omar. The US interest was first and foremost to protect North American hegemony and maintain stability on the isthmus; in Machiavellian Washington politics it mattered little if US objectives were assured by a military regime or by an elected civilian government. The subsequent North American support for the military regime makes the United States at least partially responsible for its prolonged tenure, as well as for the militarization of Panamanian politics it brought about.

Resumption of diplomatic relations indicated Washington's willingness to "play ball," but the pragmatic, self-serving US approach to relations with the Torrijos dictatorship, gradually solidifying during 1969, did not consolidate until after Torrijos emerged triumphant from the December 1969 coup attempt. The Rockefeller Mission, among other factors, increased Torrijos' worth in Washington's view. Governor Nelson Rockefeller visited Panama in May 1969 and expressed unbounded enthusiasm for the military regime, which by that time had already begun putting into effect certain populist measures. With a view to preserving stability on the isthmus, the governor advised Torrijos to continue implementing his populist program. Rockefeller also invited the dictator to visit New York City, where Torrijos took due advantage of the opportunity to publicize his government among a group of US investors.[24]

While Southern Command's opinion of the dictator had changed by December of 1969, the CIA fully subscribed to Rockefeller's thesis. US army counterintelligence, worried about the commander's move to the left, stood behind Amado Sanjur's effort to unseat Torrijos. The CIA, however, judged Torrijos a valuable US ally, his populist rhetoric "good camouflage," and his understanding with the Moscow/Havana-oriented Partido del Pueblo the best possible guarantee for stability on the isthmus.[25] Believing that US interests lay with Torrijos, "a known quality,"[26] the CIA provided logistical support for him during the internecine military dispute. Langley solicited collaboration from its agent Manuel Noriega who, as was previously mentioned, crucially assisted Torrijos' return from Mexico.

IN DECEMBER 1969 Torrijos promoted himself to general and sacked the officers who had plotted against him. Duumvirs Pinilla and Urrutia were replaced by two middle-class civilians, Demetrio

Lakas and Arturo Sucre. Noriega's loyalty was later rewarded when the commander appointed him chief of the newly-created G-2, the guard's intelligence office. More importantly for the isthmus, Torrijos now became Panama's maximum leader. The directing role he played in the guard, his political skills awakened by civic action theory and practice, and his links to opportunistic leftist politicians, permitted Torrijos to assume the leadership of the new Panamanian institutional military dictatorship. With US support, Panama now witnessed the full-steam launching of a populist agenda in an effort to consolidate and legitimize the new regime.

Notes

1. Joaquín Soler Serrano, *Personajes a fondo: Conversaciones con grandes figuras de nuestro tiempo* (Barcelona: Editorial Planeta, 1987), p. 39.

2. Labrut, *Este es Omar Torrijos* (Panama: By the Author, 1982), p. 76.

3. Ibid., pp. 165–69.

4. Richard M. Koster and Guillermo Sánchez Borbón, *In the Time of the Tyrants: Panama, 1968–1990* (New York: W.W. Norton & Company, 1990), p. 70.

5. Labrut, *Este es Omar Torrijos*, pp. 140, 169.

6. Giancarlo Soler, "Surgimiento del reformismo militar, evolución y crisis," in *Panamá: Fuerzas armadas y cuestión nacional* (Panama: Taller de Estudios Laborales y Sociales, 1988), pp. 10–11. Juan Materno Vásquez, *Mi amigo Omar Torrijos: Su pensamiento vivo* (Panama: Ediciones Olga Elena, 1989), p. 162.

7. Koster, *In the Time of the Tyrants*, p. 149.

8. Ibid., pp. 74, 88, 125.

9. Ibid., pp. 71, 124.

10. Ibid., p. 98.

11. Ibid., pp. 75, 82, 91.

12. Ibid., p. 67.

13. Ibid., pp. 71, 84.

14. Ibid., pp. 76, 101. Renato Pereira, *Panamá: Fuerzas armadas y política* (Panama: Ediciones Nueva Universidad, 1979), pp. 120–22.

15. Vásquez, *Mi amigo Omar Torrijos*, pp. 21–22.

16. Koster, *In the Time of the Tyrants*, p. 90.

17. Ibid., pp. 128–30.

18. Amado Sanjur, "La desmilitarización y la eliminación del ejército," *El Panamá América*, 11 August 1992, p. 6A.

19. Koster, *In the Time of the Tyrants*, pp. 129–32.

20. Ibid. pp. 93, 95. Humberto E. Ricord, *Los clanes de la oligarquía panameña y el golpe militar de 1968* (Panama: By the Author, 1983), pp. 84–88.

21. US Department of State, *Bulletin*, 4 November 1968, p. 470.

22. Ibid., 2 December 1968, p. 573.

23. For information on the Chiriquí insurgency, see chapter 8.

24. Koster, *In the Time of the Tyrants*, p. 119. Labrut, *Este es Omar Torrijos*, pp. 22, 41–42.

25. Koster, *In the Time of the Tyrants*, pp. 130–31.

26. Ibid., p. 131.

Chapter 7

Military Populism and US-Panamanian Relations, 1969–1981

ALAIN ROUQUIÉ HAS pointed out that a "clientelistic type of redistribution that assures the consent of the dominated is only possible in periods of prosperity."[1] Such was the case in Panama, where the 1960s proved to be a decade of sustained economic growth. Distribution of wealth in Panama, although never as inequitable as in other Latin American countries, was, however, slower than growth. This disparity caused some social tension, as evidenced by a series of strikes, mass protests, and revolutionary activities that occurred at the time. Panama's governments had proven unequal to the task of undertaking the difficult but necessary reforms leading toward effective redistribution while maintaining social peace and preserving a favorable climate for growth.[2]

Torrijos seized the opportunity that Panama's socioeconomic inequities presented to create a base of support for his military authoritarianism. Designed to please key constituencies, his development strategy was organized in corporatist fashion and featured bureaucratic expansion, toleration of official corruption, saturation of the country's credit capacity, excessive state involvement in the economy, and, paradoxically, a failure to apply effective taxation, the redistribution mechanism par excellence.[3] These characteristics, as well as Torrijos' own personality and Panama's lack of political legitimacy, gave shape to an authoritarian, populist, and personalist regime. Responsible only to the National Guard commander and general staff, Torrijos dubbed his government the "Revolution of 11 October," or *proceso de cambios revolucionarios* ("process of revolutionary changes"), and claimed it was "directed towards a national transformation to achieve the participation in national welfare and wealth of all sectors which form the republic."[4]

Workers, Peasants, and Students

The first hints of populism in the military regime occurred shortly after the takeover. Soon after 11 October, through his "progressive" collaborators, Torrijos contacted student and labor leaders "to assure them the coup was not addressed against popular interests." Haphazard populist measures were announced shortly thereafter: a freezing of the prices of essential foodstuffs and low-income rents, the transfer to the National University of funds allocated to the legislature, and the repeal of a decree which limited high-school students' participation in militant organizations such as FEP.[5]

The earliest coordinated, systematic inclusionist measures, however, came after the downfall of Boris Martínez. Predictably, they focused on labor, the peasantry, and militant student groups. In March of 1969 Torrijos appointed Rómulo Escobar, another "progressive" intellectual linked to leftist worker organizations, as labor minister. Thus began the regime's close association with organized labor. In April Escobar announced mandatory unionization and plans for the grouping of all the country's workers in a single, government-led confederation. Torrijos' rhetoric sanctioned his labor minister's approach: in a Labor Day (1 May) address delivered in the

banana-growing region of the republic, the military commander proclaimed his "solidarity" with the workers of Chiriquí Land
Company. The banana workers' union leaders—those who remained
after the dictatorship had imprisoned or exiled their more outspoken
predecessors—were treated to more than speeches for their pliancy
toward the regime's corporatist scheme. In response to their peti-
tion, Torrijos extended the union leaders' terms of office for two
more years.[6]

On 1 January 1972 new labor legislation went into effect.
According to Torrijos, the new code "succeeds in humanizing the
working conditions and gives real and effective protection to the
working man. The new code *incorporates* a great mass of workers to
its benefits"[7] including drivers, fishermen, domestics, and peddlers.
Other features included protection against arbitrary dismissal,
decentralization of labor justice, emphasis on collective bargaining,
an additional month's bonus payment for all workers, and obligato-
ry discount of union dues, the last deemed a "conquest" of the
Panamanian working class by the dictator. Torrijos justified obliga-
tory unionization and payment of union dues as follows:

> The revolution of 11 October proclaims the organization of obligato-
> ry unionization as the basis of its revolutionary policy so that [labor],
> which has endured suffering and incomprehension, may participate
> in the national destiny, in economic planning, and in general welfare.
> This obligatory unionization which the revolution of 11 October
> shall implant will permit the creation of a powerful general confeder-
> ation of workers, thus realizing the dream of all workers and union
> leaders who during many years proposed this formula against the
> incomprehension, denials, and persecution of corrupt and immoral
> governments. A general confederation of Panamanian workers will
> transform organized labor—with obligatory union dues—into an
> economically strong, civically healthy, and nationally positive organ-
> ism, because thanks to such confederation persecutions against
> unions and the constant violation of the Panamanian workers' rights
> will cease.[8]

Torrijos' agrarian policy focused on exploiting at least some of the political potential of a large but dormant rural constituency, consisting of approximately half the population of the isthmus. For this purpose, Panama's de facto ruler would frequently carry out "domestic patrolling"—official tours of the countryside during which he would personally cater to the needs of the local population and order improvements for their benefit, including immediate cash handouts —a hybrid of the Alliance for Progress' civic action program and the Iberic-American paternalist tradition. The *proceso* also institutionalized substantive policy measures in this field. It stepped up agrarian reform and technical and financial assistance for agricultural production; stimulated peasant organization, notably through a form of cooperative farmers' association modeled after the Chilean *asentamientos;* and involved the Panamanian state, for the first time, in agro-industrial projects. These innovations were accompanied by appropriate rhetoric: Torrijos expressed his faith that the agrarian program would convert "those who in the past were persecuted into men who are taken care of, those who were stepsons of a father who did not love them into the beloved children of a new republic."[9]

The first *asentamiento* was inaugurated on 14 March 1969 in Florentino, a community in the dictator's native Veraguas. In 1970 a national confederation of these *asentamientos* was created and, pursuant to an agreement between Torrijos and the Partido del Pueblo, the regime handed leadership of the confederation over to the Marxist party. But in spite of communist participation in Torrijos' agrarian policy, the country's new leader avoided making revolutionary reforms that might antagonize Panama's landowners and other important constituents such as local business and international capital.[10] The commander's discourse took care to reflect this caution:

Agrarian reform has done nothing undue: it has done nothing but support a *revolution of growing aspirations* which was to be either willingly carried out [by us] or undertaken in violent fashion, by a famished peasantry. Not even three fence wires have been trampled.

No property deed has been trampled, although some of this country's deeds are of very bad reputation and dubious provenance.[11]

On 11 October 1971, Torrijos pledged to work "at any cost, for the fifty thousand farmers whose incomes do not even reach one hundred dollars a month."[12] To finance the activities of the poorest agriculturists, Torrijos created the Agricultural Development Bank in 1973. In spite of an avowed policy of reducing Panamanian dependence on the United States, financing for the bank came mainly from the USAID. A government agency in charge of monopolizing the purchase of certain agricultural products was set up in 1974. This agency also engaged in limited retail sales of produce in Panama City and Colón, with a view to exercising pressure over the prices charged by private retailers.[13]

Most of the organized, militant, and nationalist student movement was assimilated to the regime, also to a great extent due to the good offices of Rómulo Escobar. In exchange for loyalty to Torrijos, in May 1971 the government placed the National University under the tutelage of FEP. Escobar was designated rector to guarantee compliance, in all respects, with the agreement.[14] Torrijos also appointed a number of current and former student leaders to the bureaucracy, and the government undertook to fund all "civic and political events" of the now official student federation.[15]

Local Marxists and the Urban Masses

One of the most profitable achievements of the dictatorship was its co-optation of the Marxist Partido del Pueblo, which became a pillar of the military regime until the US invasion of December 1989. Leftist students and intellectuals, in fact, concocted much of the pseudo-nationalist, socialist discourse of the regime. After the ouster of Boris Martínez, whose anti-Communist phobia had occasioned the imprisonment of Partido del Pueblo leaders, Torrijos reached a durable understanding with the Moscow-liners in 1969–1970. Although as of 1968 the party's influence in national politics was almost nil, it did have some leverage with small but highly vocal university and labor groups, which it now agreed to keep in check. In exchange, Torrijos liberated jailed party members and gave them a share of the spoils, especially in the agriculture, labor, and education ministries. The party, moreover, was officially recognized by the regime; it was, in actuality, the only political organization allowed to operate until 1978. More importantly, the pact with the Partido del Pueblo eventually paved the way for an understanding with Cuba. Fidel Castro pledged not to foment insurgency on the isthmus and, after diplomatic relations between the two states were reestablished in 1974, provided valuable international support for the regime in general and Torrijos in particular. Castro's advantage in the bargain was by no means slight: Panama became crucial in his scheme to evade the US trade embargo and obtain Yankee goods and technology. On the Panamanian side, this same scheme further lined the pockets of general staff members and selected civilian supporters of the military, who operated the companies that traded with Fidel's Cuba.[16]

The regime also sought to lure the urban masses. Public housing projects, stimulated by the creation of a national mortgage bank in 1973, provided many slum tenants with their own homes. New housing legislation, which declared leases an issue of "public order," prohibited landlords from arbitrarily terminating lease contracts or increasing rents. The Torrijos regime also gained control of two bus- and taxi-drivers' cooperatives and, through them, of the important urban transportation sector.[17]

A successful example of the dictatorship's drive for urban co-optation was its assimilation of a civic movement of the San Miguelito shanty community. The movement had originated through the efforts of the Catholic Church, which entrusted the spiritual care of the community to a group of US priests. Inspired by liberation theology, the parish priests organized a series of conscious-ness-raising programs, starting in 1963. The programs were very effective, and soon gave rise to an independent lay organization whose principal objective was material and moral improvement of the community. This organization strongly opposed the 1968 military coup, demanding, through peaceful yet intense resistance, a return to constitutional rule.

Torrijos, however, neutralized the San Miguelito opposition by promising the creation of an "experimental district," with autonomy to pursue its own development—indeed an innovation in Panama-nian politics. In July of 1969 the dictatorship created the "Special District of San Miguelito." Community development was now made the responsibility of new municipal officers and bureaucrats, direct-ly appointed by Torrijos. Those civic leaders who accepted Torrijos' suzerainty were rewarded with public offices; those who did not give in soon found that they were impotent to achieve development as they sought it, in the face of official endowment for the municipal officers' projects. By undermining the San Miguelito grassroots orga-nization, the dictatorship neutralized a strong challenge to its leader-ship.[18]

Anti-"oligarchic" discourse, directed at the old political and propertied class, represented still another effort at cultivating the popular sectors. In the words of Omar Torrijos, the military govern-ment "did not emerge by caprice or accident. It was [rather] the cul-mination of a long process of growing incapacity by the political parties to govern in honest, responsible, and orderly fashion."[19] Through the 1968 military coup, declared the maximum leader, "the oligarchy has been deprived of the political power which it held since the beginnings of the republic."[20] Torrijos' rhetoric sometimes took virulent trends:

> The businessmen who wish to throw US troops upon the Panamanian people are bad Panamanians. They wish to repeat the 1925 exploit in which North American troops set up their tents on

Santa Ana Park and occupied the rest of the country [sic] because the people had striven from their course and were disrupting order by requesting a lowering of rents and better living conditions. I do not know whom [these businessmen] are going to call now. Thank God they are not sufficiently numerous or substantial that they will not fit into an Air Force plane which can repatriate them where they are socially and mentally located: a town in the Florida peninsula, the Valley of the Fallen for all Latin American reactionaries who cannot work with their people.[21]

Domestic and Foreign Capital

Despite the dictatorship's anti-"oligarchic" and nationalist discourse, Torrijos actually stimulated the development model traditionally favored by Panama's urban propertied class. A liberal banking decree entered into force in July of 1970, and permitted the almost overnight establishment in Panama of numerous financial institutions, which accounted for the isthmus' conversion into Latin America's principal international banking center. In return, international loan capital provided ready financing for the dictator's populist scheme. Panama's foreign debt rose from $286 million in 1970 to $2.1 billion in 1980 (current figures), the latter amount representing the highest per capita indebtedness in Latin America. Significantly, the government did not allow the unionization of Panama's banking employees.[22]

Torrijos also protected his favorite local businessmen. "Nonconfrontation and class cooperation," writes a US scholar supportive of the dictator, "were the watchwords" in Torrijos' relationship to the old directing class.[23] One of the maximum leader's closest collaborators was Gabriel Lewis, a conspicuous member of what the regime tagged the "oligarchy." Another was Tomás Altamirano Duque, who controlled Panama's (and two of the hemisphere's) oldest newspapers, *The Star & Herald* and *La Estrella de*

Panama. He found shelter in Torrijos' camp after the military commander released him from prison on terms similar to those accompanying the liberation of the Partido del Pueblo leadership. Former Foreign Minister Fernando Eleta and his brother Carlos, owners of the country's oldest and largest radio and television networks, were also prominent supporters of the dictator.[24]

Torrijos was also extremely successful in co-opting foreign capital. In this endeavor he was ably assisted by Nicolás Ardito Barletta, an economist for whom a planning ministry was eventually created. In the immediate aftermath of the coup, Torrijos secured from the Chiriquí Land Company an emergency $1 million loan, in exchange for the regime's emasculation of the banana worker's union.[25] The following year Goldman Sachs & Company lent the dictatorship $30 million for development.[26] Goldman Sachs hosted Torrijos on 27 December 1969, during the dictator's visit to New York. In the premises of the international bankers' firm, Torrijos addressed a group of US businessmen with the purpose of attracting foreign capital to the country in his grip. Panama, he said, had registered an average growth rate of eight percent in the last twelve-year period, and featured "an international economic policy of market expansion, ample maritime, air, banking, legal, and labor facilities, and a cultural aptitude [sic] for international business," as well as "proven potential for mineral exploitation and export-oriented agricultural production."[27]Torrijos' wooing of international investors brought his regime favorable commentaries. *Barron's,* a specialized business publication, reported in 1978:

> The fact is that Panama's economy and management style are already dominated by U.S. attitudes and business methods at a level found nowhere else in Central America, which the unpredictable Torrijos, though often appearing to be far leftward leaning, has encouraged.[28]

Nationalism and the Canal Issue

Even as the regime cooperated with international capital, the sovereignty issue figured prominently in the dictatorship's agenda. It was directed not only against the US government's presence in the Canal Zone, but also against such traditional forms of private US economic domination in the Caribbean as banana plantations and public utilities. The regime profited immensely from its nationalist rhetoric, both in Panama and in the international arena. Domestically, the discourse offered, as James Malloy has pointed out, gratification to nationalist elements of the population long preoccupied with the issue.[29] Internationally, the issue created widespread support for the Panamanian cause among outspoken world leaders in Latin America, as well as in other Third World and Western European countries.

The regime's first apparent attack on US "imperialism" was its rejection, in August 1970, of the 1967 draft treaties, considered "unsatisfactory" for Panamanian demands by Torrijos' Foreign Office.[30] In the same year, the government refused to renew the lease on the Río Hato base, taking over the installation in December. The base was handed over to the National Guard for the establishment of Panama's first military academy.

"The imperialist claw on the canal strip is an unhappy remnant of dollar diplomacy and the big stick," the dictator told Colombian novelist Gabriel García Márquez, in a display of nationalist imagery characteristic of his canal oratory.[31] And when the State Department failed to take Torrijos' demagoguery seriously, Panama caused Washington an apparently significant diplomatic embarrassment by inviting the United Nations Security Council to meet in Panama City in March 1973. Torrijos welcomed the Security Council with a passionate inquiry: "Why are we not respected? Why are we provoked? Why are we subjected? Why do they [the United States] not let this defenseless, euphoric Panamanian people live in peace?"[32]

Except for a US veto—the first in the history of the United Nations—and a British abstention, the Security Council voted unanimously for recognition of Panamanian sovereignty in the Canal Zone. But the US veto, far from signifying the defeat of Torrijos' cause, was its springboard to celebrity. The dictator compared it to a "projectile" US policy makers "shot from Panama," offending the "feelings of all the free men of the world. . . . It was a veto of arrogance, a projectile of arrogance [and] haughtiness which indicated to small peoples" that Washington "would not permit the continuation of independence struggles."[33]

Two months later, writes Michael Conniff, "a NSC-drafted report by President Nixon to Congress stated that the time had come to establish a new relationship with Panama."[34] In February 1974, Torrijos' Foreign Minister Juan Antonio Tack and US Secretary of State Henry Kissinger signed a Joint Statement of Principles concerning the Panama Canal. New negotiations ensued, and to bolster Panamanian leverage in the process Torrijos made diplomatic overtures to Eastern-bloc countries, and joined the Latin American Economic System and the Non-Aligned Movement in 1975. Panama was also one of the founding members of the Contadora Peace Process in 1975. US-Panamanian negotiations culminated with the signing of two separate canal treaties, concerning the canal *per se* and the canal's neutrality, in 1977.[35] With the signing of the conventions, the Panamanian military dictatorship duly capitalized on the inauguration of what President Jimmy Carter termed a "new chapter" in the history of US-Latin American relations.[36]

At a substantial cost to the state, in 1972 the regime nationalized the US-owned Compañía Panameña de Fuerza y Luz, which provided electric power to Panama City and Colón.[37] Two years later, Torrijos and United Brands briefly interrupted their cozy relationship. With the onset of financial difficulties, due to the exhaustion of the dictatorship's economic model and the 1973 rise in the price of oil, Torrijos—in conjunction with other regional leaders—decided to impose a new levy on banana production. United Brands threatened to suspend its activities if the new tax was not repealed. The dictator, seizing yet another opportunity to clothe his leadership in national-ist trappings, declared a banana war "against the neocolonialism of multi-national corporations . . . which try to destabilize the political life and complicate the economic life of the country opposing the legitimate demands of the sovereign in defense of their natural resources."[38]

The "war" ended when the government and United Brands signed a new contract, whereby Panama acquired the plantations and granted the US company the right to manage them and export their produce. A considerable amount of productive land that the banana company maintained uncultivated to discourage competition reverted to the republic and allowed the creation of state banana enterprises. After this victory, Torrijos promoted the creation of a regional cartel, the Union of Banana Exporting Countries.[39]

State Involvement in the Economy

Torrijos' inclusionist policies required a greater degree of state involvement in the economy than had been previously the norm in Panama. Most notable was the expansion in the bureaucracy, which materially benefited some of the lower classes with increases in reg-ular income and new opportunities for graft. Although of dubious reliability, official figures do indicate an increase in public employ-ment: 36,000 civil servants in 1965, 56,000 in 1970, and 87,000 in 1975. Ministries and government agencies multiplied and were staffed by *recomendados* of guard officers and well-placed civilians, who used the public payroll to favor family, friends, and political clients in a manner that far surpassed the practices of the former "oli-garchy." It was indeed, as Rouquié indicates, a policy of redistribu-tion; a corrupting one, however, which in the long run slowed possibilities for national development. Meanwhile, timid attempts at sounder redistributive policies were undermined by official corruption. A rise in the tax on liquor and luxury goods, for example, was offset by the intense, government-condoned contraband in these items from the Colon Free Zone.[40]

Large-scale programs for the construction of schools, health centers, roads, and houses were also implemented; they too provided the opportunity to reward the dictatorship's favorites with government contracts or other sources of supplementary income. An example occurred with the Vista Alegre housing project in Arraiján district, close to Panama City. In 1974, the Housing Office implemented a plan to urbanize the small community with a view to providing dwellings for at least one hundred thousand residents within a decade. The local representative thought it wise that the county buy the land and resell it at a profit to the government, or parcel it out to those locals who wished to maintain their residence in Vista Alegre. But—writes George Priestley, who documented the case—when the representative "investigated purchasing the land, he found that it had been bought up by the Compañía Vista Alegre, S.A." Curiously enough, a brother of G-2 Chief Manuel Noriega, the wife of puppet President Demetrio Lakas, one of Torrijos' sisters, and the husband of a representative closely associated with Torrijos and Noriega, were all shareholders in the enterprise. "The company had bought the land, sold a portion to the Housing and Urbanization Institute (IVU), and kept another portion with which to speculate."[41]

Along with placing all public utilities under state control, during the military dictatorship Panama's government became directly involved in productive, export-oriented activities. The state acquired banana plantations and sugar mills, a citrus fruit processing plant, Panama City's slaughterhouse, and a cement factory. It set up a national radio network and inaugurated three large hydroelectric projects. The state monopolized the supply of electric power, as well as all internal communications; it intervened in journalism through its expropriation and operation of the newspapers belonging to the heirs of former President Harmodio Arias Madrid. The regime organized the workers of all these state-led enterprises, and their respective unions swelled the official labor confederation.

National Guard Professionalization and Militarization

As expected, the regime substantially endowed the military institution, which underwent significant changes. These came in response to the desire of Torrijos and the officer corps to retain all effective power, for which purpose the maintenance of absolute National Guard loyalty was essential. Alongside the creation of a general staff in 1968, the National Guard increased in size and scope, obtained more sophisticated armament, acquired numerous installations, and became more professionalized. An air force and a marine corps were created in 1969. By 1979 guard membership had risen to approximately 8,000 from approximately 4,000 in 1968. An air unit and seven light-infantry companies had been created. Military expenditure had increased from approximately $9 million in 1970 to $42 million in 1979. The guard changed obsolete US armament prevalent in 1968 for newer US, Brazilian, British, and Israeli equipment. The feather in the National Guard's hat during these years was participation in the United Nations Peacekeeping Force to the Sinai in 1973.[42]

In the Río Hato base Torrijos established the Tomás Herrera Military Institute, Panama's first military academy, as well as the Guard Formation School, which provided four-month courses to soldiers. Both were inaugurated in 1974. The Herrera Academy curriculum included interdisciplinary national development seminars as well as social science courses. The military dictatorship also introduced political orientation seminars for commissioned and noncommissioned officers. The personnel office of the National Guard brought assignment of military scholarships firmly under its control, and candidates were limited to high school majors in science. South American academies, such as those of Peru, Argentina, and Brazil, were given preference over their Central American counterparts.[43]

As observed by Guillermo O'Donnell in the Southern Cone, increased professionalization brought about a rise in the military's technocratic expectations.[44] Professionalization required the transformation of the National Guard into a full-fledged army, and to justify professionalization, the semblance of a security doctrine began to evolve. Professionalization and militarization, in the Panamanian context lacking legitimacy and an authentic defensive mission for the military, were therefore mutually reinforcing. It is no mere coincidence that the militarization of the National Police was contemporary with the professional career of José Antonio Remón, Panama's first professionally-trained soldier.

The *Torrijista* security doctrine initially focused not on the East-West struggle but on economic development and national independence. In this regard Roberto Díaz Herrera, executive secretary to the general staff, declared in 1971:

> As seldom in [Latin] America, our rifles no longer point towards the bowels of this country's dispossessed. Today, in spite of the generally unhealthy criticism woven in the country and outside against Panama's revolutionary government, our uniform is only feared in the circles which previously utilized it to frighten or profit under the threatening shadow of the bayonets. For three years we have had a military institution that is rapidly becoming an instrument of popular action, aiming against illiteracy, disease, and injustice, without overlooking the security of the state and its territorial integrity.[45]

In spite of all the innovations the military regime introduced, the National Guard continued to lack actual combat capacity. Its principal objective still remained the maintenance of internal security, although now in the context of a military dictatorship that existed to protect and enhance the widened privileges of the military caste. Under such circumstances, the guard had to defend its leaders as well as the populist program put into effect by Torrijos to gain legitimacy. Torrijos disclosed these facts in an oft-quoted 1972 letter to Senator Edward Kennedy: "Our army has been organized under the conviction that it will never have to face an invasion of foreign forces. We do not have sophisticated fighter planes or bombs of great explosive power." The National Guard's war, continued Torrijos, was a domestic issue. "We daily verify it when we see the suburbs in which our people live, parks full of unemployed citizens, and mothers seeking shelter and sustenance for their children." Panama's socio-economic situation, said the dictator, reaffirmed the military's conviction that a war had to be fought "to end the causes which propitiated such a state of affairs."[46]

The 1972 Constitution

The overall legal framework which buttressed the military regime was Torrijos' 1972 Constitution. The charter purported to provide legal legitimacy to the regime, for the de facto nature of the dictatorship made its leader insecure in the international arena.[47] But above all it represented an attempt to implant *Torrijismo,* Panama's sui generis populist militarism, institutional and personalist at the same time. A reading of the constitution's two fundamental articles evidences the document's principal raison d'être. Article 2 declared: "Public power derives from the people; it is exercised by the Government through the distribution of functions undertaken by the Executive, Legislative, and Judicial branches, which act in harmonic collaboration among themselves *and with the Public Force* [i.e., the National Guard]." Article 277 appointed Torrijos "maximum leader of the Panamanian revolution," and assigned him the exercise of a wide array of powers for six years, including "the coordination of public administration," and the right to appoint and dismiss ministers and members of the legislative commission, the comptroller-general, the attorney general, the Supreme Court magistrates, the heads of government agencies, and National Guard officers. Torrijos was also given power to direct the republic's foreign and economic policies, as well as to participate in the formulation of laws.[48]

The charter introduced new and complex power structures which were, however, generally meaningless, for real power remained with Torrijos and the guard's general staff. Proportional representation previously exercised by deputies was substituted for county representation, in spite of the very unequal population of the republic's 505 *corregimientos*. A token inclusionary measure, it supposedly sought to dignify, in classic populist style, the republic's humblest political subdivision, as well as the republic's *campesinos,* for most *corregimientos* are located in the rural areas. Torrijos claimed to have learned from his civic action experience and his "domestic patrolling" the need to "respect, listen, and consult" the "natural leaders" of the communities. From "domestic patrolling," he claimed, "emerged the idea of organizing the country, politically, with a basis on the 505 *corregimientos.*"[49]

In spite of Torrijos' claim that the new constitution placed law-making power in the hands of "the most representative community leaders,"[50] a look at the legislative responsibilities of the new assembly of *corregimiento* representatives demonstrates that its creation was merely symbolic. Representatives were to meet annually for one month; elect the president and vice-president of the republic once every six years; approve or reject international treaties negotiated by the executive; declare war or establish peace; approve or reject reforms in the country's political subdivisions proposed by the cabinet; grant amnesty to political prisoners; and write the assembly's own rules of proceedings. Responsibility for issuing laws was vested in a legislative commission, of which Torrijos, in accordance with Article 277, was a member.[51]

If representatives were given little clout at the national level they were assigned broader responsibilities—and provided budgetary allocations—at the provincial, municipal, and local levels. Provincial councils were formed in which all the province's county representatives participated, in addition to the provincial governor, military chief, and directors of national agencies. In 1972 Torrijos allocated $100,000 to each of the country's nine provincial councils, to be expended exclusively by the representatives. At the municipal level, representatives, previously known as *concejales,* had since the past century formed a council which was heir to the colonial *cabildo.* The dictatorship significantly increased municipal resources accessible to *representantes;* in 1974, for example, a $5 million AID loan for "municipal development" was made available to them. Finally, in each county the constitution created community boards, charged with fostering economic development at the grassroots level. For this sole purpose, each representative was to receive a minimum yearly grant of $1,000.[52] With such a multiplicity of funding sources within their reach, it is not surprising that public office triggered the economic advancement of many an *honorable representante.*

US Concerns for Panamanian "Consent"

Washington's approach to relations with Panama during the Torrijos years was a pragmatic one. Although US interests of hegemony and stability required protection, the United States was reluctant to impose them through outright military intervention. Beginning in the late 1920s, diplomacy had been the preferred means of carrying out US objectives. And since October of 1968 diplomacy with Panama required "playing ball" with a military regime, obnoxious as it was. Given the self-serving, co-optive nature of the *proceso,* the bottom line of US-Panamanian relations during the Torrijos years was therefore symbiosis. While the Panamanian dictatorship attempted to conceal the symbiotic relationship behind a veil of nationalist rhetoric, Washington also continually appealed to face-saving artifices to disguise its association with a regime whose policies were antagonistic to the US liberal democratic tradition. Additionally, on a few occasions moral concerns prompted condemnatory declarations, almost exclusively from the US Congress. But in essence, the close relationship was maintained throughout the dictatorship, as the uninterrupted provision of North American economic and military assistance to the Torrijos regime demonstrates.

Such reasoning as the CIA put forth in late 1969—when it sided with Torrijos, "a known quality" capable of maintaining stability on the isthmus[53]—prevailed through the Nixon, Ford, and Carter administrations. Continuous US assistance demonstrates Washington's consistent desire for a close working relationship with the military government, and assigns Washington partial responsibility for the duration, excesses, and militarization of the regime instituted in 1968. While average annual economic assistance, measured in constant US dollars, lagged behind the amount received during the last eight years of the civilian liberal regime ($37.4 million versus $61.6 million per annum), EXIMBANK credits reached an annual (constant) average of $22.7 million during the Torrijos years as compared to a mere $4.9 million between 1961 and 1968.[54]

Military assistance figures, albeit small in comparison to other recipients of US aid, are perhaps a more telling indicator of Washington's desire to preserve the National Guard's alignment with US interests. An average (constant) $1.2 million in military assistance between 1961 and 1968 rose to $2.0 million during the 1968–1981 phase of the regime. From 1 July 1969 to 30 September 1981 the guard received a (current) total of $12.7 million in military loans and grants. Most of the assistance continued to be provided in the form of MAP grants, especially for training, although there were innovations. In 1970 the guard received the first significant transfers from excess US military stocks, which reached an overall (current) total of $1.8 million during the 1968–1981 period. Equipment included airplanes, helicopters, and one patrol boat. Additionally, in 1976 the Ford Administration granted the first loan for purchases of military equipment, amounting to $500,000; the following fiscal year the same item added up to $2.5 million ($1 million in 1979, all current figures).[55]

On at least one known occasion, the United States also provided counterinsurgency assistance to the National Guard. In January 1969 Southern Command airlifted Panamanian military to Coclé Province where the National Guard brutally dealt with five student saboteurs. Finally, intelligence cooperation between the CIA and the National Guard intensified during the Torrijos years, especially after Manuel Noriega assumed direction of the G-2 in the early 1970s.[56]

Once rid of internal military opposition to his rule, Torrijos amassed sufficient power to proceed with plans to exploit the canal issue. Prior to December 1969 the Nixon Administration had rejected the military regime's advances on the subject. Washington based its refusal to negotiate with Panama on moral grounds, manifesting— as a US official leaked to the *New York Times*—reticence to "engage in long-term commitments with . . . the 'military type, provisional' government." By late 1970 these objections had disappeared, as the Panamanian regime's efforts to consolidate its rule moved rapidly forward. On 25 October a meeting between Richard Nixon and puppet Panamanian President Demetrio Lakas resulted in a declaration whereby both parties agreed to reinitiate canal negotiations. Talks, in suspension since 1967, resumed on 30 June 1971.[57]

Shortly afterwards, however, yet another US moral qualm stalled the negotiations. In July 1971, the Bureau of Narcotics and Dangerous Drugs discovered a conspiracy directed by the dictator's multifaceted elder brother to introduce heroin into the United States. Moisés Torrijos was indicted in New York in 1972, and although US diplomacy prevented the indictment from ever being pursued, formal US-Panamanian relations soured as Torrijos, in an outburst of nationalist indignation, terminated the activities of the DEA's predecessor in Panama. Thereafter, in order to ensure continuation of the talks, the Panamanian dictator opted for diplomatic blackmail.[58] In February 1974, less than one year after the 1973 Security Council met in Panama City, both negotiating parties issued a Joint Statement of Principles.

The statement contemplated joint administration and defense of the waterway as well as the expansion of the existing canal or the construction of a new one. Although publicized as a nationalist victory by the regime, the Joint Statement was, in the view of a group of experienced Panamanian jurists, little more than a reiteration of basic principles that had long been incorporated into the negotiating process. In exchange, Torrijos agreed to legalize the US military presence. The statement became the basis for the treaties which would enter into effect on 1 October 1979.[59]

Yankee ideological morality again played a starring role in US-Panamanian relations when Jimmy Carter assumed the North American presidency. Ideals of justice seemingly motivated Carter's determination to resolve the longstanding Panama Canal controversy. Incomprehensible as it may be, however, many of the means pursued to reach this lofty goal were unworthy of the cause. In order to obtain the desired diplomatic breakthrough and bring about an improvement in US-Latin American relations, the Carter Administration deliberately concealed many unsavory truths about the Torrijos dictatorship that would undoubtedly have raised eyebrows and prompted a heated debate on the morality or convenience of negotiating with a de facto, *pan o palo* dictatorial regime. Senator Robert Dole, for example, accused the Justice Department, acting on specific orders from Attorney General Griffin Bell, of ensconcing "forty four file drawers full of documents about the drug dealings of [Moisés] Torrijos and friends of the general . . . so that neither the press nor U.S. senators could get to see them."[60]

Undeterred by minutiae such as these, Carter proceeded swiftly toward conclusion of the negotiating process. Soon after the Democratic president's inauguration, a new analysis of US objectives in Panama had been put forth in Presidential Review Memorandum 1 of January, 1977. Security interests regarding the canal were defined as "having the canal open, efficiently operated, and freely accessible," not in direct US operation or control of the facility. Sabotage against canal facilities constituted a threat to these interests, but sabotage, it was concluded, was more likely to come from Panama than from a third country, such as the Soviet Union, Cuba, or another Moscow satellite. Consequently, "Panamanian consent" was deemed "the surest guarantor of the security of the canal." This "consent" was also deemed important to assure the permanence of US military bases on Panamanian soil. In this line of reasoning, "Panamanian consent" was nebulously linked to stability and order, but also to the satisfaction of the Panamanian people with their government.[61]

The analysis focused on the negative effects Panamanian instability could have on US interests. Instability might generate a situation of anarchy that could obstruct access to US installations, or it might bring to power a regime hostile to Washington's objectives, one determined to put an end to the US presence in Panama. Therefore, even though US-style representative democracy was viewed as the magic formula that would produce legitimacy anywhere in the world, the US government was unconcerned about "restoring democracy" in Panama because the military in power accepted US hegemony and were successful in imposing, through assimilation and terror, a degree of stability acceptable to US requirements. Thus, the US Congress' ideological-morality preoccupations could be avoided by sweeping the dirt under the rug, and official US security interests would be satisfied by the military regime, as long as the regime was able to keep the Panamanian people quiescent.

On 7 September 1977 in Washington, President Carter and Commander Torrijos signed the Panama Canal Treaty and the Treaty Concerning the Permanent Neutrality and Operation of the Panama Canal, two international conventions that replaced all previously existing agreements on the waterway. The treaties' main features closely resembled those of the 1967 "three-in-one" drafts: abrogation of the 1903 perpetuity clause; joint US-Panamanian management of the canal until the year 2000 and sole Panamanian responsibility for administration thereafter; a regime of neutrality to assure the canal would be available to ships of all nations at all times; joint US-Panamanian guarantee of said neutrality, through shared responsibility for canal defense; and the US right to maintain military bases on the isthmus of Panama, in order to permit the fulfillment of canal defense obligations. The new treaties "based on partnership," the Carter Administration expected, "would give the United States the rights we need, restore the crucial ingredient of Panamanian *consent,* and strengthen our mutual interest in a well run and secure canal."[62]

After the signing, the canal treaties met with fiery opposition in the United States. The Carter Administration responded by lobbying in their favor and by pressuring the Torrijos dictatorship to implement political reform so as to appear more acceptable to the US public. In consequence, the military regime organized a plebiscite which returned a two-thirds majority in favor of the treaties, notwithstanding scattered accusations of vote-rigging. Torrijos also hosted a visit by a group of US senators, who exacted from him promises of democratization. Liberalization eventually caused the regime some embarrassment: as reports of the dictatorship's human rights abuses became more widely diffused, the US House of Representatives voted to deny military assistance to Panama in March of 1979. Military and economic aid did drop significantly in fiscal year 1980, but grants for military training were not suspended. Since the coup, moreover, Panama had already received some $360 million (current) in US loans and grants.[63]

In February 1978, a month before the Senate was to consider the treaties, President Carter addressed the US public to vouch for Panama's military dictatorship:

Panama and her people have been our historical allies and friends. The present leader of Panama has been in office for more than 9 years, and he heads a stable government which has encouraged the development of free enterprise in Panama. Democratic elections will be held this August to choose the members of the Panamanian Assembly, who will in turn elect a President and a Vice-President by majority vote.[64]

Senate approval came in March, but not without reservations. The most significant of these was the so-called DeConcini Condition, named for the junior senator from Arizona who proposed it. The amendment gave the United States the unilateral right of military intervention in Panama "to take such steps as it deems necessary . . . to reopen the Canal or restore the operations of the Canal, as the case may be," if the canal were closed or its operations interfered with.[65] The condition exceeded what Panama had been prepared to surrender under the civilian liberal regime in 1967, in effect deepening Panama's political dependence on the United States.

The new conventions also abetted the National Guard's expansion, under US aegis. Article IV of the Panama Canal Treaty required the upgrading of the guard in order to participate jointly with the United States in the defense of the waterway. It contemplated the establishment of a combined US-Panamanian military board charged "with consulting and cooperating on all matters pertaining to the protection and defense of the Canal, and with planning for actions to be taken in concert for that purpose."[66] Pursuant to the treaty, Panama and the United States entered into an Agreement for Economic and Military Cooperation, dated 7 September 1978. Accordingly, Washington concurred in issuing repayment guarantees, for a total of $50 million over a ten-year period, under the Foreign Military Sales Program, "in order to facilitate the extension of loans" to Panama "for the purpose of financing the purchases . . . of defense articles and defense services."[67] With the ban on military assistance approved by the House of Representatives in 1979, however, the first installment of the military credits stipulated in the agreement was not made available until after Torrijos' death.[68]

GIVEN THAT THE crudeness of the military coup's true objective— the preservation of the corporate privileges and status of the National Guard—would have been difficult to justify to the Panamanian people, the military regime attempted to give meaning and substance to its direct political involvement by resorting to a populism of sorts. The policy focused on three basic aspects: favoring the masses through a sui generis redistribution of wealth, including making graft available to more sectors of society; favoring the propertied class through official encouragement of service activities and expanding the opportunities for profit of key businessmen and foreign capital; and appealing to Panamanian nationalists by adopting a pseudo-nationalist foreign policy aimed at obtaining control of the Panama Canal and the Canal Zone. Individuals or sectors not co-opted by these measures were dealt with in repressive fashion. The policy was not essentially new, although it was indeed more far-reaching than similar ones implemented before. It resembled the authoritarian populism of José Antonio Remón and even that of Arnulfo Arias himself, particularly during his first administration. All these experiences were basically modern-day versions of the old Iberic-American, *pan o palo,* approach to governance. The following declaration by Omar Torrijos, dictator between 1969 and 1981, gives testimony in this regard:

> Panama cannot be managed under the sectarian, dogmatic schemes now in vogue. To direct Panama the country must be understood as a large family; it cannot be directed rationally because its problems are interconnected. A great capacity for tolerance, pardon, and firmness is required, such as is applied by *a good father, who gives his son the club when he deserves it, and knows when to be compassionate.*[69]

Recognizing the military coup as a fait accompli, the United States looked with favor upon the military dictatorship because of the regime's ability to preserve stability in a country that played host to important US assets. Determined to solve the pending canal problem through a new treaty both acceptable to Panama and guaranteeing US interests, within the overall contexts of containment and hegemony, Washington ignored the unsavory aspects of the dictatorship as well as its anti-US rhetoric. US interests, conditioned to the Panamanian environment, translated into close relations—including close military cooperation—between Panama and Washington, especially during the Carter Administration (1977–1981).

Notes

1. Alain Rouquié, *The Military and the State in Latin America*, trans. Paul E. Sigmund (Berkeley: University of California Press, 1987), p. 36.

2. Andrew Zimbalist and John Weeks, *Panama at the Crossroads: Economic Development and Political Change in the Twentieth Century* (Berkeley: University of California Press, 1991), pp. 30, 33.

3. Ibid., p. 34.

4. Michele Labrut, *Este es Omar Torrijos* (Panama: By the Author, 1982), p. 23.

5. Renato Pereira, *Panamá: Fuerzas armadas y política* (Panama: Ediciones Nueva Universidad, 1979), pp. 123–24.

6. Richard M. Koster and Guillermo Sánchez Borbón, *In the Time of the Tyrants: Panama, 1968–1990* (New York: W.W. Norton, 1990), p. 124. Labrut, *Este es Omar Torrijos*, p. 22. Pereira, *Panamá: Fuerzas armadas y política*, p. 127. Juan Materno Vásquez, *Mi amigo Omar Torrijos: Su pensamiento vivo* (Panama: Ediciones Olga Elena, 1989), p. 277. Rómulo Escobar had been appointed in early 1969 as one of the Electoral Tribunal's magistrates.

7. Labrut, *Este es Omar Torrijos*, p. 52; emphasis added.

8. Ibid., p. 23.

9. Ibid., p. 44.

10. George Priestley, *Military Government and Popular Participation in Panama: The Torrijos Regime, 1968–1975* (Boulder: Westview Press, 1986), pp. 57-58.

11. Labrut, *Este es Omar Torrijos*, pp. 62; italics added to emphasize resemblance with Alliance for Progress rhetoric.

12. Pereira, *Panamá: Fuerzas armadas y política*, pp. 136–37.

13. Priestley, *Military Government*, p. 60.

14. Labrut, *Este es Omar Torrijos*, p. 23. Priestley, *Military Government*, p. 28.

15. Pereira, *Panamá: Fuerzas armadas y política*, p. 136.

16. Koster, *In the Time of the Tyrants*, pp. 143–45.

17. Vásquez, *Mi amigo Omar Torrijos*, p. 317. Pereira, *Panamá: Fuerzas armadas y política*, pp. 176–77.

18. Priestley, *Military Government*, pp. 36–50.

19. Vásquez, *Mi amigo Omar Torrijos*, p. 196.

20. Ibid., p. 53.

21. José de Jesús Martínez, *Idearia: Omar Torrijos* (San José: EDUCA, 1982), p. 44. In 1925 President Rodolfo Chiari solicited US military intervention to suppress a renters' strike which appeared to threaten a principal source of income of the propertied class. US troops consequently occupied Panama City and Colón. See Julio E. Linares, *Enrique Linares en la historia política de Panamá, 1869–1949: Calvario de un pueblo por afianzar su soberanía* (Panama: By the Author, 1989), pp. 239–40.

22. Zimbalist, *Panama at the Crossroads*, pp. 33, 35. República de Panamá, Contraloría General de la República, *Panamá en cifras,* 1974 and 1982 eds. (Panama: Dirección de Estadística y Censo), chart 343–05.

23. Priestley, *Military Government*, p. 119.

24. Koster, *In the Time of the Tyrants*, pp. 80, 89, 118, 120–21, 219.

25. On Torrijos dealing of the banana workers' labor union, see chapter 8 of this book.

26. Koster, *In the Time of the Tyrants*, pp. 122, 124.

27. Labrut, *Este es Omar Torrijos*, pp. 41–42.

28. Zimbalist, *Panama at the Crossroads*, p. 41.

29. James M. Malloy, "Authoritarianism and Corporatism in Latin America: The Modal Pattern," in *Authoritarianism and Corporatism in Latin America*, ed. James M. Malloy (Pittsburgh: University of Pittsburgh Press, 1977), p. 14.

30. Pereira, *Panamá: Fuerzas armadas y política*, p. 135. Vásquez, *Mi amigo Omar Torrijos*, p. 154.

31. Labrut, *Este es Omar Torrijos*, p. 119.

32. Ibid., p. 124.

33. Ibid., pp. 124–25.

34. Michael L. Conniff, *Panama and the United States: The Forced Alliance* (Athens: The University of Georgia Press, 1992), p. 130.

35. Labrut, *Este es Omar Torrijos*, p. 125. Priestley, *Military Government*, p. 90.

36. US Department of State, *American Foreign Policy: Basic Documents, 1977–1980* [hereafter AFP] (Washington Government Printing Office, 1983), p. 1384.

37. Koster, *In the Time of the Tyrants*, p. 138.

38. Labrut, *Este es Omar Torrijos*, pp. 99.

39. Ibid., pp. 101–07. Vásquez, *Mi amigo Omar Torrijos*, pp. 292–93.

40. Priestley, *Military Government*, pp. 129, 110. Vásquez, *Mi amigo Omar Torrijos*, p. 215. Rouquié, *The Military and the State*, p. 37.

41. Priestley, *Military Government*, p. 106.

42. Stockholm Peace Research Institute, *World Armaments and Disarmaments: SIPRI Yearbook* [hereafter SIPRI Yearbooks] (Oxford: Oxford University Press), 1972–1980 issues. Luis Puleio, *Militarismo, presencia y política* (Panama: Fuerzas de Defensa de Panamá, 1988), p. 89.

43. Pereira, *Panamá: Fuerzas armadas y política*, pp. 150–51.

44. Guillermo O'Donnell, "Toward an Alternative Conceptualization of South American Politics," in *Promise of Development: Theories of Change in Latin America*, ed. Peter F. Klarén and Thomas J. Bossert (Boulder: Westview Press, 1986), pp. 253–57.

45. Pereira, *Panamá: Fuerzas armadas y política*, p. 152.

46. For the text of the letter, see Vásquez, *Mi amigo Omar Torrijos*, pp. 175–80.

47. Koster, *In the Time of the Tyrants*, p. 213.

48. Ramón E. Fábrega and Mario Boyd Galindo, *Constituciones de la República de Panamá: 1972, 1946, 1941, 1904* (Panama: By the Authors, 1981), pp. 7, 96-97; emphasis added. The dignity of "maximum leader" and the duties assigned to the said office expired in 1978, and were not renewed. A 1983 constitutional reform rewrote Article 2 and excluded the Public Force from collaborating in the exercise of public power.

49. Labrut, *Este es Omar Torrijos*, p. 154.

50. Ibid., p. 156.

51. Priestley, *Military Government*, p. 76.

52. Ibid., pp. 82, 99.

53. See chapter 6 of this book.

54. US Agency for International Development, *US Overseas Loans and Grants and Assistance from International Organizations* [hereafter AID Reports] (Washington, DC: GPO), issues corresponding to US fiscal years 1976–1983. Constant figures (1982–1984=100) were calculated with data provided in the *President's Report on the Economy, 1993* (Washington: GPO, 1993).

55. SIPRI yearbooks; AID Reports.

56. Koster, *In the Time of the Tyrants*, pp. 118-19, 131-32, 175, 235-37. For the incident in Coclé Province, see Chapter 8.

57. Ibid., p. 182. Carlos Manuel Gasteazoro, Celestino Andrés Araúz, and Armando Muñoz Pinzón, *La historia de Panamá en sus textos*, vol. II (Panama: Editorial Universitaria, 1980), p. 57.

58. Koster, *In the Time of the Tyrants*, pp. 185–86.

59. Conniff, *Panama and the United States*, p. 131. Gasteazoro, *La historia de Panamá en sus textos*, p. 58.

60. Koster, *In the Time of the Tyrants*, p. 189.

61. Margaret E. Scranton, *The Noriega Years: U.S.-Panamanian Relations, 1981–1990* (Boulder: Lynne Rienner Publishers, 1991), pp. 20–21.

62. AFP, p. 1381; emphasis added.

63. AID Reports.

64. AFP, p. 1411.

65. Ibid., p. 1413.

66. Ibid., p. 1389.

67. US Department of State, *U.S. Treaties and Other International Agreements, 1978–1979*, vol. 30, pt. 2 (Washington: GPO, 1980), pp. 1825–26.

68. AID Reports.

69. Labrut, *Este es Omar Torrijos*, p. 24; emphasis added.

Chapter 8

Pan o Palo *and the Results of Torrijos' Dictatorship*

WHILE THE TORRIJOS dictatorship was more inclusionist than repressive, its authoritarian nature mandated the application of violence whenever co-optive measures did not succeed in dismantling threats to the guard's control. And while figures for human rights casualties under Torrijos are lower than the number of violations committed by authoritarian and totalitarian regimes elsewhere, the Torrijos dictatorship institutionalized human rights violations as a government policy. Panama had not undergone a similar experience since the end of Colombian sovereignty in the early 1900s. Torrijos' human rights violations were, indeed, a break with the past.

Torrijos' Repressive Measures, 1969–1981

Immediately following the coup, the guard suspended the 1946 constitution, dissolved the National Assembly, censored the press, and expropriated opposition media, most notably Editora Panama América, owned by the Arias family, which published three major dailies.[1] Most of the prominent *Arnulfista* politicians who had not fled with the deposed president to the safety of the Canal Zone were imprisoned in Panama City's ghastly Modelo jail, or in the National Guard headquarters. Militant labor leaders of the banana union that had promoted strikes against the Chiriquí Land Company in the earlier 1960s suffered a comparable fate. The military regime ruled by decree until 1972, when the new constitution, which provided for a semblance of a legislative branch, entered into force.

Reactions to the coup differed widely, further evidencing the illegitimacy of the political system. While the ostracized Liberals welcomed the coup, expecting they would become its major beneficiary, many Panamanians remained indifferent or expressed relief. By 1968 politics had degenerated into what many perceived as a crude scramble for control of the national treasury. The military overthrow, they thought, would put an end to chaos. But there was also substantial opposition, and it surfaced quickly. Arnulfo Arias had a huge, devoted following, and the National Guard was by no means a popular institution, as Torrijos himself recognized. In addition to the corruption of its officer corps, the guard's history of smashing popular movements made it inimical to numerous elements of Panamanian society.

These sectors called for action against the coup, but were split in their objectives. Their divisiveness, therefore, rendered their actions ineffective. On 13 October there was a shoot-out in the Calidonia tenement district of Panama City, in which three guardsmen died.[2] University students convoked a demonstration against the regime on 14 October; the protest was harshly repressed by the guard, which violated university autonomy in handling the protesters. On 18 October a Popular Front Against the Dictatorship was formed which called for a general strike on the 21st. The guard immediately responded by persecuting Popular Front leaders. Although many sectors did join the movement, the Popular Front strike lost momentum after the departure of Arnulfo Arias from the Canal Zone on the

23rd. University students, however, were back on the streets on 3 November, the anniversary of Panama's secession from Colombia, and on 12 December, the anniversary of the rejection of the 1947 Defense Sites Agreement with the United States. They were treated with the guard's usual ferocity which, after the latter occasion, included the six-month closure of the National University.

Under the command of Ariosto González, a *campesino* of the mountainous region bordering Costa Rica, a small number of *Arnulfista* guerrillas began operations in Chiriquí Province on 12 October 1968 and continued through October of the following year. Captured guerrillas received Manuel Noriega's special treatment. Noriega, a lieutenant at the David garrison, distinguished himself for the cruelty he exercised in the repression of the guerrillas. Promoted to captain in February 1969, by October of the same year he was already a major and had been given military command of Chiriquí in reward for having eradicated insurgency in the province. Terror was his strategy. "Peasants were beaten, were staked out naked for days, under the high sun, were murdered out of hand, had their poor ranchos burned to the ground and their families put outside at the height of the rains. Manuel Noriega was teaching Chiricanos not to help the guerrillas."[3] The experience of the guerrilla Enrique Moreno, a one-time bodyguard of Arnulfo Arias, is even more eloquent. Moreno was abducted in Costa Rican territory by orders of Noriega.

The kidnappers included Orejita Ruiz and Sergeant Villamil, the Guardia's top thugs at that time. Since Moreno put up a struggle, Ruiz shot him twice, once through each thigh, with his .38, then proceeded to steal his watch and all his money. By dawn on Sunday, December 1 [1968], Moreno was in the cuartel at David, but it was Tuesday afternoon before he had food or medical attention. He was kept outdoors in a patio, handcuffed, leashed round the neck like a beast, entirely naked. There he lay, under sun and rain, in his own blood and excrement, kicked and beaten with hoses during interrogation, till the scandal resulted in his receiving more humane treatment—a year in La Modelo and then exile.[4]

Military harassment, however, was not reserved exclusively for Panamanians. The National Guard also attacked any unimportant foreigner it suspected of opposing its rule. One Yankee surnamed Kimball, who provided insurgency training to the guerrillas, was captured in early 1969 and tortured under Manuel Noriega's instructions, until he died four or five months later. Noriega also arrested a US Peace Corps couple he suspected were aiding the guerrillas and subjected them to a harrowing ordeal. En route from the mountains to David, the provincial capital, "Noriega requisitioned a horse and let Mrs. Freivalds ride it. . . . He had her carry the squad's automatic rifle and wear a green Guardia cap. If there were snipers about, she'd draw their fire."[5] The only protest actions like these provoked from a US official came from the consul in David. In his letter of resignation from the foreign service, Jerry L. Dodson wrote:

> Since the coup of October 11, 1968, the National Guard has deposed the constitutionally-elected President, dissolved the National Assembly, destroyed one judicial system, closed down the national university, and instituted a reign of terror throughout the Republic of Panama. American citizens have been arrested on a large scale for no apparent reason. In a large number of these cases, the National Guard has denied consular access to the citizens. There have been numerous cases of mistreatment as well.
>
> It is my contention that our government must bear at least some responsibility for the behavior of the Guard due to our support for that organization. Moreover, I feel that we are acting against the best interests of the United States by alienating the enlightened sector of Panamanian society, not to mention that of Latin America as a whole.[6]

Outside Chiriquí there was an isolated episode of subversion in Quije, a village of Coclé Province. The National Guard learned of a plan by five university students to blow up a nearby hydroelectric plant. The military surprised the saboteurs, three of whom were killed in the exchange of fire. The remaining two, "one a woman named Dora Moreno, were taken to the village and tortured awhile, then machine-gunned for the instruction of the locals."[7]

On 3 November 1969 the last political prisoners were released from Modelo jail. The destinies of these prisoners reflected Torrijos' understanding with the Moscow-line Partido del Pueblo, as well as his failure to co-opt the intransigent Peking-liners. The imprisoned members of the Partido del Pueblo were sent to exile in Chile. The seven uncompromising, revolutionary Maoists, however, were dispatched to the inhuman penal colony at Coiba island. Their leader, Floyd Britton, had fought in the Cerro Tute uprising in 1959, which Torrijos had been ordered to put down. As opposed to other former insurgents, however, Britton refused to give in to the dictator. "A gala welcome was laid on" for the Maoists as they arrived in Coiba, "a terrible beating administered by seven G-2 agents before some three hundred prisoners." Britton and his companions were thrown against a wall,

> then clubbed and punched and karate chopped, and when on the ground kicked. . . . After that, Britton was singled out for beating, was beaten daily or more often, at the guards' whim. It was clear they'd been told his survival was not required. . . . At one point, he was handcuffed, and the cuffs tied to a horse's tail, and the horse whipped round and round. . . . On another occasion, his companions were brought for a look at him after a beating session. He lay huddled in a corner of the hut gasping heavily, his eyes monstrously bulged from blows to his head. "This is how we deal with communists," the guard said proudly.

> Under these beatings, Britton deteriorated rapidly, particularly because of damage to his kidneys. He had great difficulty urinating. He passed large quantities of blood. No doctor was on the island, and none was sent for. On the twelfth or thereabouts, the seven political prisoners were sent to different camps. On the twenty-ninth, they were returned to [the central camp] to receive attention from a med-

ical team sent out from the mainland. All but Britton. When the six were together, they noted his absence, and a short while later a trusty . . . came and said Britton was dead. A decision, evidently, was taken that in no way was the medical team to see him. Later [they learned] that Floyd Britton had died delirious, and that at the end he weighed hardly a hundred pounds.[8]

The military reorganization which the coup triggered included two significant additions to the guard's organizational chart. One was the anti-subversive Macho de Monte Brigade, created in April 1969.[9] The other, whose influence on Panamanian society was to be far more pervasive, was the G-2, the intelligence office of the National Guard. Notorious for its viciousness, the G-2 was assigned as a reward to Noriega for his loyalty during the December 1969 attempt to unseat Torrijos. One of the office's first crimes was the murder of attorney Rubén Miró on 31 December 1969. Miró, a brilliant but mentally unstable lawyer, had been involved in the Remón case following the assassination of the former president.

In June 1971, a Colombian priest serving in the remote Santa Fe district of Veraguas Province, disappeared after having been arrested by two guardsmen with warrants for his arrest. Since his appointment in 1968, the Reverend Héctor Gallego had conducted successful social work in the region in accordance with Catholic doctrine and liberation theology. But his activities had antagonized the local *gamonal*, a first cousin to Omar Torrijos. The dictator himself was also annoyed, for Father Gallego's *conscientización* appeared to undermine Torrijos' constituency-building policy: in the eyes of the military commander, the priest appeared as a rival to Torrijos' self-anointed role of national liberator. A reliable account indicates that, on orders from Torrijos, G-2 Chief Noriega disposed of Gallego by throwing him alive from a helicopter into the sea. The "disappearance" of Father Gallego caused a wave of indignation in Panama—especially among the Catholic clergy and faithful—which, however, the military regime managed to withstand.

In addition to the propagandist effects of his inclusionist measures, Torrijos prevented the increase of opposition through tight control of the mass media. Torrijos' media policy, in fact, is one of the clearest examples of his *pan o palo* approach to government. "Press is controlled by the dictatorship either by its ownership by members of the government or by business associates or the dictator," indicated a 1978 human rights report.[10] Those journalists and broadcasters who favorably publicized the regime were given *pan*. Those it was impossible to co-opt, like the Arias heirs, were given *palo*—expropriation, persecution, exile. After taking over their assets, the government would deliver their property to malleable administrators. In the case of *El Panamá América*, Torrijos created ERSA, a supposedly private publishing house which, nevertheless, was directly and indirectly funded by the state throughout the military regime. For two decades ERSA sang the dictatorship's praises until the 1989 invasion caused it to be returned to its lawful proprietors.

The deterioration of Panama's economy after 1973, however, was to many Panamanians more palpable than Torrijos' populism. While canal treaty negotiations remained an issue—that is, until March of 1978, when the conventions were approved by the US Senate—Torrijos would argue that Panama was "locked in a deadly struggle" against Washington and thus any form of dissent sabotaged Panama's cause.[11] Under this logic, in 1976, a number of prominent citizens who had voiced opposition to the regime, especially regarding its economic policy, were rounded up and, in violation of the constitution, sent to exile. After treaty approval, on the eve of the June 1978 visit to Panama by Jimmy Carter and other Latin American presidents, a National Guard intelligence squad broke up an anti-US demonstration by university students, killing two by gunfire. In another incident of political violence that year, security forces picked up and tortured twelve supporters of Arnulfo Arias in the town of Capira. One of the *Arnulfistas* died as a result of the inhumane treatment. It transpired that the arrested had refused to attend the government-organized welcome celebration in honor of Carter and the other dignitaries.[12]

Human rights violations continued to be a policy of the regime despite Torrijos' pledges of democratization made to visiting US senators in the fall and winter of 1977. The following year a long overdue visit of the Inter-American Commission on Human Rights of the Organization of American States reported on the "grave situation of human rights in Panama." Among many other violations, the commission documented

> torture by the National Guard by such tactics as: electric shocks to vital parts of the body, ears, genital organs and the anus . . . holding prisoners incommunicado for an indeterminate length of time; physical beatings of male or female prisoners, most often with a hose; fondling of private parts of female prisoners and threats of rape; and subjecting prisoners to long interrogation periods while depriving them of rest, sleep, food or water.[13]

Palo was, it is evident, the regime's alter ego.

The Legacy of Omar

The co-optive and repressive policies of the Torrijos dictatorship had transcendent effects on Panamanian life. Economically and socially, Torrijos' *pan* measures did provide some degree of lower-class advancement, and the legislation he introduced transformed Panama into an important international banking center. Early agricultural policies also stirred an increase in domestic food production.[14] But the positive aspects of Torrijos' populism pale beside its overall negative effects. Economic deterioration was the major result of the dictatorship's redistribution policies, aimed not at authentic human development, but at buying support for the regime. Economic mismanagement and widespread graft, financed by foreign capital, brought alarming indebtedness and, as a consequence, an actual deepening of dependence.

Corruption became much more generalized, a factor that had not only economic, but psychosocial and moral dimensions as well. Torrijos was a flagrant nepotist who filled the bureaucracy with family and friends, most of whom utilized their official positions to plunder the national treasury. The illegal traffic in narcotics and arms, in which the National Guard had subtly and intermittently been involved since the 1940s, acquired large-scale dimensions after 1968. Both activities increased the revenue of individual officers; Panama, for instance, became the Sandinistas' chief source of weapons in 1978-1979, providing the guard's officers (Manuel Noriega notoriously among them) with supplementary sources of income.[15]

Millions were syphoned from the state's coffers by regime favorites in celebrated frauds such as Transit, S.A., an illegal, private taxing company in the Colon Free Zone; Cerro Colorado, a huge copper mine from which no copper was ever extracted; and Panama City's new international airport, named *Omar Torrijos Herrera* after the dictator's death. Overall, the *asentamiento* plan was a failure, most of all due to graft and mishandling. Immense quantities of money were poured into the cooperatives and squandered by their respective directing boards, all of whom drew salaries from the state. The National Guard's general staff additionally looted millions of dollars worth of fixed assets after 1 October 1979, when the Panama Canal treaties came into effect. The dictatorship assigned valuable property transferred by the United States, which Panama could well have put to excellent use for purposes of national development, to individual favorites or other unproductive users, such as the National Guard.[16]

Mismanagement and corruption, furthermore, reduced possibilities for diversification, which Panama's economy urgently required. The stress on service activities, for which Panama has an undoubted comparative advantage, in fact intensified during the Torrijos regime, in spite of the official nationalist rhetoric and state intervention in agriculture and industry. According to the authors of a recent economic history of Panama, the service sector's share in the republic's GDP rose from 55.2 percent in 1968 to 73.5 percent in 1980.[17]

After the 1973 oil crisis, which further depleted the regime's populist model, Torrijos dealt with economic problems in ways that contradicted his inclusionist discourse. New government policies, outlined in a 1974 declaration, favored capital over labor. The fundamental goals of the regime's economic policy as put forth in the *Declaración de Boquete* were defined as "the increase of production, productivity and employment."[18] As the focus on official redistribution policies—excepting corruption—evanesced, a neo-liberal emphasis on growth took its place. The government pledged to subsidize agricultural and industrial loans, implement harvest insurance, create an industrial development bank, stimulate profit reinvestment, reduce government spending, establish a specialized office to deal with investors' complaints, facilitate bureaucratic procedures for investment, and promote agroindustrial, construction, service, and mining projects. The following year new legislation was written which rescinded many of the benefits assigned to labor in the 1972 code. A combination of governmental inefficiency and improbity, however, once more prevented the desired economic take-off and aggravated the populace's woes. A Catholic Church study reported that 38 percent of Panamanian households lived in poverty in the early 1980s, and nearly one quarter lacked resources to satisfy their basic dietary needs.[19]

Politically, whereas prior to 1968 Panama's sovereignty grievances remained essentially a bilateral matter, Torrijos' populism led to the "internationalization" of the Panama Canal issue. The dictatorship also successfully negotiated new canal treaties that were superior in many respects to the status quo ante. But the new agreements were very similar to the Robles-Johnson drafts initialed ten years before, despite the important international developments the 1967–1977 decade had witnessed, as well as the heightened level of nationalist rhetoric, all of which the treaty fell short of addressing. In the view of one Panamanian international-relations specialist, the treaties were inefficacious in satisfying Panama's loftiest goals of neutrality and sovereignty. While the US guarantee and the Yankee military presence made the canal's neutrality questionable in practice, the Senate condition authorizing US intervention anywhere on the isthmus to protect the neutrality regime hung over Panama's sovereignty as a Damoclean sword and ultimately provided the Bush Administration with a justification—dubious as it may have been—for the 1989 invasion.[20]

Another by-product of the 1977 treaties was Panama's increased militarization. Disguised as a partnership for defense, the militarization of the National Guard was stimulated by the Carter Administration in an effort to bring about Panamanian "consent." In actuality, what Washington sought through joint defense was to assure the dictatorship's satisfaction with the role assigned the isthmus within the overall context of US hegemony. The United States succeeded for a time in this regard, bolstering the National Guard's pride while it served as Washington's pawn.

Torrijos' *proceso,* its supporters argue, served to contain the potentially radical tendencies of militant components of Panamanian society, such as labor unions, student groups, civic associations, and leftist political parties.[21] To evaluate correctly the dictator's contribution to Panamanian stability, however, it is necessary to ask if any of these groups would have radicalized had the civilian liberal regime continued after 1968. Seen in this light, Torrijos' inclusionist policies are suspect contributions to Panamanian stability. Prior to 1968 political violence, although certainly an issue, was neither systemic nor institutionalized as in many other Latin American countries. Moreover, the political system, in spite of its flaws and, above all, its lack of legitimacy, had usually been able to accommodate all shades of the political spectrum. More realistically, the *proceso* had the effect of emasculating previously militant sectors and thus reducing prospects for the legitimization and democratization of Panamanian politics. The *proceso,* in short, subordinated the republic to the whims of Torrijos and the general staff of the National Guard.

The results of labor reform nicely illustrate this point. The *proceso* made workers passive recipients of a bounty mercifully bestowed upon them by the National Guard and its commander. The voluntary subjection of labor leaders to the dictator reached such a level that even a loyal Torrijos aide like Juan Materno Vásquez would in coming years remark:

> A new type of labor leader arose: that of promoter of micro-unions. It became the common practice of these leaders to place themselves at the head of a group of organized workers with the purpose of obtaining some sort of representation before capital and the government, but specifically before General Torrijos. The new leaders blackmailed employers with strikes and intimidated owners with the threats of seizure. . . . They became constant litigants before the Labor Office . . . the key positions of which they soon came to control. . . . They repeatedly declared to Omar their revolutionary demagoguery and their unrestricted support for his fight against the oligarchy and Yankee imperialism. . . . So enticed were they by the general's munificence that he [Torrijos] had no difficulty whatsoever in obtaining from them the famous vote of confidence for the issuance of Law 95 of 1975, which drained the substance from the 1972 Labor Code.[22]

Above all, *Torrijismo,* like the liberal regime, Arias' *Panameñismo,* and Remón's authoritarian populism before it, failed at imparting legitimacy to the Panamanian polity. Although the dictatorship did enjoy popularity during its initial years, economic woes, aggravated by mismanagement and corruption, as well as the regime's authoritarian, repressive policies, generated bitter resentment. Heavy-handed repression and the threat of force to keep dissent in check violated human rights. There is no need to labor the point that institutionalized human rights abuses, apart from being illegal, deteriorate the quality of life a society can offer.

The exhaustion of the nationalist cause after treaty approval in 1978 left the regime, in the view of many, without a raison d'être. The culmination of canal treaty negotiations removed a convenient distraction from the national scene, making more Panamanians aware of the distressing political and economic reality of their country. Opposition to the regime increased, stimulated by a "democratic opening" which the Carter Administration encouraged starting in 1977. Torrijos apparently gave in to Carter to avoid further embarrassment and to preserve the US source of financial assistance. By that time, moreover, the dictator was sufficiently confident that the degree of militarization he had brought about would prevent the replacement of his regime by authentically civilian, democratic rule. He thus permitted the return of exiles and a semblance of democratic politics through renewed, though limited, party activity and independent media. A constitutional reform put through by the government in 1978 contemplated a return to the system of proportional representation and direct presidential elections in 1984. Furthermore, a 1978 law "rehabilitated" the activities of political parties.[23]

Opposition to the regime increased toward the end of Torrijos' dictatorship, and manifested itself particularly on two occasions. The first was the return of former President Arnulfo Arias, on 10 June 1978, after nearly a decade in exile. A huge crowd of well over one hundred thousand came out to receive him, signifying that a substantial portion of the Panamanian people did not identify with the regime. A year later, on 9 October 1979, the largest demonstration Panama had yet seen assembled to repudiate an educational reform the government intended to impose.[24]

To counter the dissidence the "democratic opening" was expected to produce, the military launched its own political organization, the Partido Revolucionario Democrático or PRD. A corporatist organization, it had labor, business, student, women, and countless other "fronts." "The Revolutionary Democratic Party, which will be in charge of guaranteeing the continuity of the *proceso,*" declared the dictator, "is a party grounded on true ideological reasons."[25] Time proved that the PRD could more accurately be defined as a motley crowd of opportunists, whose only amalgam was a common desire to cling to the perquisites of power they had obtained under the military regime. As such, it was the political section of the National Guard, and a source of still more graft and pull.[26]

WITH THE DICTATOR'S death in a mysterious plane crash on 31 July 1981, the Torrijos phase of Panama's twenty-one-year military regime came to an end. The "maximum leader" left Panama more politically divided, economically dependent, socially distraught, and morally corrupted than when he took over. Furthermore, his disappearance set loose the ambition of individual general staff members, which since 1969 Torrijos had succeeded in arbitrating.[27] Under the continued dominance of a powerful military caste implanted in power by the 1968 military coup and institutionalized by Omar Torrijos, more troubles were still ahead for Panama.

Notes

1. Unless otherwise indicated, the information in this section is taken from Richard M. Koster and Guillermo Sánchez Borbón, *In the Time of the Tyrants: Panama, 1968–1990* (New York: W.W. Norton & Co., 1990) chaps. 3–8.

2. The shoot-out was led by Walter Sardiñas, an Uruguayan adventurer, who later joined the *Arnulfista* guerrillas. After the guerrillas disbanded, Sardiñas fled to Costa Rica, where he was murdered on Torrijos' orders. Koster, *In the Time of the Tyrants*, p. 102.

3. Ibid., p. 106.

4. Ibid., p. 108.

5. Ibid.

6. "Recordemos . . . para que no vuelva a suceder," a supplement to *La Prensa*, 20 April 1992.

7. Koster, *In the Time of the Tyrants*, p. 119.

8. Ibid., p. 127.

9. Labrut, *Este es Omar Torrijos*, p. 18. The *macho de monte* is a fierce animal of the tropical jungles.

10. US, Congress, House, Committee of Foreign Affairs, *Hearings Before the Subcommittee on International Organizations: Text of the Human Rights Watch No, 4, February 1979*, 96th Cong., 1st sess., 2, 10 May; 21 June; 12 July; 2 August 1979, p. 396.

11. Koster, *In the Time of the Tyrants*, p. 222.

12. US Congress, *Hearings*, p. 397.

13. Ibid., p. 395.

14. Zimbalist, *Panama at the Crossroads*, p. 111.

15. Koster, *In the Time of the Tyrants*, pp. 140, 123, 226.

16. Ibid., pp. 218, 239, 151–52, 193.

17. Zimbalist, *Panama at the Crossroads*, p. 28.

18. Vásquez, *Mi amigo Omar Torrijos*, p. 79.

19. Ibid., pp. 79–82. Zimbalist, *Panama at the Crossroads*, pp. 37, 40.

20. See Carlos Bolívar Pedreschi, *De la protección del canal a la militarización del país* (Panama: By the Author, 1987), pp. 32–34.

21. Pereira, *Panamá: Fuerzas armadas y política*, p. 170.

22. Vásquez, *Mi amigo Omar Torrijos*, pp. 278–79.

23. Koster, *In the Time of the Tyrants*, pp. 201–02. Vásquez, *Mi amigo Omar Torrijos*, p. 136. Priestley, *Military Government*, p. 121.

24. Koster, *In the Time of the Tyrants*, p. 235.

25. Labrut, *Este es Omar Torrijos*, p. 159.

26. Koster, *In the Time of the Tyrants*, pp. 261–71, 302, 307–08.

27. Ibid., p. 238.

Chapter 9

The Noriega Dictatorship, 1981–1989

THE 1980S WITNESSED Panama's increased militarization, mostly under the direction of Manuel Noriega. The new dictator also pursued a *pan o palo* approach to governance, albeit in a less institutionalized, more primitive, autocratic fashion. Noriega himself defined it as the "three p's" policy in October of 1989: *plomo, palo y plata,* or bullets for the enemy, the club for the indecisive, and money for the friend.[1] At the same time, under Noriega a Panamanian variant of the national security doctrine gained momentum. The ideology, which manifested itself for the first time under Torrijos, served as a justification for the maintenance of military privileges, which now broadened to include extensive narcotics trafficking and money laundering.

The Reagan Administration initially supported Noriega for his ability to maintain an acceptable level of stability on the isthmus, as well as for the dictatorship's collaboration with the US containment effort in Central America, Washington's main regional concern in the first half of the decade. When Panama's legitimacy problem erupted in its most vocal and prolonged form in June of 1987, Washington was faced with a serious instability crisis, which appeared to threaten US interests as outlined in the 1977 canal treaties. But even in the face of widespread domestic opposition to his rule, Noriega proved a stubborn foe. When an environment of increased US-Noriega tensions developed in 1988 and 1989, Washington decided, as in 1904, that a Panamanian military was antagonistic to its hegemonic pursuits of stability and responsiveness. On this occasion, however, diplomatic pressure and US military threats did not suffice. Only through large-scale military action, which took the form of Operation Just Cause, were Noriega and the military regime finally defeated.

National Security and Narco-Corruption

Manuel Noriega was born in 1934.[2] An orphan (his mother died shortly after childbirth and his father never assumed responsibility for him), the boy was raised by a family friend in a Panama City slum. Despite the adverse circumstances surrounding his childhood, Noriega attended the National Institute, then Panama's finest public high school. He dreamed of becoming a psychiatrist, but had to opt for a military career due to lack of resources. In the late 1950s, Noriega's elder brother Luis Carlos, who was employed in a subordinate position in the foreign office, alerted his sibling of a scholarship opportunity to Peru's Chorrillos Military Academy. With the support of Foreign Minister Aquilino Boyd, the young Noriega was awarded a place at Chorrillos.[3]

In Peru Noriega became an informant for the CIA. After graduation, he joined the National Guard; in 1966 he was commissioned as a lieutenant at the Chiriquí garrison, initially under Omar Torrijos. Torrijos charged him with setting up a military intelligence unit in the province to monitor the activities of the banana workers' union, which had incurred the hostility of the Chiriquí Land Company.[4] In

The apogee of narco-militarism. Seated from left to right: Nánder Pitty, advisor to the PDF commander; Manuel Noriega; puppet president Eric Arturo Delvalle (1985–1988); Francisco Rodríguez, comptroller general and Noriega's last puppet president (September–December 1989). Standing behind is Dulcidio González, a business leader. *Photograph by courtesy of Tatiana Padilla / El Siglo, Panamá.*

this new capacity, Noriega intensified his links to the CIA. The lieutenant's brutality also surfaced at the time. As mentioned in the preceding chapter, he was involved in the murder of a labor organizer. Additionally, he is reported to have raped a teenage girl and viciously beaten her younger brother. Torrijos, who bailed him out on both occasions, found him useful after October 1968 in the eradication of the *Arnulfista* insurgency. Noriega's loyalty in December 1969 brought about his promotion to the rank of lieutenant colonel, in charge of the G-2, early in the following decade.

After Omar Torrijos' death in a plane crash on 31 July 1981, a power struggle ensued within the National Guard. Torrijos was succeeded by the guard's chief of staff, Florencio Flórez, who was sacked a year later by his subordinates. Rubén Paredes assumed command of the military institution, with Manuel Noriega as deputy. Endeavoring to follow in José Antonio Remón's footsteps, Paredes resigned as commander in August 1983, with both eyes on the May 1984 presidential elections. His deputy, now a general, succeeded him. Once in absolute control of the military, Noriega dropped Paredes as official presidential candidate, and replaced him with Nicolás Ardito Barletta, at the time a World Bank vice-president. The dictator imposed his candidate as president following a massive vote fraud.

Almost immediately after his replacement of Paredes, Noriega put through the assembly a new law which further enhanced the legal status of the Isthmian military, renamed Defense Forces of the Republic of Panama (or Panamanian Defense Forces, PDF). The law contained several dispositions that reflected its national-security orientation. Given that the security ideology purports to rationalize the exercise of absolute power by the army, the actual purpose of Noriega's militarization was to provide justification, based on Panama's responsibility for protecting the canal and defending its neutrality regime, for the continued rule of the military institution.[5]

The Latin American national security doctrines emerged as a response by the region's military to the threat of social revolution within the Cold War context.[6] It stemmed from geopolitical analysis and the latter's organic view of the world, in which the state is seen as a live being, containing within itself all the elements necessary to assure the fulfilling existence of its subjects. In order to achieve this objective—the fulfillment of human happiness—the state grows and strives to strengthen itself, lest it be obliterated by another power. And the threat—either external or internal—of annihilation is ongoing. In the variant of the doctrine prevalent in the Southern Cone, the menace was identified with Soviet Communism. Other variants, such as the Peruvian one and the fledgling Panamanian one under Torrijos, linked the threat more directly to underdevelopment and dependency. Whatever the ever-present danger, however, national security is required to protect the state from extinction. Therefore, a national security system under military direction must be in place to direct each one of the activities undertaken within the state.

Several elements contributed to the development of the doctrines of national security. First and foremost is the South American military tradition, in which the armed forces are identified with the nation-building process and are thus seen as the only organization able to maintain the cohesiveness of the state. European, especially German, military principles also had influence as did, after 1945, French counterinsurgency theory and US national security and containment doctrines.

Although the military regimes inspired by this ideology never succeeded in applying it in its entirety, the doctrines did influence the policies such regimes implemented. Notorious were the suppression of liberal democratic institutions, the extension of military control over vast segments of national activity, and the perpetration of thousands of cases of human rights abuses, including the torture and murder of suspected subversives and so-called "internal enemies."

Noriega's law of August 1983 mandated that the PDF assume responsibility for national defense and public security, including the regulation of private security agencies, the sale of weapons, and vehicular traffic control, as well as the prevention of contraband, drug traffic, prostitution, and illegal immigration. The organization was also charged with the defense of the Panama Canal, in conjunction with the US Southern Command, as stipulated by the 1977 treaties. For these purposes, the law incorporated a number of already existing agencies into the PDF: the National Guard, the air force, the coast guard, the canal defense force, the police force, the traffic bureau, the national investigations bureau (successor to the former secret service), and the immigration service. Separated from the Ministry for Government and Justice, on which the National Guard had been previously dependent, the military institution was granted administrative autonomy.

The ideology of national security also imbued other clauses. Article 11 specified that the PDF could require from government agencies, private corporations, or individuals, information relative to national defense or public security. Article 12 charged the PDF with "recommending" the delimitation of those portions of national territory to be considered "strategic." The institution had the duty of organizing the citizenry for the defense of national sovereignty and independence, in case they were threatened. "Collaborating" in natural-resource conservation was another responsibility. Information related to national security was to be considered secret, and could not be divulged without express permission of the president of the republic, who retained the symbolic role of supreme chief of the PDF. The president, however, could order officer promotions only in accordance with the "advice" of the PDF commander-in-chief.

The commander could be replaced by the president only due to death, retirement, "manifest or grave disobedience of the constitutional or legal orders," or "manifest incapacity." Appointments to the general staff were to be made exclusively by the commander. A whole section devoted to "officer formation and military improvement" was also included in the law. Finally, the military honor provisions, as well as the prohibitions on mockery and whistle-blowing contained in Remón's 1953 law, were maintained.

Although the law was violatory, in letter and spirit, even of Torrijos' 1972 constitution, Noriega ambiguously justified it as necessary due to domestic and regional developments. Not least among these were the responsibilities imposed upon Panama by the canal treaties. In defending his legislation, the dictator actually resorted to the same justification other national security ideologues had clung to: "military government is necessary because the nation is involved in a total war."[7] Noriega's convoluted discourse expressed his views as follows:

> We find ourselves at a critical point in our history combining vital events such as the forthcoming elections for president of the repub-

lic, which will fully complete the democratization of the Panamanian state.

In the international arena [the law is justified] by the generalized, concatenated, and growing conflict in the Central American countries, from whose consequences and decisions Panama cannot escape, taking into account, above all, the proximity of the democratic nation of Costa Rica. Lacking a security infrastructure, Costa Rica is geopolitically located beside the central point—questioned by the rest of the Central American countries [Nicaragua]—where the theater of operations between ideological opponents is found.

Furthermore, at the international-relations level, progress in the implementation of the Torrijos-Carter Treaty dictates the decrease of US military forces and the increase in Panamanian forces.[8]

While Panama's military budgets reached the $100 million mark by the mid 1980s, membership in the PDF had risen to 15,400 in 1989. By the end of the decade, 3,500 servicemen were assigned to two battalions, eight infantry companies, one special force, two public order companies, one engineering company, and one company of cavalry troops. Army equipment included reconnaissance vehicles, mortars, and rocket launchers. The coast guard had 400 men, six patrol craft, four mechanized landing craft, and one former US medium landing ship. The air force had 500 soldiers, and planes and helicopters from Chile, Spain, Argentina, Brazil, Great Britain, Israel, and the United States. Additional equipment received from the Northern Colossus included one AN/TPS-70 air defense radar, the first of six for the Caribbean region, and five counterinsurgency A-37B Dragonfly Fighters, the first combat aircraft in the air force. On 13 June 1984 Peru and Panama signed an agreement whereby Peruvian navy personnel were to train the PDF's coast guard.[9]

Panama also began to play an increasing role in regional military affairs. The 1984–85 *Military Balance* announced that the Central American Defense Council (CONDECA), now composed of the security forces of Guatemala, Honduras, El Salvador, and Panama, was being revived. Among the council's plans was the creation of a common military training center.[10]

The expanded function of the Panamanian military as well as its overarching control over national life are comprehensible in the light of the purposes of the regime. The military took power, as was previously stressed, to guarantee the continued enjoyment of privileges, including the supplementation of army officers' income with illicit revenue. Throughout the military regime, these alternate sources of income expanded concomitantly to include widespread drug and arms trafficking, as well as money laundering. These activities greatly enriched Noriega and his supporters. Reportedly, the dictator first became involved in the drug traffic in the early 1970s, during his tenure as intelligence chief. He later diversified into arms supply to the Sandinistas during the Nicaraguan civil war. His relationship to the Medellín drug cartel is said to have begun in 1981, when he effectively mediated a dispute between the cocaine lords and the Colombian M-19 guerrilla. Thereafter, he permitted—in collusion with unscrupulous local bankers—the use by the cartel of Panama's international banking center to launder drug money. This activity earned him immense profits, which were shared by associates in the PDF, the national government, and the private sector. Noriega, in effect, could well have claimed authorship of Alfredo Stroessner's dictum, "It is necessary to foment criminality because criminality produces complicity and complicity produces loyalty."[11]

Noriega the Asset

Following a decade of perceived defeatism in global affairs—the Vietnam syndrome, basically shaped by the withdrawal of US forces from Southeast Asia and the subsequent "loss" of that region to Soviet communism—the Reagan Administration, bent on enhancing Washington's position worldwide, defined its Central American policy in terms of containment. The United States was to demonstrate its might by stamping out the supposedly pervasive Soviet and Cuban influence in the region. The strategy focused on maintaining hegemony over the other Central American states, especially El Salvador, through US assistance for suppressing insurgency against client regimes, and on returning Nicaragua to the US orbit through the destabilization of the Sandinista regime. In this last endeavor the Reagan Administration went to great lengths, even breaking US law to provide support for the *contras*.[12]

Obsessed with overthrowing the Nicaraguan Sandinistas, the Reagan Administration defined US interests in Panama in terms of the *contra* effort. North American military bases, originally established to fortify the canal and predicated on the security importance of the waterway itself, now definitively established their primacy over all other concerns. These military installations did more than extend the US defensive perimeter to the south and provide the opportunity for maintaining a substantial armed force capable of rapid deployment to other Latin American countries in case of emergency. Noriega allowed the United States furtive undertakings inconsistent with Panama's purported role as a sovereign, non-aligned republic, with the US tradition of abiding by the law, and with the Panama Canal treaties of 1977. These activities included US training of *contras* and other "Central American personnel" in North American military bases in Panama, as well as National Security Agency (NSA) and CIA "listening operations."[13]

By maintaining what Washington could define as an acceptable level of stability in Panama—believed essential to the protection of US interests in the country—and by responding to US objectives in Central America, Noriega behaved, in Washington's eyes, as the perfect client ruler. And US hegemony did not prove onerous for the dictator. On the contrary, Washington was surprisingly permissive: requiring only receptivity to the above-mentioned objectives, the United States overlooked Noriega's shadier activities.[14]

Noriega also performed other valuable services for the United

States. He consistently spied on the Nicaraguan regime and shared the information with the CIA; he supplied the *contras* with weapons; and he sabotaged a Sandinista arsenal in 1985. The dictator is also reported to have contributed $100,000 to the *contras'* war chest.[15] For a Reagan Administration that considered any means available towards the end of eliminating Nicaragua's socialist regime to be valid, Noriega's contributions were a godsend. In his testimony before the Senate Armed Services Committee submitted on 23 February 1984, Commander-in-Chief Paul F. Gorman of the US Southern Command expressed the Reagan Administration's contentment with Noriega as follows:

> Within the past two years Panama has come forward as a leader in regional politics and security arrangements. Panamanian leaders have stated unequivocally that their security begins at the northern frontier of Costa Rica and have offered to be of direct assistance to the Costa Rican security forces in improving their professionalism. . . . The Panamanians at this point in time have invited us back into all of the various military areas, from which we were excluded by the terms of the treaty, for combined training. At the moment U.S. forces operate throughout the Republic of Panama with Panamanians and have indeed conducted with them combined operations throughout Latin America. There is a degree of partnership that is striking and growing year by year.[16]

Other US interests on the isthmus were believed to be safely secure under Noriega, given his "stabilizing" grasp on Panama's national life. US operation of, and access to, the canal, still in the 1980s an important sea line of communication, depended to a large extent on Panama's stability and "consent," as did other secondary interests such as DEA drug interdiction efforts; the unhindered operation of the trans-Isthmian oil pipeline; the use by a substantial portion of the US merchant marine of the Panamanian flag of convenience; Panamanian alignment with (or at least lack of opposition to) the United States in international forums; and the uninterrupted and profitable operations of US investment firms in Panama.[17]

For his services to the Reagan Administration, Noriega was handsomely recompensed by Washington. The United States provided his regime with economic and military aid, and voted in favor of loans to Panama by multilateral lending agencies. This occurred in spite of the US government's knowledge of human rights abuses, widespread official corruption, intelligence and commercial links to Cuba, and the increasing militarization of Panamanian life.[18] AID data for the period from 1 October 1981 to 1 July 1987 (when Washington suspended all US assistance to Panama) indicate an annual average, in constant 1982–1984 dollars, of $7.4 million in military assistance to the PDF, an extraordinary increase when compared to the average of the Torrijos years ($2 million). More than half the assistance came in the form of MAP grants ($24.7 million in current dollars). Additionally, of the $50 million loan guarantee package agreed to in 1978, three issues of $5 million (current) each were made available between 1982 and 1984; a fourth one, of $3.8 million (current), came in 1987. Last but not least, Washington favored the Noriega dictatorship with Security Supporting Assistance for a (current) total of $63.2 million in fiscal years 1985 and 1986. Not since the early 1960s had Panama received security supporting funds.[19]

In other regards, the Reagan Administration warmly endorsed Panama's fraudulent 1984 election, rigged by Noriega to assure the continuation of his dictatorship.[20] US Secretary of State George Shultz attended the inauguration of Nicolás Ardito Barletta, Noriega's choice for president of Panama, and once more indicated the Reagan Administration's support for the regime:

> What a great pleasure it has been for me personally to be a witness at the inauguration of President Barletta. . . . As far as the United States is concerned, we look forward to working closely with the Government of Panama, and, of course, we *encourage very strongly the movement in the direction of democracy* and the establishment of a democracy here as in other parts of our hemisphere.[21]

But the United States not only financed and publicly endorsed the Noriega regime. It also ignored the dictator's illegal economic activities, such as money laundering and narcotics and arms trafficking, which he undertook, in effect, to the detriment of US security interests.[22]

The 1987–1989 "Crisis"

Panama's illegitimacy problem became apparent once more in June of 1987, when the largest protest movement since the establishment of the military regime began. The popular protests gave rise to a political and economic situation known locally as the "crisis." This "crisis," in addition, transformed Noriega and his dictatorship into an embarrassment and a threat for the second administration of Ronald Reagan, as well as for that of his successor, George Bush. The situation ultimately deteriorated to such a level that the Bush Administration opted for armed force to remove Noriega from power and destroy the PDF's war potential, which previous US governments had been so willing to endow.

Domestic opposition to the military regime reached considerable heights after the massive vote fraud of 1984, but especially after the brutal torture and decapitation of a Noriega opponent, Hugo Spadafora, in 1985, a murder personally ordered by the dictator. Prior to his death, Spadafora had openly accused Noriega of drug trafficking and money-laundering.[23] When efforts to obtain an impartial trial were frustrated by the Panamanian judiciary's complete submission to Noriega, Spadafora's brother Winston decided to take his crusade to Washington, denouncing the crime in the Organization of American States (OAS), the US Congress, and the North American news media.

Efforts by other Panamanians to publicize the corrupt, antidemocratic character of the military regime also intensified at this time.

Former President Arnulfo Arias leading a protest rally against the military dictatorship in 1987. *Photograph by courtesy of Guillermo Sánchez Borbón / La Prensa, Panamá.*

Altogether, they resulted in investigations by the US Congress, the media, and certain Miami and Tampa federal agencies involved in drug interdiction. The immediate consequence of these investigations was Noriega's exposure in several June 1986 issues of the *New York Times* as a brutal narco-military dictator, followed by high-profile coverage of his illegal activities by most US newspapers and television networks.[24]

Even as such reporting was making it more difficult for "politically-correct" US government figures to endorse openly Noriega, the dictator's utility to the Reagan Administration within the Central American context faded away after disclosure of the Iran-Contra scandal in November 1986 exposed the administration's illegal covert activities against the Sandinistas. At the same time, with increased concern in the United States over the dangers of widespread narcotics addiction, the drug issue began to displace containment as a North American security priority. Aware of these developments, administration officials endeavored to capitalize on the drug problem. Narcotics rapidly gained a place among major US foreign policy objectives, particularly in the coca-producing Andean nations of Peru and Bolivia, in Colombia, the premier cocaine manufacturer, and in countries providing support services for the drug trade, such as Panama.[25]

In its Isthmian policy, however, Washington was by no means cohesive. While influential members of the Congress such as senators Helms, Kennedy, D'Amato, and Kerry looked with mounting apprehension at the relationship with Noriega, the State and Defense departments, the CIA, and (ironically) the DEA still held that continued support for the dictator was the best assurance for securing US interests on the isthmus.[26] Internal developments in Panama and the results of investigations by two Florida grand juries would change the still positive evaluations of Noriega as guarantor of US interests and hegemony. In early June 1987 *La Prensa,* a major Panamanian daily, published an interview with a former chief of staff of the Defense Forces in which the retired military officer accused Noriega of electoral fraud, corruption, and the murder of Hugo Spadafora. A few days later a number of civic groups opposed to the regime formed the National Civic Crusade, which called for a campaign of civil disobedience against Noriega's dictatorship.

Noriega retaliated by stepping up repression and adopting a pseudo-nationalist rhetoric which attributed all opposition to a US-directed plan to prevent the fulfillment of the canal treaties. Repression notwithstanding, the protests continued, even after Black Friday, when hundreds of demonstrators were harassed, beaten, arrested, and submitted to diverse forms of torture. The dictator coupled his repressive measures and anti-US discourse with new approaches to Cuba and (in yet another example of political cunning) the Sandinistas, a development which attracted particular attention from US policy makers.[27] On 30 June 1987 Assistant

Secretary of State for Inter-American Affairs Elliott Abrams interpreted Noriega's new stance as follows:

> The calls for democracy in Panama have already prompted some curious reactions. Fidel Castro's press has rallied to support the Panamanian military leaders against the people of Panama. Last week, Nicaragua's Comandante Daniel Ortega even went himself to Panama to praise the "brave and decisive" actions taken to repress opposition. I imagine everyone here saw that photo of General Noriega in happy comradeship with his Sandinista visitors. Praise from the Communist dictators of Cuba and Nicaragua is a telling sign that Panama needs international democratic support.[28]

On 30 June 1987 Noriega orchestrated a mob attack against the US embassy which, in the words of a State Department spokesman, caused "significant damage to U.S. diplomatic property and ... put U.S. diplomatic personnel at risk."[29] This anti-US demonstration was the dictator's response to a Senate Resolution of 26 June calling for "free elections and for 'the current commander of the Panama Defense Forces and any other implicated officials to relinquish [their] duties' pending an independent investigation into allegations of electoral fraud, political murder, and drug trafficking."[30] The US Congress also suspended all forms of US aid to the republic until a civilian government, respectful of human rights, was established.[31]

Pressure then began building in the United States for more decisive action against Noriega. Added to the rise of instability in Panama, it led to a re-evaluation of the US stake on the isthmus. North American interests were now isolated from broader regional objectives to focus on the US rights and obligations pursuant to the canal treaties. In this new light, Noriega's control of the country now became antithetical to Washington's hegemonic demands of stability and responsiveness, essential in the fulfillment of the US role as outlined in the 1977 agreements.[32]

Policy reformulations notwithstanding, a consensus among most of official Washington was not reached until after the disclosure of

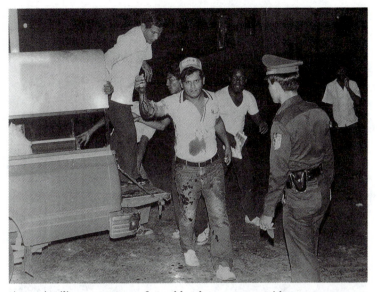

An anti-military protester after a bloody encounter with pro-government forces, 1988. *Photograph by courtesy of Guillermo Sánchez Borbón / La Prensa, Panamá.*

the Miami and Tampa indictments on 5 February 1988. Acting independently of other agencies involved in policy towards Panama, US attorneys in both cities handed down indictments against Manuel Noriega and other collaborators for profiting from drug trafficking and protecting drug traffickers. Unanimity was achieved, therefore, out of political necessity, for no US agency could bear to appear to be protecting a suspected criminal.[33]

President Reagan then opted for economic sanctions, secret negotiations, and clandestine undertakings aimed at destabilization, for Noriega had drifted from US hegemony. US policy, in effect, focused at this stage against the PDF commander, not against the PDF as a whole, the links with which Washington still considered valuable. Shortly after the Florida indictments, Assistant Secretary of State Elliott Abrams suggested to puppet President Eric Delvalle that he fire Noriega. Delvalle complied on 25 February, but the dictator then

Anti-military protesters face Noriega's riot police in Panama City's Calle 50, 1988. *Photograph by courtesy of Guillermo Sánchez Borbón / La Prensa, Panamá.*

had the National Assembly sack the puppet president instead. After this development, Washington declared Delvalle to be Panama's "constitutional" president and withdrew recognition from the Noriega regime.[34]

The Reagan Administration subsequently applied economic pressure. In early March Washington included Panama among the list of states that refused to collaborate with North American drug interdiction efforts. US representatives to multilateral lending agencies were thus required to vote against Panama's loan applications. The administration also prevented Noriega's government from transferring Panamanian funds deposited in New York, and prohibited US agencies, including the Panama Canal Commission, from making payments to the regime. On 23 March, Washington nullified Panama's preferred commercial status under the Caribbean Basin Initiative and the Generalized System of Preferences. Meanwhile, an unsuccessful internal PDF coup attempt took place on 16 March. Shortly thereafter, Noriega created the so-called Dignity Battalions, with Cuban assistance. Reminiscent of Juan Eligio Alzuru's Compañía de Desguazadores, the paramilitary force's objective was to terrorize the domestic opposition and defend the country from a feared US military intervention.[35]

The economic sanctions caused an acute cash shortage in Panama, where the US dollar is legal tender, forcing the closure of banks and the freezing of deposits. They did not, however, produce Noriega's downfall. The dictator was able to meet his fortnightly payroll by resorting to abundant supplies of drug money which found a safe haven as ever in Noriega's Panama.[36]

Early in April President Reagan invoked the International Emergency Economic Powers Act (IEEPA) against the republic, prohibiting all payments from private US citizens and corporations to Panama and freezing the Panamanian government's assets in the United States. The IEEPA, nevertheless, was not implemented until 25 May, pending the outcome of discussions between Deputy Assistant Secretary of State Michael Kozak and Noriega, with a view to the latter's "voluntary removal from office."[37]

Subsequent US actions came in covert form. In early July the president authorized "Panama 3," for which the CIA recruited Eduardo Herrera, a colonel in the PDF. The operation was meant to harass Noriega in order to provoke a PDF attack against US military personnel or installations in Panama, after which US punitive measures could be implemented. The plan was never put in practice, however, due to misgivings among members of Congress and the Joint Chiefs of Staff (JCS).[38]

Panamanian impotence against the Defense Forces, in addition to US half-heartedness, intra-governmental conflicts, and political opportunism, forestalled Noriega's departure, but did not prevent serious damage to Panama's economy. By one ostensibly conservative calculation, unemployment had risen to 20 percent by mid-1988.

"The legacy of the U.S. campaign," in the opinion of two economic historians, "proved to be a scarcely weakened Noriega, a decimation of the Panamanian banking system, a shattered private sector, and untold misery for the country's poor."[39]

From late July until the end of 1988, Washington's drive against Noriega assumed minimal proportions. President Reagan and Vice-President Bush strove to keep the Noriega affair quiescent with a view to preserving the integrity of Bush's presidential campaign, vis à vis the accusations of Democratic candidate Michael Dukakis regarding his opponent's dealings "with drug-running Panamanian dictators." George Bush, as CIA director in 1976, and then as vice-president in 1983, had met with Noriega to request his renewed cooperation with US intelligence efforts. At a time when US public opinion was fully aware that the United States had supported the Panaman-ian dicta-torship even as the Reagan Administration had reliable information on Noriega's human rights violations, drug-trafficking activities, and intelligence cooperation with Cuba, Dukakis' accusations had a neg-ative effect on the Republican candidate's image.[40]

After Bush's inauguration in January of 1989, his administration's efforts to solve the Panama crisis were seemingly channeled toward the May 1989 Panamanian elections. The new president approved "Panama 4," another covert operation that provided the Panamanian opposition ticket with $10 million, basically for propaganda activities and fraud prevention. When the opposition triumphed by a land-slide, Noriega annulled the elections. The subsequent failure of an OAS mission in brokering the dictator's removal and the establish-ment of a transition government, in addition to the collapse of a sec-ond army coup attempt on 3 October, contributed to the Bush Administration's "wimp" reputation. While US credibility eroded, undermining Washington's global and regional preponderance, con-frontations between Noriega's forces and US military escalated to a "point of no return." Washington became convinced that the only answer to its mounting difficulties in Panama and to its domestic

Manuel Noriega greeting supporters, 1989. *Photograph by courtesy of Tatiana Padilla / El Siglo, Panamá.*

public relations problem lay with overwhelming military action, not only against the dictator, but against his army as well.[41]

On 16 December 1989 a PDF patrol shot a US Marine Corps lieutenant; another US serviceman and his wife were later detained and abused by Noriega's military. Linked to a declaration, the day before, by a spurious National Assembly, which found Panama to be "in a state of war so long as the United States continues its policy of aggression," these actions were interpreted by the Bush Administration as "unwarranted acts of aggression" in the light of Noriega's "declaration of war."[42] The right to self-defense contemplated by the charters of the United Nations and the OAS, as well as the US duty to protect the Panama Canal under the 1977 treaties, were invoked to launch Operation Just Cause in the early hours of 20 December 1989.[43] According to President Bush, the objectives of Just Cause were four: "to safeguard the lives of Americans, to defend democracy in Panama, to combat drug trafficking, and to protect the integrity of the Panama Canal Treaty."[44] The invasion, in which twenty-six thousand US soldiers participated, ultimately destroyed the war potential of the PDF and captured Noriega, who was flown to Miami to face the 1988 indictments. These objectives, however, were not fulfilled without renewed suffering and destruction: between $1 and $2 billion in economic losses and, more distressingly, a death count that ranges anywhere from 200 to 5,000.[45]

It is obvious that the Bush Administration undertook Just Cause to preserve national security interests. The 1977 canal treaties not only sanctioned the US military presence in Panama but moreover provided that "vessels, aircraft, vehicles and equipment of U.S. forces may move freely through Panamanian territory, air space, and water when performing official duties, without charge or any other impediment."[46] Noriega's hostile actions against US personnel arguably threatened US treaty rights which, as President Reagan recalled in 1987, were "the law of the land."[47] And although Noriega never moved to sabotage the canal, Washington could not completely rule out this possibility given the unpredictable nature of the military regime.

But above all, the US military presence in Panama, like the US commitment to assume primary defense of the canal until the year 2000, is a symbol of Washington's power and hegemony. Noriega's anti-Yankee actions, including rhetoric, approaches to Castro and the Sandinistas, and harassment of US military and diplomatic personnel, were more than a threat to the security of US citizens. They indicated the dictator's defiance of US hegemony, an intolerable attitude from the leader of a client state at a crucial moment in history. In effect, with the Soviet Union retreating and reducing its international involvement, Washington strove to prove that the United States was still a first-class world power determined to demonstrate that it would not suffer slaps to its face. And with regards its Central American policy, Washington still considered the Sandinista regime a threat to US national security, and was in the process of contributing to its defeat in the 1990 elections so as to assure the rise to power of the Nicaraguan opposition.

That at the root of US perceptions of the Panamanian problem lay the global issue of great power status is proven by the attitudes of officials dedicated to safeguarding US national security. In August 1989 Defense Secretary Richard Cheney had refused to consider JCS Chairman William Crowe's suggestion of moving the Southern Command to Florida. "'Big political problem,' Cheney responded. 'No matter how it was dressed up, it would look like the United States was running. Just can't do it, no matter what the merits,' the Secretary told his Chairman."[48] And in the aftermath of the failed 3 October coup, Colin Powell, the new JCS chairman, is reported to have declared "Great powers should not be at the mercy of a gang that couldn't shoot straight," referring to the PDF.[49] Moreover,

> In his eighty days as JCS chairman, Powell had changed, and the world had changed. The Soviet bloc was crumbling and America's strategic focus was shifting. When he was National Security Adviser, he had agreed with his predecessor at JCS, Admiral Crowe, that Panama was of secondary importance. But now, he felt that America should hang out a shingle saying "Superpower lives here." In thinking and talking through their options that night [16 December 1989], Powell and his military advisers began to feel strongly that a move against Noriega was called for. The next day, they would go to the president and recommend implementation of the full plan.[50]

Finally, on the eve of the invasion, Air Force Chief Larry Welch opined that "the choice for the United States was either to get out of Panama entirely or get in all the way. Given the international responsibility to protect the Panama Canal, the United States could not retreat to a Panama equivalent of Guantanamo Bay. . . . So in that sense there was no choice."[51] In summary, it is obvious that, as the authors Paterson, Clifford and Hagan put it, "on one familiar issue American leaders remained bold: the projection of U.S. power abroad. The Cold War may have waned, but the United States intended to act globally to protect its interests."[52]

Given the Bush Administration's concern with its "wimp" reputation in its handling of the Panamanian "crisis," and given the US global and regional hegemonic concerns, an invasion would simultaneously serve to reconfirm US superiority in world affairs, intimidate the Sandinistas, substitute a regime antagonistic to US interests in Panama for a pliant one, and advance George Bush's self-proclaimed standard-bearing role in the "war against drugs," an area in which, to say the least, his record was weak. Despite the sweeping destruction it brought about in Panama, in the fulfillment of all four objectives Just Cause proved successful.

The Noriega Legacy

While the discussion of Torrijos' record engenders some scholarly debate, the results of the Noriega dictatorship are all too clearly negative.[53] Recent studies, such as that of Andrew Zimbalist and John Weeks, bluntly describe the last phase of the military regime as a period of "shrinking incomes, escalating unemployment, and growing political corruption and instability."[54] As the US Marshall's prisoner No. 41586, Noriega left his country in a state of political, economic, social, and moral disarray such as Panama had never previously known. It will take many years before the isthmus recovers from his legacy.

Omar Torrijos' death in 1981 occurred in the midst of a short-lived cycle of modest economic growth. Starting in 1978, the entry into force of the canal treaties, the transshipment of Alaskan oil, the rise in the activities of the Colón Free Zone, and the increased laundering of drug money infused Panama's service economy with large amounts of cash. Growth, however, did not trickle down easily: while in 1980 unemployment stood at 9 percent of the active work force, 67 percent of rural dwellers and 43 percent of their urban counterparts were classified as being unable to satisfy their basic needs.

Domestic and foreign developments prompted the end of the

growth cycle. The Latin American debt crisis reduced the purchasing power of the region's countries, to which the free zone's re-exports were directed. The US Congress' approval of a December 1981 law that permitted offshore banking in the United States reduced the attraction of Panama's international banking center. More importantly, governmental incompetence and corruption did serious damage to the country's fiscal condition. Typical of the military regime's approach to governance was a Social Security housing fraud in which top-level military and civilian favorites embezzled an approximate $100 million between 1981 and 1982.[55]

Fiscal difficulties increased the military regime's dependence on multilateral lending agencies. Predictably, the International Monetary Fund and the World Bank demanded the application of austerity and economic liberalization measures in order to continue providing the funds necessary to keep the budget afloat. The demands of these multilateral lending agencies, however, never focused on defense spending or the curtailment of official corruption. In consequence, other sectors were forced to bear the burden of the regime's irresponsibility.

Without resources to finance them, the regime had to repudiate Torrijos' inclusionist measures. In March of 1986 the National Assembly approved a package of laws which further debilitated workers' rights as contemplated in the 1972 code, initiated agricultural deregulation, and reduced tariffs on a number of imported goods. The neo-liberal emphasis also hit government services related to Panama's productive capabilities. Essential infrastructure transferred under the canal treaties, such as the Panama Railroad and the ports of Cristóbal and Balboa, was practically abandoned to the elements. Failure to preserve the jungle areas surrounding the canal translated into intensified deforestation, which threatens to put canal operations and drinking water supplies at risk in the near future. Even as these developments occurred, the debt-service share of government spending increased, by conservative calculations, from 29 percent in 1982 to 48 percent in 1986.

Unemployment, a basic indicator of a country's socio-economic performance, rose significantly during the decade, from 10 percent in 1984 to 12 percent in 1985. It was to escalate further as a consequence of domestic instability, economic sanctions, and the destruction brought about by Just Cause. After December 1989, the country's unemployed comprised, by one count, an appalling 30–35 percent of the work force, with higher figures in the urban areas.

The dismantling of Torrijos' populism, the country's economic woes, the increased militarization of national life indicated by the PDF's empire-building, and the political instability and frustration the dictatorship generated explain why, as opposed to Torrijos, few Panamanians remember Noriega fondly. The turnover in figurehead presidents illustrates the primitiveness of the dictatorship. Six incumbents occupied the presidential chair in eleven years, between 1978 and 1989, representing an average incumbency of one year and ten months each.[56] The dictator also furthered terror as an administrative instrument. Hugo Spadafora's brutal murder was perhaps the most publicized of a series of institutionalized acts of violence and torture. Noriega dealt viciously with his opponents in the 1984 elections, as well as during the 1987-1989 "crisis" years. The treatment given the opposition candidates on 10 May 1989, when the Dignity Battalions beat the rightfully elected president and vice-president with iron rods, exemlifies *palo* as well as any other incident in Latin America's long history of official repression.[57]

But Noriega also gave *pan,* or *plata,* as he preferred to call it, in more direct fashion. Under his tenure Panama had the unworthy honor of becoming one of the world's primary money laundering centers. From the various testimonies before the 1988 hearings of the US Senate's Subcommittee on Terrorism, Narcotics, and International Communications, "it appears that total laundering through Panama exceeded $10 billion a year in the mid-1980s."[58] All those involved received a piece of the pie: drug traffickers, couriers, local military, government employees and bankers, and above all, the dictator himself. The unchecked authoritarian control Noriega exercised over Panamanian life also permitted the diversification of the military caste's economic activities:

Either Noriega or the Defense Forces controlled and/or owned numerous Panamanian activities, inter alia: shipping and shipbuilding; two duty-free airport companies selling liquor and general merchandise; Transit S.A., the company regulating traffic in and out of the [Colon Free Zone]; gambling casinos; Arwell, the government advertising agency; Banco Cafetero; Banco Patria; extensive real estate; overland trucking; the newspaper chain Ersa; and Explonsa, an explosives producer. In addition, his brother-in-law, Ramon Sieiro, ran Marinac; this business grossing $20 million a year sold identity cards to crew members and officers of the 15,000-odd ships flying the Panamanian flag. Noriega also ran a multimillion-dollar operation of providing phony passports and visas to Asians and Cubans for entry into the United States. According to an estimate appearing in the New York Times, during the first eleven months of 1989 alone Noriega's visa sales to Hong Kong emigrants produced more than $130 million in revenue.[59]

NORIEGA MUST BE HELD responsible for Panama's destructive conflict with the United States. In a show of extreme personalism, by refusing to remove himself voluntarily from power even when faced with the hatred of his countrymen and manifest US opposition, the dictator brought upon the isthmus prolonged and unjustifiable suffering. The dictator obviously miscalculated the preponderant significance of hegemony in Washington's policy making. It is utterly ironic that by intending to scare the Yankees into inactivity, he pushed them to his capture and imprisonment. The fact that in his personal dispute with the Northern Colossus he brought the country in his grip to disaster is, however, far more substantial: it is indicative of the urgent need the Panamanian people have of legitimizing their polity.

Notes

1. Margaret E. Scranton, *The Noriega Years: U.S.-Panamanian Relations, 1981-90* (Boulder: Lynne Rienner Publishers, 1991), p. 192.

2. The information on Noriega's background is taken from Richard M. Koster and Guillermo Sánchez Borbón, *In the Time of the Tyrants: Panama, 1968-1990* (New York: W.W. Norton & Company, 1990), pp. 20-24.

3. Aquilino Boyd figured in the May 1989 elections as vice-presidential candidate in the official slate. He had previously served the Torrijos dictatorship as ambassador to the United Nations.

4. Andrew Zimbalist and John Weeks, *Panama at the Crossroads: Economic Development and Political Change in the Twentieth Century* (Berkeley: University of California Press, 1991), p. 138.

5. José Comblin, *The Church and the National Security State* (Maryknoll, New York: Orbis Books, 1979), p. 70. Carlos Bolívar Pedreschi, *De la protección del canal a la militarización del país* (Panama: By the Author, 1987), p. 43.

6. For informative analyses of the National Security Doctrine, see Genaro Arriagada, "Ideology and Politics in the South American Military: Argentina, Brazil, Chile, and Uruguay," a paper presented at the March 1979 colloquium of the Latin American Program of the Woodrow Wilson International Center for Scholars (Washington: Smithsonian Institution, 1979); Roberto Calvo, "The Church and the Doctrine of National Security," *Journal of Inter-American Studies and World Affairs* 21, pt. 1 (February 1979): 69-87; Augusto Varas, *Militarization and the Arms Race in Latin America* (Boulder: Westview Press, 1985), chapter 21 and Comblin, *The Church and the National Security State*. For insight into a fledgling Panamanian Security ideology, See Luis Puleio, *Militarismo, presencia y política* (Panama: Fuerzas de Defensa de Panamá, 1988).

7. Comblin, *The Church and the National Security State*, p. 76.

8. República de Panamá, "Ley No. 20 de 29 de septiembre de 1983, por la cual se dicta la Ley Orgánica de las Fuerzas de Defensa de la República de Panamá," *Gaceta Oficial*, No. 19.909, 30 September 1983.

9. International Institute for Strategic Studies [IISS], *The Military Balance* (London: Brassey's, 1983-90 issues). Stockholm Peace Research

Institute [SIPRI], *World Armaments and Disarmaments: SIPRI Yearbook* (Oxford: Oxford University Press, several issues, 1980–1990).

10. IISS, *The Military Balance, 1984–1985* (London: Brassey's, 1985).

11. Zimbalist, *Panama at the Crossroads*, pp. 74–75. Koster, *In the Time of the Tyrants*, pp. 283–300. The quote is from Paul C. Sondrel, "Totalitarian and Authoritarian Dictators: A Comparison of Fidel Castro and Alfredo Stroessner," *Journal of Latin American Studies* 23, pt. 3 (October 1991): 599–620. Koster and Sánchez put Noriega's personal wealth at $1 billion; Ricord at $500 million. Koster, *In the Time of the Tyrants*, p. 20. Humberto E. Ricord, *Noriega y Panama: Orgía y aplastamiento de la narcodictadura* (México: By the Author, 1991), p. 620.

12. For a discussion of the Reagan Administration's Central American policy, see Thomas Carothers, "The Reagan Years: The 1980s," in *Exporting Democracy: The United States in Latin America*, ed. Abraham F. Lowenthal (Baltimore: The Johns Hopkins University Press, 1991); Walter LaFeber, *Inevitable Revolutions: The United States in Central America* (New York, W.W. Norton & Co., 1984); Lester D. Langley, *America and the Americas: The United States in the Western Hemisphere* (Athens: The University of Georgia Press, 1989); and Thomas W. Walker, *Reagan Versus the Sandinistas: The Undeclared War on Nicaragua* (Boulder: Westview Press, 1987).

13. Scranton, *The Noriega Years*, pp. 9, 13–14.

14. Michael L. Conniff, *Panama and the United States: The Forced Alliance* (Athens: The University of Georgia Press, 1992), pp. 154–55. Koster, *In the Time of the Tyrants*, pp. 23, 34, 37–38, 120, 175, 326.

15. Conniff, *Panama and the United States*, pp. 151–52. Zimbalist, *Panama at the Crossroads*, pp. 75, 139–40.

16. US Department of State. American Foreign Policy: *Current Documents, 1984* (Washington: GPO, 1986), p. 1027.

17. Steve C. Ropp, *Panamanian Politics: From Guarded Nation to National Guard* (New York: Praeger, 1982), pp. 106–13. Scranton, *The Noriega Years*, pp. 20–21.

18. Conniff, *Panama and the United States*, p. 148. Koster, *In the Time of the Tyrants*, pp. 80–321. John Weeks and Phil Gunson, *Panama: Made in the USA* (London: The Latin American Bureau (Research and Action), 1991), pp. 41–50. Zimbalist and Weeks note that in his deposition before the

US Senate Subcommittee on Terrorism, Narcotics and International Communications in March of 1988, former National Security Council staff member Norman Bailey testified that "by 1981 there already existed 'available to any authorized official of the U.S. government . . . a plethora of human intelligence, electronic intercepts and satellite and overflight photography that taken together constituted not a 'smoking gun' but rather a twenty-one cannon barrage of evidence' of Noriega's involvement in crime and drugs." Zimbalist, *Panama at the Crossroads*, pp. 74-75.

19. US Agency for International Development, *US Overseas Loans and Grants and Assistance from International Organizations* [hereafter AID Reports] (Washington, DC: Government Printing Office), issues corresponding to US fiscal years 1981-1989. Constant figures (1982-1984=100) were calculated with data provided in the *Economic Report of the President, 1993* (Washington: GPO, 1993).

20. Koster, *In the Time of the Tyrants*, p. 301. Lawrence Whitehead, "The Imposition of Democracy," in *Exporting Democracy: The United States in Latin America*, ed. Abraham F. Lowenthal (Baltimore: The Johns Hopkins University Press, 1991), p. 368.

21. US Department of State. *American Foreign Policy: Current Documents, 1984* (Washington: GPO, 1986), p. 1089, emphasis added.

22. US Department of State. American Foreign Policy: *Current Documents, 1987* (Washington: GPO, 1988), p. 222. Koster, *In the Time of the Tyrants*, pp. 284-93. Scott B. MacDonald, *Mountain High, White Avalanche: Cocaine and Power in the Andean States and Panama* (New York: Praeger, 1989), pp. 102-11. Weeks, *Panama: Made in the USA*, pp. 49-55.

23. For details of this gruesome case, see *In the Time of the Tyrants*, chap. 1.

24. Kevin Buckley, *Panama: The Whole Story* (New York: Simon & Schuster, 1991), p. 53. Koster, *In the Time of the Tyrants*, pp. 358-59.

25. Peter Dale Scott and Jonathan Marshall, *Cocaine Politics: Drugs, Armies, and the CIA in Central America* (Berkeley: University of California Press, 1991), pp. 4-19. Bob Woodward, *The Commanders* (New York: Simon & Schuster, 1991), pp. 95, 114-16.

26. Koster, *In the Time of the Tyrants*, pp. 340-41. Woodward, *The Commanders*, p. 133.

27. Koster, *In the Time of the Tyrants*, pp. 322–52.

28. US Department of State, *American Foreign Policy: Current Documents, 1987* (Washington: GPo, 1988), p. 711.

29. Ibid., p. 794.

30. Ibid., p. 792.

31. Scranton, *The Noriega Years*, p. 117.

32. Weeks, *Panama: Made in the USA*, p. 66. Zimbalist, *Panama at the Crossroads*, pp. 144–45.

33. US Department of State. *American Foreign Policy: Current Documents, 1988* (Washington: GPo, 1988), p. 745. Weeks, *Panama: Made in the USA*, p. 62.

34. Scranton, *The Noriega Years*, p. 131.

35. Ibid., pp. 15, 136–37.

36. Zimbalist, *Panama at the Crossroads*, p. 82.

37. Scranton, *The Noriega Years*, p. 139.

38. Ibid. , pp. 153–56.

39. Zimbalist, *Panama at the Crossroads*, p. 149.

40. Scranton, *The Noriega Years*, p. 156. Conniff, *Panama at the Crossroads*, p. 157. Koster, *In the Time of the Tyrants*, pp. 355–68. Weeks, *Panama: Made in the USA*, pp. 62, 71–80. Zimbalist, *Panama at the Crossroads*, p. 146–50.

41. See the official US declarations on the Panamanian "crisis" in the 1987, 1989, and 1989 issues of the US Department of State, *American Foreign Policy: Current Documents* (Washington: GPO). Bruce W. Watson and Peter G. Tsouras, eds., *Operation Just Cause: The US Intervention in Panama* (Boulder: Westview Press, 1991), pp. 52-54. Woodward, *The Commanders*, pp. 86–87, 114–16, 127–30, 169.

42. Scranton, *The Noriega Years*, p. 197.

43. US General Accounting Office, *Panama: Issues Relating to the U.S. Invasion* (Washington: GAO, 1991), pp. 1–5.

44. *Public Papers of the Presidents of the United States: George Bush, 1989* (Washington: GPO, 1990), p. 1724.

45. Zimbalist, *Panama at the Crossroads*, p. 154. Evidencing unbelievable negligence, neither the US Southern Command nor the Endara Government have seriously investigated the number of Panamanian casualties Just Cause produced.

46. US General Accounting Office, *Panama: Issues Relating to the US Invasion* (Washington: GPO, 1987), p. 4.

47. US Department of State, *American Foreign Policy: Current Documents, 1987* (Washington: GPO, 1987), p. 4.

48. Thomas Donnelly, Margaret Roth, and Caleb Baker, *Operation Just Cause: The Storming of Panama* (New York: Lexington, 1991), p. 88.

49. Woodward, *The Commanders*, p. 103.

50. Donnelly, *Operation Just Cause*, pp. 96–97.

51. Woodward, *The Commanders*, p. 106.

52. Thomas G. Paterson, Garry J. Clifford, and Kenneth J. Hagan, *American Foreign Policy: A History, Since 1900,* 3d ed. (Lexington, MA: D.C. Heath and Company, 1991), pp. 718–19.

53. The information in this section is taken basically from Zimbalist, *Panama at the Crossroads*, chapters 6–7.

54. Ibid., p. 121.

55. For details on the Social Security housing fraud, see Koster, *In the Time of the Tyrants*, pp. 258–71.

56. The figurehead presidents were: Aristides Royo (1978–1982), Ricardo de la Espriella (1982–1984), Jorge Illueca (1984), Nicolás Ardito Barletta (1984–1985), Eric Arturo Delvalle (1985–1988), Manuel Solís Palma (1988–1989), and Francisco Rodríguez (1989).

57. For a compilation of the 1968–1989 military regime's human rights abuses, see "Recordemos . . . para que no vuelva a suceder," a supplement to *La Prensa*, 20 April 1992.

58. Zimbalist, *Panama at the Crossroads*, p. 78.

59. Ibid., p. 76.

Epilogue

The Public Force, 1990–Present

FOLLOWING THE US INVASION of 20 December 1989, Panama's new government placed the republic's security apparatus under civilian rule. Known since as the Public Force (PF), the organization, however, has been characterized by inefficiency. While corruption has also permeated its ranks, its subordination to civilian authorities, as during the 1903–30 period, has been guaranteed only by the threat of US military action against it in case of rebellion. A PF uprising against the Endara Administration in December 1990, checked by the US Southern Command, so demonstrates. As the ongoing problem of militarism indicates, the issue of illegitimacy persists, aggravated by Torrijos' and Noriega's negative legacies. Given Panama's past experiences, in the absence of a US commitment to intervene, the isthmus might yet see another episode of institutional militarism.

JUST CAUSE destroyed the Noriega dictatorship and placed Guillermo Endara, the candidate elected by the Panamanian people in May of 1989, in the presidency. The Endara Government, however, soon proved its incompetence, especially in its manifest inability to lead the country towards the achievement of a truly legitimate political system. Endara and his collaborators failed to understand the mandate the winning coalition had received at the polls to lead Panama's transition from dictatorship to a true democracy. An efficient restructuring of Panama's legal, judicial, and administrative systems should have been the government's major concern. The circumstances called for a reinstatement of the 1946 constitutional charter overthrown by the National Guard in 1968, as well as for the election of a constituent assembly to reorganize and reform the political institutions of the republic.

Despite these obvious requirements, the civilian government decided to abide by the 1972 charter dictated by Omar Torrijos. Undemocratic legislation left in place by the dictatorship was also maintained. Like Torrijos before him, Endara was apparently moved by a desire to obtain legitimacy *para ingles ver,* for most Latin American governments were quick to question the legitimacy of an administration empowered by virtue of the US invasion. The civilian regime thus failed to understand that legitimacy is a quality generated by internal consensus, not foreign acceptance. Furthermore, although the governing coalition widely announced the prompt establishment of a *concertación nacional,* or process of national accord—which could have produced an authentic legitimization of the polity—such a process never materialized. The *concertación* plan soon faded away, giving way to the authoritarianism, nepotism, venality, and personalism which have traditionally characterized Panama's politics.[1]

Contrary to what was hoped, therefore, no true break with the negative practices of the past took place. Resilience in the political realm was coupled with ineffective attempts to reform the security apparatus. The new government formally abolished the PDF and replaced it with the PF. The force was made dependent on the Ministry for Government and Justice, headed by Ricardo Arias Calderón, Panama's Christian Democrat leader.

But instead of calling for urgent international support—even, if necessary, in the form of a United Nations Peacekeeping Force—to reorganize the security institution, the government resorted to reforming it on a basis of supposedly uncorrupted elements of the former PDF. With the ostensible purpose of rapidly assuming control of the national territory, one of the necessary conditions for international recognition, the government promised these unblemished elements a place in the PF if they pledged to subordinate themselves to the civilian regime. As a further lure, military ranks were maintained in the new, ostensibly civilian, organization. Most of the PDF's rank and file, as well as middle officer corps, joined the PF, which in early 1990 was composed of approximately 13,000 members. In the face of widespread public concern for the integration of the force with former Noriega personnel, Minister Arias Calderón disclosed his naive approach to governance as follows: "Some persons have asked if it would be possible to create a new Public Force with people who served the old Defense Forces. I say it is possible, because I am a Christian and I believe no one is condemned to [be a victim of] his past."[2]

In February of 1990 the administration issued a cabinet decree giving legal basis to its security policy. Considering it the "demand of an overwhelming majority of the Panamanian people" that the Defense Forces be formally abolished and that "the vestiges of militarism—and its sequel of human rights violations, repression, disrespect for the popular will and democratic institutions, and burden to the public treasury—disappear," the cabinet ordered the organization of the "Public Force of the Panamanian State, with technical and professional responsibility for safeguarding public security and national defense." The force's performance was to be at all times subordinated to the constitution and laws of the republic, "with full respect for human rights, as well as for the protection and support of democratic institutions." To reinforce these precepts, all members of the PF were required to take an oath of loyalty to the constitution and laws of the republic, under the authority of the president, prior to assuming their functions. The total membership of the institution was to be determined by the National Assembly, as a percentage of the republic's population.[3]

The force was divided into three national, centralized services, each with an independent chief: the National Police, the National Air Service, and the National Marine Service. The national investigations bureau, renamed the Technical Judicial Police, was also temporarily assigned to the Ministry for Government and Justice. Leslie Loaiza, a "proud" former officer of the military regime's secret service, was appointed director. In July of 1991, the National Assembly passed a law that put the Judicial Police under the authority of the Attorney General's Office, beginning on 1 January 1992.[4] Finally, in March of 1990 a fifth security force was created, the Institutional Protection Service, to assume the functions of the former presidential guard. This service was placed under the responsibility of the cabinet chief of staff.[5]

The National Police was assigned normal police duties in consultation and coordination with civilian authorities, to whose orders it was to be at all times subordinated. The creation of special units within the police for the protection of international borders, national territory, and the Panama Canal, in accordance with the 1977 treaties, was also contemplated. The air and marine services were entrusted with supporting government agencies in development programs, rescue activities, and general security functions. Additionally, the Marine Service was charged with collaborating in the prevention of piracy, contraband, and illegal immigration and fishing.

The PF decree also stipulated the creation of a Public Security and National Defense Council to advise the executive in such matters. The council's day-to-day business was to be managed by an executive secretary, a post for which President Endara selected Menalco Solís, a partner in the president's law firm, and a former minister in charge of the treasury and planning portfolios under the

Noriega dictatorship. As expected, this appointment, as well as similar ones, alienated many *civilistas* from the Endara Administration.[6]

Washington was quick to provide assistance to the PF in the form of equipment and training. Through the Foreign Military Sales Program and Security Supporting Assistance, the Bush Administration provided a large number of vehicles in 1990. In the same year, Southern Command advisors implemented a series of courses and seminars for members of the "new" force. During 1990 and 1991, the International Criminal Investigative Assistance Program (ICITAP), a US agency devoted to police instruction, allocated $13.2 million for training of Panama's PF; $10 million was scheduled to be spent in 1992. In December 1991 a Department of State document praised Panama's sustained advancement in the establishment of a "professional, civilian police agency."[7]

Direction of the new security institution was a controversial matter from the start. The highest-ranking, reputedly unpolluted officer of the PDF, Roberto Armijo, was appointed to direct the PF. But Armijo, who had participated in acts of repression in 1979—was asked to resign a few days later, when the Ministry for Government discovered that his bank records were impossible to justify on the basis of his PDF salary. He was replaced by Eduardo Herrera, the PDF colonel whom the CIA approached in 1988 to direct "Panama 3." Herrera had also served previously as Noriega's ambassador to Israel and had coordinated the dictatorship's repression during Black Friday, the infamous 1987 episode of arrest, beating, and torture of hundreds of *civilistas*. As the new director's deputy, Endara appointed another ex-PDF officer, Aristides Valdonedo. Valdonedo was fired in May of 1990 after being accused of committing acts of torture and arson during the Noriega phase of the military regime.[8]

Eduardo Herrera, after February 1990 director of the National Police, did not last long either, for in August, while on leave abroad, he was retired without explanation. Another purge followed, in which numerous officers were also retired and dismissed, and the ranks of general, colonel, and lieutenant-colonel were eliminated. Herrera was replaced by another of Noriega's officers, whom the government discharged in September of the same year after he publicly slandered the publisher of *La Prensa*.

The government now became convinced it was time to place the police under civilian direction, for which purpose it designated a Christian Democrat attorney, Ebrahim Asvat, as chief. Asvat, who since July 1990 had occupied an administrative position within the organization, had to face a number of rebellion threats from police officers in collusion with former PDF members. On 18 October President Endara and Attorney General Rogelio Cruz denounced the existence of a plan for a PF uprising, of which the government supposedly had knowledge prior to Eduardo Herrera's retirement. Six days later Herrera, upon arriving from yet another private trip, declared to the press his opposition to the administration's "demilitarization" policy. Underscoring his belief that "in every country an armed force is necessary," he claimed the Panamanian "military" felt increasing frustration towards the government. The Attorney General's Office subsequently placed Herrera under arrest.[9]

Rumors and accusations of an impending PF insurrection became a reality on 4 December 1990, when two policemen, in a surprise helicopter action, abducted Herrera from prison and took him to a police barracks to lead a revolt against the government. The PF's insubordination was planned to coincide with a protest march of civil servants and opposition groups which the government had labeled as "destabilizing," for which reason the administration had threatened public employees with summary dismissal if they participated. Although Herrera claimed to be only a spokesman of police requests for fringe benefits, the political orientation of his movement was evidenced by a personalist, Bolívar-type "Proclamation to the People of Panama" published in a local daily on 5 December:

> In the dramatic circumstances which Panama is presently undergoing, which combine one of the worst socio-economic crises with the

moral disrepute of the government, I reaffirm my patriotic vocation, bound to the anguish of a people who have no work and who are forced to demand and defend their trampled social rights. We cannot but publicly express our solidarity with the people's struggle against unemployment and misery, our identification with their demands for an honest and efficient government, our adhesion to their dreams and hopes.[10]

The police movement, however, was of short duration, for on 5 December, at the request of the Endara Administration, US troops subdued the rebellious officers and returned Herrera to custody.

Ebrahim Asvat remained as director until April 1991 when a split occurred within the government coalition and President Endara expelled the Christian Democrats from his administration. An *Arnulfista* attorney, Gonzalo Menéndez Franco, was then appointed police chief, but had to resign a few months later when he participated in a partisan political event, in express violation of the decree which constituted the Public Force. The director of the Judicial Police, Oswaldo Fernández, was then nominated to head the National Police.

Although Panama's principal security force has been under the direction of civilian attorneys for nearly four years, vestiges of militarism still remain. The Endara Administration's overwhelming unpopularity caused the massive rejection of a constitutional reform in a plebiscite held in November 1992. One of the reform's features was an article which expressly stated, "the Republic of Panama shall not have an army."[11] While the disposition would have been mostly symbolic, it would have indeed represented a majoritarian desire to do away with the militarist past. Government incompetence, however, obfuscated the serious debate and consideration of national issues. In other regards, both the air and marine services continue to be headed by former PDF officers. Moreover, direction of the Police Academy—inaugurated by the Endara Administration to train future policemen for performance in a supposedly democratic setting—was entrusted to Luis Puleio, Noriega's national security ideologue.[12] The inefficacy and self-serving nature of Panama's civilian politicians have, therefore, maintained the germ of militarism alive on the isthmus.

SINCE ITS CREATION in 1990, the Public Force has demonstrated its utter incapacity to comply with the duties it was assigned. The breakdown in law and order has been manifest, with violence occurring throughout the national territory with a frequency Panamanians were unfamiliar with. While 1990 criminal statistics tripled those of 1989, figures for the first half of 1992 increased alarmingly in comparison to data for the previous year. A distressing socioeconomic situation, coupled with drug trafficking, arms proliferation and, perhaps more significantly, a "subculture of corruption and militarism," explains the rise in criminality. Noriega's departure set loose the underworld forces the former dictator held in firm grip during his tenure. With the PF overwhelmingly composed of ex-PDF members, its commitment to public security, honesty, and the rule of law is, not surprisingly, weak. Reflecting on Panama's woeful reality, Isthmian attorney and scholar Humberto Ricord has written:

> The political corruption initiated by the plutocratic oligarchy in the 1940s and the orgy of crimes, frauds, and repression which Panama experienced during Torrijos' military dictatorship and Noriega's narco-dictatorship, for a long period of twenty-one years, created a national, generalized *modus vivendi,* a true subculture of corruption and repressive militarism; a subculture of degradation, collective immorality, which progressively invaded the interstices, medulla, spine, and skin of Panama's society.[13]

Notes

1. On the mistakes, incompetence, and venality of the Endara Administration, see Humberto E. Ricord, *Noriega y Panamá: Orgía y aplastamiento de la narcodictadura* (México: By the Author, 1991), part 9.

2. Ibid., pp. 546, 548, 552.

3. República de Panamá, "Decreto de Gabinete No. 38 de 10 de febrero de 1990, por el cual se organiza la Fuerza Pública," *Gaceta Oficial*, No. 21.479, 20 February 1990, pp. 2–7.

4. República de Panamá, "Decreto de Gabinete No. 42 de 17 de febrero de 1990, por el cual se reforma y adiciona el Decreto de Gabinete No. 38 de 10 de febrero de 1990," *Gaceta Oficial*, No. 21.485, 1 March 1990, pp. 2–3.

5. República de Panamá, "Ley No. 16 de 9 de julio de 1991, por la cual se aprueba la ley orgánica de la Policía Técnica Judicial como una dependencia del Ministerio Público," *Gaceta Oficial*, No. 21.830, 16 July 1991, pp. 1–25.

6. The appointments of Loaiza and Solís are but two examples. The most salient designation of a military-regime figure was that of Rogelio Cruz to the crucially sensitive post of attorney general. Cruz not only served as private secretary to puppet president Ricardo de la Espriella, but also as secretary to the board of the First Interamericas Bank, a financial institution with links to a notorious Colombian drug trafficker. The solicitor general ordered Cruz's removal in December of 1992, pending the outcome of a suit brought against the attorney general for alleged illegality in the liberation of frozen bank accounts presumed to contain laundered funds.

In April 1991 Endara appointed Omaira Correa, a former deputy of the pro-military *Partido Laborista,* as mayoress of Panama City. Correa was suspended from office in May of 1993 for allegedly utilizing municipal funds for partisan purposes.

7. Ricord, *Noriega y Panamá*, pp. 549, 562. Betty Brannan Jaén, "Optimismo oficial," *La Prensa*, January 1992.

8. Richard M. Koster and Guillermo Sánchez Borbón, *In the Time of the Tyrants: Panama: 1968–1990* (New York: W.W. Norton, 1990), pp. 229–30. Ricord, *Noriega y Panamá*, pp. 543–64.

9. Ricord, *Noriega y Panamá*, p. 640.

10. Ibid., p. 648.

11. República de Panamá, "Acto Legislativo No. 1 de 29 de junio de 1992, por el cual se sustituye el preámbulo, se introducen nuevos preceptos y se reforman el contenido y la denominacion de varios títulos, capítulos y artículos de la Constitución Política de la República," *Gaceta Oficial*, No. 22.070, 3 July 1992, pp. 1–46.

12. Orlando Mendieta, "Sancionan oficiales de policía," *El Panamá América*, 19 June 1992, p. 1A. In his book *Militarismo, presencia y política* (Panama: Fuerzas de Defensa de Panamá, 1988), Luis Puleio manifests himself as a panegyrist of the military regime, Omar Torrijos, and Manuel Noriega. "The Panamanian armed forces were born with the republic and will die with it," he wrote about the PDF (p. 148). Former dictator Manuel Noriega he described in the following terms: "General Noriega is a military man with projection, who is updated in all aspects of war and peace. As a man and a soldier, and given the post he fulfills, Noriega is receptive to dialogue and open in manner; he possesses high human sensitivity and believes in friendship and in one's pledged word. Reading provides him with mental broadness for accurate discernment in the exercise of his daily responsibilities as commandant" (p. 140). Puleio was removed as director of the Police Academy in January 1993, following the public uproar caused by the death of a police cadet as the result of harsh military training. Rainelda Mata Kelly, "Academia de policía," *La Prensa*, 22 January 1993, p. 15A.

13. Ricord, *Noriega y Panamá*, p. 621.

Conclusion

On 8 May 1994, four years after the restoration of civilian rule, the Panamanian electorate returned a "recycled" PRD to power. The election of the military dictatorship's political party—previously described in this book as a motley crowd of opportunists—is explained by several traits of the Panamanian political culture, which have here been addressed. On the one hand, the supposedly democratic, *civilista* political parties, torn apart by personalism and factional battles for control of the loot, proved incapable of preserving their 1989 alliance against the military dictatorship. The incompetence, nepotism, and venality of the Endara Administration further alienated the *civilista* parties from many of its former sympathizers, who proffered their support to a "third force"—supposedly unrelated to the PRD or the traditional politicians—led by *salsa* singer Rubén Blades. While not adding directly to the PRD, the popularity of this "third force" reduced the possibilities for the triumph of a *civilista* candidacy. Finally, the PRD appealed to its clientele (amounting roughly to one fourth of the country's population of 2.5 million) which, true to the Latin American political tradition, favors a paternalist regime, despite the authoritarianism and corruption that usually have accompanied such systems in Latin America.

It is still too early to determine whether the PRD's return to power will signify a re-establishment of militarism. While it is a fact that the party served the military, obsequiously, to fulfill civil appointments during the 1968–1989 military dictatorship, it is also true that since the US invasion the Panamanian security force are no longer in control of the state. Likewise, despite the close links which continue to exist between the deposed PDF command and the PRD leadership, the party does not seem to be under the control of military figures.

Torrijos' party, therefore, seems to have freed itself from its military creators. Ultimately, the re-militarization of Panamanian politics will depend not on which party governs, but on the governing party's ability to generate political legitimacy. Enduring political illegitimacy, as this book has attempted to demonstrate, will only produce breaks with legality, of which militarism was the most pernicious in Panamanian history.

PANAMA'S EXPERIENCES OF militarism stand in direct contradiction to the liberalism that inspired Panama's constitutional structure since independence from Spain, both under Colombian sovereignty (1821–1903) and after the isthmus' emergence as an independent republic in 1903. Militarism was contrary to the letter of Panama's liberal constitutional regime (except, perhaps, between 1972 and 1983, when a constitutional disposition mandating the participation of the military in the exercise of public power was in force). This study argues that militarism emerged because the political regime is illegitimate and the political culture is authoritarian.

Crucial in understanding Panamanian militarism is the concept of *legitimacy*. Because political actors have not subscribed loyally to the liberal regime stipulated in the country's constitutions, Panama's post-1821 history is marred by breaks with legality: electoral fraud, attempts at forcible change, and militarism. The authoritarian political tradition inherited from Spanish colonialism determined, to a large extent, the recourse to militarism. Iberian rule was anything but democratic or liberal. It was a divine-right polity which required absolute submission to a father-like monarch, with little place for pluralism or dissent. Authoritarianism, moreover, dictates the use of force to maintain stability, when stability is deemed by the state's authorities to be threatened by dissent. However foreign to our late twentieth-century concept of proper governance Spanish monarchical authoritarianism might be, it was legitimate until the early 1800s—and legitimacy is the quality which explains the absolutist regime's longevity and relative stability. It was the loss of monarchical legitimacy and the failure of the rule of law to assume its place that spelled the beginning of a period of instability characterized, among other features, by militarism throughout all of Spanish America and, not least of all, in Panama.

Other internal and external factors contributed to determine the shape Panamanian militarism would assume. An attitude of permissiveness toward official corruption, coupled with socially and racially flexible recruiting policies, made the military since colonial times a viable avenue of social and economic advancement for ambitious individuals from the masses, in a society in which wealth and conditions of birth weighed more than talent or capabilities. Personalism, which surfaced at the breakdown of the absolutist regime, endeavored to replace the monarch's legitimacy by concentrating authority in the *caudillo,* a leader of the people who, more often than not in the nineteenth century, based his exercise of power on military victories. Last but not least, the reality of US hemispheric superiority, manifest since the mid-1800s, either discouraged or abetted the political preponderance of the Panamanian military, depending on the policies favored by Washington in its quest to establish, consolidate, and protect its hegemony.

Since its formal establishment in 1846, US hegemony over

Panama has been expressed basically through requirements of stability and responsiveness to specific US interests. While these have shifted from railroad to canal to military bases, stability has remained Washington's primary preoccupation. In an effort to eschew instability, the United States initially opposed domestic militarism. The need for stability later determined, in the 1940s, an ostensibly neutral policy towards the Panamanian military, for the pursuit of hegemony demanded a certain regard for an institution that, in Washington's eyes, held the key to local stability. Starting in the 1960s, with a change in the regional and global environments, Washington adopted a policy of close association with the Isthmian armed force, which in effect contributed to reinforcing domestic militarism. The policy proved costly, as the need for Just Cause in December of 1989 illustrates. Hence, the US role as a determinant of Panamanian militarism has been inconsistent, even as US hegemony has remained uninterrupted throughout the 150-year-old US-Panamanian relationship.

This study has endeavored to distinguish between institutional militarism—the predominance, in national politics, of a military institution—and the more primitive phenomenon of predatory militarism which preceded it. Predatory militarism, evident during the nineteenth century, strove to use military force for the advancement of purely personal or partisan interests, and antedated the monopolization of military power by an armed institution. Institutional militarism, on the other hand, endeavored to further corporate interest vested in an institution that had effectively assumed the country's monopoly of force. In Panama—as elsewhere in Latin America—the age of predatory militarism came to an end with the full incorporation of the isthmus into the international economy. Panamanian institutional militarism emerged toward the middle of the twentieth century, after the United States demonstrated its reluctance to arbitrate political disputes stemming from domestic politicians' disinclination to subscribe to the liberal regime's constitutional arrangements.

Institutional militarism, which characterizes nearly fifty years of Panama's modern history, blended elements of the Spanish and Colombian pasts with modern developments. The National Police, the National Guard, and the Defense Forces each held an effective monopoly of military force; at the same time, their political preponderance was marked by corruption and personalism, as manifested by the leadership of José Antonio Remón (1947–55), Omar Torrijos (1968–81), and Manuel Noriega (1981–89). Strengthened by domestic traditions and US assistance, the Panamanian military assumed direct political power in 1968, and retained it until the 1989 US invasion dislodged them from power. The fact that the National Guard acted out of self-preservation explains the military regime's imperative of elaborating an approach to government labeled *Torrijista* by its supporters. Very much imbedded in the Iberic-American tradition, its distinguishing features were co-optation and repression, disguised, however, within an institutional mantle of nationalist populism, especially during the Torrijos dictatorship. Although Noriega abandoned several of his predecessor's more institutionalized inclusionist policies, thereby reverting to a more primitive style of governance, his dictatorship was also fundamentally *pan o palo*. Noriega could not have described it better when he proclaimed his policy of the "three p's": *plomo, palo y plata*.

Historically, the interludes of militarism demonstrate not only an age-old lack of political legitimacy, but moreover that the militarist option existed since the early 1800s and extends to our day. They also effectively expose US hegemonic interests as a principal factor helping determine not only the fate of domestic militarism, but the course of Panamanian history as a whole. Politically, Panama's militarist experiences were futile, for they were unsuccessful in developing legitimacy. Furthermore, they provided opportunities for US interference, propelled by the North American interest in maintaining stability on the isthmus. Economically, militarism was pernicious, being propelled, as it was, by personal or corporate rather than truly national interest. More difficult to assess, because of their subjective character, are the moral consequences of the phenomenon. But the fact that Panamanian society is currently pervaded by what an Isthmian scholar has described as a "subculture of corruption and militarism"[1]—a subculture which effectively abates possibilities for authentic national development—indicates that, in its moral dimensions, the legacy of militarism has been even less favorable.

Notes

1. Humberto E. Ricord, *Noriega y Panamá: Orgía y aplastamiento de la narcodictadura* (México: By the Author, 1991), p. 621.

Bibliography

Government Documents and Other Primary Sources

Economic Report of the President, 1993. Washington, D.C.: GPO, 1993.

International Institute for Strategic Studies. *The Military Balance 1990–1991.* London: Brassey's, 1990.

———. *The Military Balance 1989–1990.* London: Brassey's, 1989.

———. *The Military Balance 1988–1989.* London: Brassey's, 1988.

———. *The Military Balance 1987–1988.* London Brassey's, 1987.

———. *The Military Balance 1986–1987.* London: Brassey's, 1986.

———. *The Military Balance 1985–1986.* London: Brassey's, 1985.

———. *The Military Balance 1984–1985.* London Brassey's, 1984.

———. *The Military Balance 1983–1984.* London Brassey's, 1983.

Public Papers of the Presidents of the United States: George Bush, 1989– Washington GPO, 1990.

República de Panamá. Contraloría General de la República. *Panamá en cifras, 1977–1981.* Panama: Direccíon de Estadística y Censo, 1982.

———. Contraloría General de la República. *Panamá en cifras, 1969–1973.* Panama: Direccíon de Estadística y Censo, 1974.

———. "Ley No. 43 de 23 de diciembre de 1953, por la cual se declaran ilícitas y violatorias de la Constitución Nacional en la República, las actividades totalitarias tales como el Comunismo," *Gaceta Oficial,* No. 12.255, 24 December 1953.

———. "Ley No. 44 de 23 de diciembre de 1953, por la cual se crea la Guardia Nacional y se subroga la Ley 79 de 1941," *Gaceta Oficial,* No. 12.255, 24 December 1953.

———. "Ley No. 20 de 29 de septiembre de 1983, por la cual se dicta la Ley Orgánica de las Fuerzas de Defensa de la República de Panamá." *Gaceta Oficial*, No. 19.909, 30 September 1983.

———. "Decreto de Gabinete No. 38 de 10 de febrero de 1990, por el cual se organiza la Fuerza Pública." *Gaceta Oficial*, No. 21.479, 20 February 1990.

———. "Decreto de Gabinete No. 42 de 17 de febrero de 1990, por el cual se reforma y adiciona el Decreto de Gabinete No. 38 de 10 de febrero de 1990 *Gaceta Oficial*, No. 21.485, 1 March 1990.

———. "Ley No. 16 de 9 de julio de 1991, por la cual se aprueba la Ley Orgánica de la Policía Técnica Judicial como una dependencia del Ministerio Público." *Gaceta Oficial*, No. 21.830, 16 July 1991.

———. "Acto Legislativo No. 1 de 29 de junio de 1992, por el cual se susti-tuye el preámbulo, se introducen nuevos preceptos y se reforman el contenido y la denominación de varios títulos, capítulos y artículos de la Constitución Política de la República." *Gaceta Oficial*, No. 22.070, 3 July 1992.

Stockholm Peace Research Institute. *World Armaments and Disarma-ments: SIPRI Yearbook*. Oxford: Oxford University Press, 1990.

———. *World Armaments and Disarmaments: SIPRI Yearbook*. Oxford: Oxford University Press, 1986.

———. *World Armaments and Disarmaments SIPRI Yearbook*. Oxford: Oxford University Press, 1985.

———. *World Armaments and Disarmaments: SIPRI Yearbook*. Oxford: Oxford University Press, 1980.

———. *World Armaments and Disarmaments: SIPRI Yearbook*. Oxford: Oxford University Press, 1979.

———. *World Armaments and Disarmaments: SIPRI Yearbook*. Oxford: Oxford University Press, 1978.

———. *World Armaments and Disarmaments: SIPRI Yearbook*. Oxford: Oxford University Press, 1977.

———. *World Armaments and Disarmaments: SIPRI Yearbook*. Oxford: Oxford University Press, 1976.

———. *World Armaments and Disarmaments: SIPRI Yearbook*. Oxford: Oxford University Press, 1975.

———. *World Armaments and Disarmaments: SIPRI Yearbook*. Oxford: Oxford University Press, 1972.

US Agency for International Development. *US Overseas Loans and Grants and Assistance from International Organizations, July 1, 1945–September 30, 1990*. Washington: GPO, 1991.

———. *US Overseas Loans and Grants and Assistance from International Organizations, July 1, 1945–September 30, 1985*. Washington: GPO, 1986.

———. *US Overseas Loans and Grants and Assistance from International Organizations, July 1, 1945–September 30, 1982*. Washington: GPO, 1983.

———. *US Overseas Loans and Grants and Assistance from International Organizations, July 1, 1945–September 30, 1977*. Washington: GPO, 1978.

———. *US Overseas Loans and Grants and Assistance from International Organizations, July 1, 1945–September 30, 1976*. Washington: GPO, 1977.

———. *US Overseas Loans and Grants and Assistance from International Organizations, July 1, 1945–June 30, 1975*. Washington: GPO, 1976.

US Central Intelligence Agency. *Agreement of Arnulfo Arias Madrid and the Communist Party for Joint Action Against the Government*. Cable, 13 January 1964. Available in the Declassified Documents Research system (hereafter DDRS), document No. 1988-65.

———. *Involvement of Major Victor Mata of the National Guard in Coup Plans of Arnulfo Arias and the Communists*. Cable, 13 January 1964, DDRS 1988-67.

US Congress. House. Committee on Foreign Affairs. *Hearings Before the Subcommittee on International Organizations: Text of the Human Rights Watch No. 4, February 1979*. 96th Cong., 1st sess., 2, 10 May; 21 June; 12 July; 2 August 1979.

US Congress. House. Committee on Foreign Operations and Monetary Affairs. *Hearings Before the Subcommittee of the Committee on Government Operations: U.S. Aid Operations in Latin America*. 87th Cong., 1st sess., 9 December 1961.

US Congress. House. Committee on Foreign Operations. *Hearings Before the Foreign Operations and Government Information Subcommittee: U.S. Aid Operations in Latin America Under the Alliance for Progress.* 90th Cong., 2d sess., 24 January 1968.

US Department of Defense. Cable, commander-in-chief of the US Southern Command to the Joint Chiefs of Staff, January 1964. DDRS 1983-1652.

———. Cable, White House to commander-in-chief of the US Southern Command, January 1964. DDRS 1983-1658.

US Department of State. *American Foreign Policy: Basic Documents, 1977–1980.* Washington: GP0, 1983.

———. *American Foreign Policy: Current Documents, 1984.* Washington: GPO, 1986.

———. *American Foreign Policy: Current Documents, 1987.* Washington: GPO, 1988.

———. *American Foreign Policy: Current Documents, 1988.* Washington: GPO, 1989.

———. *American Foreign Policy: Current Documents, 1989.* Washington: GPO, 1990.

———. *Bulletin,* 4 November 1968.

———. *Bulletin,* 2 December 1968.

———. *Foreign Relations of the United States, 1919,* vol. 2. Washington: GPO, 1934.

———. *Foreign Relations of the United States, 1931,* vol. 2. Washington: GPO, 1946.

———. *Foreign Relations of the United States, 1946,* vol. 11. Washington: GPO, 1969.

———. *Foreign Relations of the United States, 1950,* vol. 2. Washington: GPO, 1976.

———. *Foreign Relations of the United States 1952-1954,* vol. 4. Washington: GPO, 1983.

———. *Foreign Relations of the United States, 1955-1957,* vol. 7. Washington: GPO, 1987.

———. *IRA/ARA Contingency Study: Panama.* DDRS 1989-2180.

———. *Records of the Department of State Relating to Internal Affairs of*

Panama, 1910–1929. Available in the Department of State Decimal File. Washington: National Archives Microfilm Publications, 1965, microfilm M-697, roll no. 1.

———. *Report,* 1961. DDRS 1983-2029.

———. Telegram, Ambassador Charles Adair to Secretary of State Dean Rusk, March 1968. DDRS 1981-372A.

———. Telegram, Secretary of State Dean Rusk to Ambassador Charles Adair, March 1968. DDRS 1981-371C.

———. *Telegram,* Taylor to Assistant Secretary of State Thomas Mann, 5 March 1964. DDRS 1981-572C.

———. *Treaties and Other Agreements of the United States of America: 1776–1949,* vol. 6. Washington: GPO, 1971.

———. *Treaties and Other Agreements of the United States of America: 1776–1949,* vol. 10. Washington: GPO, 1972.

———. *U.S. Treaties and Other International Agreements,* vol. 3, pt. 4, 1952. Washington: GPO, 1955.

———. *U.S. Treaties and Other International Agreements,* vol. 13, pt. 3, 1962. Washington: GPO, 1963.

———. *U.S. Treaties and Other International Agreements, 1978–1979,* vol. 30, pt. 2. Washington: GPO, 1980.

US General Accounting Office. *Panama: Issues Relating to the U.S. Invasion.* Washington: GAO, 1991.

US National Security Council. *Walter W. Rostow to President Lyndon B. Johnson.* Memorandum, undated. Available through the Declassified Documents Research System, document No. 1991-527.

Books and Articles

Alfaro, Ricardo J. *Vida del general Tomás Herrera.* Edición conmemorativa. Panama: Universidad de Panamá, 1960.

Araúz, Celestino Andrés. *Belisario Porras y las relaciones de Panamá con los Estados Unidos.* Panama: Ediciones Formato Dieciséis, 1988.

Araúz, Celestino Andrés, and Pizzurno, Patricia. *El Panamá Hispano (1501–1821)*. Panama: Diario La Prensa, 1991.

———. "Historia de Panamá: El Estado Federal de Panamá," a supplement to *La Prensa*, 8 January 1992.

———. "Historia de Panamá: La Guerra de los Mil Días en Panamá," a supplement to *La Prensa*, 8 April 1992.

———. "Historia de Panamá: Años de crisis y el golpe de Acción Comunal (1928–32)," a supplement to *La Prensa*, 9 December 1992.

———. "Historia de Panamá: Harmodio Arias y la consolidación de la República," a supplement to *La Prensa*, 17 February 1993.

———. "Historia de Panamá: Convulsión y reformismo (1936–1941)," a supplement to *La Prensa*, 17 March 1993.

Arias, Tomás. *Memorias de don Tomás Arias, fundador de la República y triunviro*. Panama: Talleres Gráficos de Trejos Hnos., Sucs., 1977.

Arosemena, Mariano. *Apuntamientos históricos (1801–1840)*. Edited by Ernesto J. Castillero R. Panama: Ministerio de Educación, 1949.

Arriagada, Genaro. "Ideology and Politics in the South American Military: Argentina, Brazil, Chile, and Uruguay," a paper presented at the March 1979 colloquium of the Latin American Program of the Woodrow Wilson International Center for Scholars. Washington: Smithsonian Institution, 1979.

Barber, Willard F., and Ronning, C. Neale. *Internal Security and Military Power: Counterinsurgency and Civic Action in Latin America*. Columbus: Ohio State University Press, 1966.

Beluche, Isidro. *Independencia y secesión de Panamá*. Panama: By the Author, 1965.

Benjamin, Jules R. "The Framework of U.S. Relations with Latin America in the Twentieth Century: An Interpretive Essay." *Diplomatic History* 11 (Spring 1987): 91-112.

Black, Jan Knippers. *Sentinels of Empire: The United States and Latin American Militarism*. New York: Greenwood Press, 1986.

Brannan Jaén, Betty. "Optimismo oficial," *La Prensa*, January 1992.

Buckley, Kevin. *Panama: The Whole Story*. New York: Simon & Schuster, 1991.

Bushnell, David. *The Making of Modern Colombia: A Nation in Spite of Itself*. Berkeley: University of California Press, 1993.

Calvo, Roberto. "The Church and the Doctrine of National Security." *Journal of Inter-American Studies and World Affairs* 21, pt. 1 (February 1979): 69–87.

Cantarino, Vicente. *Civilización y cultura de España*. 2d ed. New York: Macmillan Publishing Company, 1988.

Carothers, Thomas. "The Reagan Years: The 1980s." In *Exporting Democracy: The United States in Latin America*, edited by Abraham F. Lowenthal. Baltimore: The Johns Hopkins University Press, 1991.

Case, Robert P. "El entrenamiento de los militares latinoamericanos en los Estados Unidos." *Aportes* 6 (October 1967).

Castillero, Ernesto J. *Panamá y Colombia, historia de su reconciliación: Capítulos de historia diplomática en los albores de la República de Panamá*. Panama: Instituto Nacional de Cultura, 1974.

Coleman, Kenneth M. "The Political Mythology of the Monroe Doctrine: Reflections on the Social Psychology of Hegemony." In *Latin America, the United States, and the Inter-American System*, edited by John D. Martz and Lars Schoultz. Boulder: Westview Press, 1980.

Comblin, José. *The Church and the National Security State*. Maryknoll, New York: Orbis Books, 1979.

Conniff, Michael L. *Panama and the United States: The Forced Alliance*. Athens: The University of Georgia Press, 1992.

Donnelly, Thomas; Roth, Margaret; and Baker, Caleb. *Operation Just Cause: The Storming of Panama*. New York: Lexington, 1991.

Fábrega, Ramón E. and Boyd Galindo, Mario. *Constituciones de la República de Panamá: 1972, 1946, 1941, 1904*. Panama: By the Authors, 1981.

Farley, Philip J.; Kaplan, Stephen S.; and Lewis, William H. *Arms Across the Sea*. Washington: The Brookings Institution, 1978.

Figueroa Navarro, Alfredo. *Dominio y sociedad en el Panamá colombiano*. 3d ed. Panama: Editorial Universitaria, 1982.

Fuerzas de Defensa de Panamá. *Fuerzas de Defensa: Fuerzas Armadas de Panama*. Santiago de Chile: Editorial Sipimex, 1987.

Gasteazoro, Carlos Manuel; Araúz, Celestino Andrés; and Muñoz Pinzón,

Armando. *La historia de Panamá en sus textos*. Panama: Editorial Universitaria, 1980.

Goytía, Victor F. *Las constituciones de Panamá*. 2d. ed. Panama: By the Author's Estate, 1987.

Grow, Michael. *The Good Neighbor Policy and Authoritarianism in Paraguay: United States Economic Expansion and Great Power Rivalry*. Lawrence: Regents Press of Kansas, 1981.

Healy, David. *Drive to Hegemony: The United States in the Caribbean, 1898–1917*. Madison: The University of Wisconsin Press, 1988.

Huertas Ponce, Esteban, ed. *Memorias y bosquejo biográfico del general Esteban Huertas, prócer de la gesta del 3 de noviembre de 1903*. Panama: Ediciones Continentales 1959.

Jaén Suárez, Omar. "El siglo XVII y las permanencias estructurales," in "Visión de la nacionalidad panameña," a supplement to *La Prensa*, 6 August 1991.

Koster, Richard M. and Sánchez Borbón, Guillermo. *In the Time of the Tyrants: Panama, 1968–1990*. New York: W.W. Norton, 1990.

Kuethe, Allan J. *Military Reform and Society in New Granada, 1773–1808*. Gainesville: The University Presses of Florida, 1978.

Labrut, Michele. *Este es Omar Torrijos*. Panamá: By the Author, 1982.

LaFeber, Walter. *Inevitable Revolutions: The United States in Central America*. New York: W.W. Norton & Co., 1984.

Langley, Lester D. *America and the Americas: The United States in the Western Hemisphere*. Athens: The University of Georgia Press, 1989.

Linares, Julio E. *Enrique Linares en la historia política de Panamá, 1869–1949: Calvario de un pueblo por afianzar su soberanía*. Panama: By the Author, 1989.

MacDonald, Scott B. *Mountain High, White Avalanche: Cocaine and Power in the Andean States and Panama*. New York: Praeger, 1989

Malloy, James M. "Authoritarianism and Corporatism in Latin America: The Modal Pattern." In *Authoritarianism and Corporatism in Latin America*, edited by James M. Malloy. Pittsburgh: University of Pittsburgh Press, 1977.

Martínez, José de Jesús. *Ideario: Omar Torrijos*. San José: EDUCA, 1982.

Mata Kelly, Rainelda. "Academia de policía," *La Prensa*, 22 January 1993, p. 15A.

McCain, William D. *The United States and the Republic of Panama*. Durham: Duke University Press, 1937.

Mellander, Gustavo A. *The United States in Panamanian Politics: The Intriguing Formative Years*. Danville, Illinois: The Interstate Printers & Publishers, 1971.

Mendieta, Orlando. "Sancionan oficiales de policía," *El Panamá América*, 19 June 1992, p. 1A.

Montaña Cuéllar, Diego. *Colombia: País formal y país real*. Buenos Aires: Editorial Platina, 1963.

O'Donnell, Guillermo. "Toward an Alternative Conceptualization of South American Politics." In *Promise of Development: Theories of Change in Latin America*, edited by Peter F. Klarén and Thomas J. Bossert. Boulder: Westview Press, 1986.

Pach, Chester J. *Arming the Free World: The Origins of the United States Military Assistance Program, 1945-1950*. Chapel Hill: The University of North Carolina Press, 1991.

Paterson, Thomas G.; Clifford, Garry J.; and Hagan, Kenneth J. *American Foreign Policy: A History, Since 1900*. 3d ed. Lexington, MA: D.C. Heath and Company, 1991.

Pedreschi, Carlos Bolívar. *De la protección del canal a la militarización del país*. Panama: By the Author, 1987.

Pereira, Renato. *Panamá: Fuerzas armadas y política*. Panama: Ediciones Nueva Universidad, 1979.

Pérez Venero, Alex. *Before the Five Frontiers: Panama from 1821-1903*. New York: AMS Press, 1978.

Petras, James; Erisman, H. Michael; and Mills, Charles. "The Monroe Doctrine and U.S. Hegemony in Latin America." In *Latin America: From Dependence to Revolution*, edited by James Petras. New York: John Wiley & Sons, 1973.

Pippin, Larry LaRae. *The Remon Era: An Analysis of a Decade of Events in Panama, 1947-1957*. Stanford: Institute of Hispanic American and Luso-Brazilian Studies, 1964.

Priestley, George. *Military Government and Popular Participation in Panama: The Torrijos Regime, 1968–1975*. Boulder: Westview Press, 1986.

Puleio, Luis. *Militarismo, presencia y política*. Panama: Fuerzas de Defensa de Panamá, 1988.

"Recordemos . . . para que no vuelva a suceder," a supplement to *La Prensa*, 20 April 1992.

Ricord, Humberto L. *Los clanes de la oligarquía y el golpe militar de 1968*. Panama: By the Author, 1983.

———. *Noriega y Panamá: orgía y aplastamiento de la narcodictadura*. México: By the Author, 1991.

———. *Panamá en la Guerra de los Mil Días*. Panama: By the Author, 1989.

Ropp, Steve C. *Panamanian Politics: From Guarded Nation to National Guard*. New York: Praeger, 1982.

Rouquié, Alain. *The Military and the State in Latin America*. Translated by Paul E. Sigmund. Berkeley: University of California Press, 1987.

Sanjur, Amado. "La desmilitarización y la eliminación del ejército," *El Panamá América*, 11 August 1992, p. 6A.

Schoultz, Lars. *Human Rights and United States Policy toward Latin America*. Princeton: Princeton University Press, 1981.

———. *National Security and United States Policy Toward Latin America*. Princeton: Princeton University Press, 1987.

Scott, Peter Dale and Marshall, Jonathan. *Cocaine Politics: Drugs, Armies, and the CIA in Central America*. Berkeley: University of California Press, 1991.

Scranton, Margaret E. *The Noriega Years: U.S.-Panamanian Relations, 1981–1990*. Boulder: Lynne Rienner Publishers, 1991.

Sepúlveda, Mélida Ruth. *Harmodio Arias Madrid: El hombre, el estadista y el periodista*. Panama: Editorial Universitaria, 1983.

Soler, Giancarlo. "Surgimiento del reformismo militar, evolución y crisis." In *Panamá: Fuerzas armadas y cuestión nacional*. Panama: Taller de Estudios Laborales y sociales, 1988.

Soler Serrano, Joaquín. *Personajes a fondo: Conversaciones con grandes figuras de nuestro tiempo*. Barcelona: Editorial Planeta, 1987.

Sondrel, Paul. "Totalitarian and Authoritarian Dictators: A Comparison of Fidel Castro and Alfredo Stroessner." *Journal of Latin American Studies* 23, pt. 3 (October 1991): 599–620.

Sosa, Juan B., and Arce, Enrique J. *Compendio de historia de Panamá.* Edited by Carlos Manuel Gasteazoro. Panama: Editorial Universitaria, 1971.

Varas, Augusto. *Militarization and the International Arms Race in Latin America.* Boulder: Westview Press, 1985.

Vásquez, Juan Materno. *Mi amigo Omar Torrijos: Su pensamiento vivo.* Panamá: Ediciones Olga Elena, 1989.

Véliz, Claudio. *The Centralist Tradition of Latin America.* Princeton: Princeton University Press, 1980.

Walker, Thomas W. *Reagan Versus the Sandinistas: The Undeclared War on Nicaragua.* Boulder: Westview Press, 1987.

Watson, Bruce W. and Tsouras, Peter G., eds. *Operation Just Cause: The U.S. Intervention in Panama.* Boulder: Westview Press, 1991.

Weeks, John and Gunson, Phil. *Panama: Made in the USA.* London: The Latin American Bureau (Research and Action), 1991.

Whitehead, Lawrence. "The Imposition of Democracy." In *Exporting Democracy: The United States in Latin America,* edited by Abraham F. Lowenthal. Baltimore: The Johns Hopkins University Press, 1991.

Wiarda, Howard. *Corporatism and National Development in Latin America.* Boulder: Westview Press, 1981.

———. "Toward a Framework for the Study of Political Change in the Iberic Latin Tradition: The Corporative Model." *World Politics* (January 1973): 206–35.

Woodward, Bob. *The Commanders.* New York: Simon & Schuster, 1991.

Zimbalist, Andrew, and Weeks, John. *Panama at the Crossroads: Economic Development and Political Change in the Twentieth Century.* Berkeley: University of California Press, 1991.

Zúñiga Guardia, Carlos Iván. *El desarme de la Policía Nacional de 1916.* Panama: Ediciones Cartillas Patrióticas, 1973.

Index

Monographs in International Studies

Titles Available from Ohio University Press, 1996

Southeast Asia Series

No. 56   **Duiker, William J.** Vietnam Since the Fall of Saigon. 1989. Updated ed. 401 pp. Paper 0-89680-162-4 $20.00.

No. 64   **Dardjowidjojo, Soenjono.** Vocabulary Building in Indonesian: An Advanced Reader. 1984. 664 pp. Paper 0-89680-118-7 $30.00.

No. 65   **Errington, J. Joseph.** Language and Social Change in Java: Linguistic Reflexes of Modernization in a Traditional Royal Polity. 1985. 210 pp. Paper 0-89680-120-9 $25.00.

No. 66   **Binh, Tran Tu.** The Red Earth: A Vietnamese Memoir of Life on a Colonial Rubber Plantation. Tr. by John Spragens. 1984. 102 pp. (SEAT*, V. 5) Paper 0-89680-119-5 $11.00.

No. 68   **Syukri, Ibrahim.** History of the Malay Kingdom of Patani. 1985. 135 pp. Paper 0-89680-123-3 $15.00.

No. 69   **Keeler, Ward.** Javanese: A Cultural Approach. 1984. 559 pp. Paper 0-89680-121-7 $25.00.

No. 70   **Wilson, Constance M. and Lucien M. Hanks.** Burma-Thailand Frontier Over Sixteen Decades: Three Descriptive Documents. 1985. 128 pp. Paper 0-89680-124-1 $11.00.

No. 71   **Thomas, Lynn L. and Franz von Benda-Beckmann,** eds. Change and Continuity in Minangkabau: Local, Regional, and Historical Perspectives on West Sumatra. 1985. 353 pp. Paper 0-89680-127-6 $16.00.

No. 72   **Reid, Anthony and Oki Akira,** eds. The Japanese Experience in Indonesia: Selected Memoirs of 1942–1945. 1986. 424 pp., 20 illus. (SEAT, V. 6) Paper 0-89680-132-2 $20.00.

No. 74   **McArthur M. S. H.** Report on Brunei in 1904. Introduced and Annotated by A. V. M. Horton. 1987. 297 pp. Paper 0-89680-135-7 $15.00.

No. 75   **Lockard, Craig A.** From Kampung to City: A Social History of Kuching, Malaysia, 1820–1970. 1987. 325 pp. Paper 0-89680-136-5 $20.00.

* Southeast Asia Translation Project Group

Africa Series

Latin America Series

Ordering Information

Individuals are encouraged to patronize local bookstores wherever possible. Orders for titles in the Monographs in International Studies may be placed directly through the Ohio University Press, Scott Quadrangle, Athens, Ohio 45701-2979. Individuals should remit payment by check, VISA, or MasterCard.* Those ordering from the United Kingdom, Continental Europe, the Middle East,. and Africa should order through Academic and University Publishers Group, 1 Gower Street, London WC1E, England. Orders from the Pacific Region, Asia, Australia, and New Zealand should be sent to East-West Export Books, c/o the University of Hawaii Press, 2840 Kolowalu Street, Honolulu, Hawaii 96822, USA.

Individuals ordering from outside of the U.S. should remit in U.S. funds to Ohio University Press either by International Money Order or by a check drawn on a U.S. bank.** Most out-of-print titles may be ordered from University Microfilms, Inc., 300 North Zeeb Road, Ann Arbor, Michigan 48106, USA.

Prices are subject to change.

* Please add $3.50 for the first book and $.75 for each additional book for shipping and handling.

** Outside the U.S. please add $4.50 for the first book and $.75 for each additional book.

Ohio University
Monographs in International Studies

The Ohio University Center for International Studies was established to help create within the university and local communities a greater awareness of the world beyond the United States. Comprising programs in African, Latin American, Southeast Asian, Development and Administrative studies, the Center supports scholarly research, sponsors lectures and colloquia, encourages course development within the university curriculum, and publishes the Monographs in International Studies series with the Ohio University Press. The Center and its programs also offer an interdisciplinary Master of Arts degree in which students may focus on one of the regional or topical concentrations, and may also combine academics with training in career fields such as journalism, business, and language teaching. For undergraduates, major and certificate programs are also available.

For more information, contact the Vice Provost for International Studies, Burson House, Ohio University, Athens, Ohio 45701.

61 /1–100   AF
SWO#–175891   PC#–90
CUS#–6776   DUE–02/11

LIBRARY
IHE UNIVERSITY OF TEXAS
AT BROWNSVILLE
Brownsville, TX 78520-4991